# 50 Hikes in the Sierra Nevada

# 50 *Hikes*
# in the
# Sierra Nevada

### Hikes and Backpacks from Lake Tahoe
### to Sequoia National Park

First Edition

JULIE SMITH

**The Countryman Press**
Woodstock, Vermont

**AN INVITATION TO THE READER**
Over time trails can be rerouted and signs and
landmarks altered. If you find that changes have
occurred on the routes described in this book,
please let us know so that corrections may be
made in future editions. The author and publisher
also welcome other comments and suggestions.
Address all correspondence to:

   Editor, *50 Hikes*™ Series
   The Countryman Press
   P.O. Box 748
   Woodstock, VT 05091

LIBRARY OF CONGRESS
CATALOGING-IN-PUBLICATION DATA
HAS BEEN APPLIED FOR.
ISBN 0-88150-810-9

Maps by Mapping Specialists Ltd.,
   © The Countryman Press
Book design by Glenn Suokko
Text composition by PerfecType
Cover photograph by the author
Interior photographs by the author

Copyright © 2009 by Julie Smith

First Edition

Published by The Countryman Press
P.O. Box 748
Woodstock, VT 05091

Distributed by W. W. Norton & Company Inc.
500 Fifth Avenue
New York, NY 10110

Printed in the United States of America

10 9 8 7 6 5 4 3 2 1

For Rick,
I owe you.


*Climb the mountains and get their good tidings. Nature's peace will flow into you as sunshine flows into trees. The winds will blow their own freshness into you, and the storms their energy, while cares will drop off like autumn leaves.*

—John Muir

# Acknowledgments

First off, thank you to Kermit Hummel and Kim Grant of The Countryman Press for entrusting me with this project, and to Jennifer Thompson, Lisa Sacks, and Bill Bowers for their guidance throughout the publishing process. Thanks to all the park rangers who offered their insight, answered my questions, and pointed me in the right direction. To all the amazing people I met along the trail ready to share a smile and bit of conversation (and that group of senior ladies trekking up Little Lakes Valley—you rock!). Thanks to Larry and Peggy and all the nice people at Grant Lake, my base in the Eastern Sierra, for sharing their campfires and fresh trout. To my red-pen-wielding, grammatical goddess of a sister, Annette, who will always be my first set of eyes, most honest critic, and best friend. Thank you to my mom and dad for introducing me to Nature's magnificence and for their constant support along *all* the trails of my life. Last, but most certainly not least, thanks to Rick for supporting me in this endeavor and being my companion on practically every hike in this book. I couldn't have done it without you.

# 50 Hikes in Sierra Nevada at a Glance

| | HIKE | AREA |
|---|---|---|
| **Gold Country** | 1 Monroe Ridge and Monument Trail Loop | Marshall Gold Discovery SHP |
| | 2 American Canyon Trail | Auburn State Recreation Area |
| | 3 Humbug Trail | Malakoff Diggins SHP |
| | 4 Sierra Buttes | Tahoe National Forest |
| | 5 Round Lake Loop | Lakes Basin Recreation Area |
| | 6 Feather Falls | Plumas National Forest |
| **Lake Tahoe** | 7 Loch Leven Lakes | Tahoe National Forest |
| | 8 Mount Judah Loop | Tahoe National Forest |
| | 9 Rubicon Trail | DL Bliss and Emerald Bay State Parks |
| | 10 Tahoe Meadows | Humboldt-Toiyabe National Forest |
| | 11 Crag Lake | Desolation Wilderness |
| | 12 Cascade Falls and Granite Lake | Desolation Wilderness |
| | 13 Mount Tallac | Desolation Wilderness |
| | 14 Echo Lake to Lake Aloha | Desolation Wilderness |
| **Trans-Sierra Passes** | 15 Round Top Lake Loop | Mokelumne Wilderness (Carson Pass) |
| | 16 Meiss Meadow to Round Lake | Eldorado National Forest (Carson Pass) |
| | 17 Granite Lake | Mokelumne Wilderness (Carson Pass) |
| | 18 Bull Run Lake | Carson-Iceberg Wilderness (Ebbetts Pass) |
| | 19 Calaveras Big Trees State Park – South Grove | Calaveras Big Trees State Park (Ebbetts Pass) |
| | 20 Sonora Pass | Emigrant Wilderness (Sonora Pass) |
| | 21 Sardine Falls | Humboldt-Toiyabe National Forest (Sonora Pass) |
| | 22 Bennettville Trail | Inyo National Forest (Tioga Pass) |
| | 23 Twenty Lakes Basin | Hoover Wilderness (Tioga Pass) |

## Legend

**TYPE:**
D   Day hike
O   Overnight

**DIFFICULTY RATINGS:**
E   Easy
M   Moderate
S   Strenuous

| TYPE | RT DISTANCE | RATING | ELEVATION |
|------|-------------|--------|-----------|
| D | 3.0 | E-M | +620'/-620' |
| D | 4.8 | M | +2'/-1,058' |
| D | 5.4 | M | +145'/-947' |
| D | 5.0 | M-S | +1,556'/-57' |
| D | 4.0 | E | +470'/-470' |
| D | 8.4 | M-S | +2,228'/-2,228' |
| D | 6.0 | M | +1,199'/-223' |
| D | 5.0 | M | +1,445'/-1,445' |
| D | 5.4 | E | +765'/-511' |
| D | 1.3; 3.4 | E; E | +74'/-74'; +286'/-247' |
| D/O | 10.0 | M | +1,290'/-27' |
| D | 1.4; 2.2 | E; M | +111'/-211'; +776'/-33' |
| D | 9.2 | S | +3,295'/-0' |
| D/O | 6.8 | M | +914'/-174' |
| D | 5.0 | M | +1,214'/-1,214' |
| D | 10.0 | M | +464'/-1,012' |
| D/O | 4.0 | E | +597'/-44' |
| D/O | 7.4 | M | +1,023'/-521' |
| D | 5.4 | E | +800'/-800' |
| D | 8.6 | M-S | +1,640'/-502' |
| D | 2.0 | E | +324'/-18' |
| D | 3.9 | E | +359'/-0' |
| D/O | 4.5 | E-M | +600'/-600' |

# 50 Hikes in Sierra Nevada at a Glance

| | HIKE | AREA |
|---|---|---|
| Eastern Sierra | 24 Green Lake | Hoover Wilderness |
| | 25 Virginia Lakes Basin | Hoover Wilderness |
| | 26 Mono Lake | Mono Basin National Forest Scenic Area |
| | 27 San Joaquin Ridge | Inyo National Forest |
| | 28 Devils Postpile to Rainbow Falls | Devils Postpile National Monument |
| | 29 Little Lakes Valley to Gem Lake | John Muir Wilderness |
| | 30 Blue Lake | John Muir Wilderness |
| | 31 Long Lake | John Muir Wilderness |
| | 32 Big Pine Lakes Basin to Second Lake | John Muir Wilderness |
| | 33 Lone Pine Lake | John Muir Wilderness |
| Yosemite NP | 34 Wapama Falls | Yosemite National Park |
| | 35 Panorama Trail | Yosemite National Park |
| | 36 Half Dome | Yosemite National Park |
| | 37 Clouds Rest | Yosemite National Park |
| | 38 Cathedral Lakes | Yosemite National Park |
| | 39 Waterwheel Falls | Yosemite National Park |
| | 40 Gaylor Lakes | Yosemite National Park |
| | 41 Chilnualna Falls | Yosemite National Park |
| Sequoia/Kings Cyn NP | 42 Mist Falls | Kings Canyon National Park |
| | 43 Boole Tree | Sequoia National Forest |
| | 44 Redwood Mountain Grove | Kings Canyon National Park |
| | 45 Little Baldy | Sequoia National Park |
| | 46 Tokopah Falls | Sequoia National Park |
| | 47 Lakes Trail to Heather Lake | Sequoia National Park |
| | 48 Circle Meadow | Sequoia National Park |
| | 49 Crescent and Log Meadows Loop | Sequoia National Park |
| | 50 Eagle Lake | Sequoia National Park |

## Legend

**TYPE:**
D   Day hike
O   Overnight

**DIFFICULTY RATINGS:**
E   Easy
M   Moderate
S   Strenuous

| TYPE | RT DISTANCE | RATING | ELEVATION |
| --- | --- | --- | --- |
| D/O | 6.2 | M | +1,004'/-63' |
| D | 6.0 | M-S | +1,282'/-1' |
| D | 2.0; 0.75 | E; E | +357'/-357'; +31'/-31' |
| D | 4.5 | M | +1,044'/-51' |
| D | 3.5 | E | +455'/-347' |
| D/O | 7.1 | M | +760'/-73' |
| D/O | 6.3 | M-S | +1,383'/-76' |
| D/O | 4.2 | M | +955'/-43' |
| D/O | 9.0 | M-S | +2,314'/-22' |
| D | 5.5 | M-S | +1,852'/-195' |
| D | 5.0 | E | +581'/-515' |
| D | 8.2 | M-S | +900'/-4,000' |
| D/O | 14.0; 16.4 | S++; S++ | +4,953'/-216' |
| D | 14.4 | S | +2,355'/-696' |
| D | 6.5 | M | +1,010'/-294' |
| O | 16.4 | M-S | +592'/-2,375' |
| D | 3.5 | M-S | +1,039'/-198' |
| D | 8.0 | S | +2,257'/-165' |
| D | 8.0 | E-M | +638'/-0' |
| D | 2.5 | M | +809'/-809' |
| D/O | 7.2 | M | +1,465'/-1,465' |
| D | 3.4 | M | +764'/-110' |
| D | 3.8 | E | +683'/-3' |
| D/O | 8.2 | M-S | +2,210'/-229' |
| D | 4.0 | E | +694'/-694' |
| D | 2.5 | E | +570'/-570' |
| D/O | 6.8 | S | +2,202'/-11' |

50 Hikes in the
Sierra Nevada

# Contents

## V. YOSEMITE NATIONAL PARK

## VI. SEQUOIA AND KINGS CANYON NATIONAL PARKS

# Introduction

From a skyline of serrated granite to a delicate carpet of spring wildflowers, the Sierra Nevada mountain range is a land of sensory extremes. Full of sharp edges, rough textures, and fragile biota, these mountains, when taken all together, form some of the most sublime landscapes in the world.

The Sierra is a perpetually changing natural masterpiece filled with boundless perspectives. Whether you're perched atop Mount Whitney with an ocean of snow-capped spires lapping against your feet or spying a black bear and her cub saunter across a blossoming meadow, each vantage has its own intoxicating panorama.

The Sierra Nevada is the longest single mountain range in the contiguous United States. This prominent geographic feature runs almost entirely within the eastern portion of California, briefly spilling into Nevada near Lake Tahoe. The range contains the deepest lake, the tallest waterfall, the largest living tree, the deepest gorge, and the highest mountain in the continental United States.

The oak woodland-covered foothills of the western Sierra, beginning around 1,000 feet in elevation, give way to mixed conifer forests and pine stands, ultimately culminating at stark, treeless mountaintops above 14,000 feet, where little will grow but lichen and moss. This wide range of elevation, climate, and topography results in a remarkable diversity of flora and fauna. Climbing the Sierra Nevada is comparable to making a trip from the deserts of the southwestern United States to arctic Canada—1,000 feet of elevation gain roughly corresponding to traveling 300 miles northward. Each dramatic shift in elevation includes a different set of denizens, all adapted to their specific niches.

The cultural history of the Sierra Nevada has transitioned from peaceful coexistence with early Native American inhabitants, to deleterious mining, logging, and grazing by European-American settlers, to a conservation movement spearheaded by naturalist John Muir. Through his writing and political activism, he became a pivotal figure in preserving the integrity of the Sierra and the creation of our national parks system.

Today, much of the Sierra Nevada is maintained as a patchwork of federal- or state-designated parks, forests, monuments, and wilderness areas. Most notably, Yosemite, Kings Canyon, and Sequoia National Parks are found tucked amid the range's rock outcroppings and forested slopes.

The most intimate way to experience this vast range is under your own power. The Sierra is crisscrossed by an extensive trail network—from sections of the rugged, 2,650-mile Pacific Crest Trail (PCT) to paved interpretive nature walks, there is something for everyone. With a plethora of fantastic opportunities, choosing 50 hikes was challenging, but I think you will find this book includes a pleasant mix of classic Sierra treks and lesser-known, less-frequented gems just waiting for you to explore.

As you roam the Sierra trails, whether you find yourself on a remote ridge of the Mokelumne Wilderness or on a bustling trail in Yosemite Valley, be in awe—listen to the trees, touch the polished granite, fill your lungs with sweet mountain air, watch a butterfly dance. Most important, be present in that moment amid Nature's brilliance and know what it means to be home.

## GEOGRAPHY

The Sierra Nevada, Spanish for "snowy mountains," stretches more than 400 miles from the southern edge of the Cascade Range in northern California to Tehachapi Pass. Spanning between 40 and 80 miles wide, the Sierra are bounded by the Central Valley to the west and the Great Basin to the east.

The beauty and unique geography of the Sierra are the results of a complex combination of volcanic activity, tectonic processes, and glacial erosion. When dinosaurs roamed the Earth, an arc-shaped chain of volcanoes erupted where the present-day Sierra Nevada stands. During repeated volcanic episodes that occurred over millions of years, some molten rock erupted at the surface as lava, but most solidified deep below the Earth's crust, forming granite. Over time, the volcanoes eroded, exposing the deep-seated granitic rock that forms the backbone of the range.

Less than five million years ago, through a combination of uplift of the Sierran block along its eastern margin and down-dropping of the Great Basin to the east, the Sierra Nevada began to rise. The range is a massive tilted block of Earth's crust that rises abruptly in the east and slopes gently westward toward the Central Valley.

This asymmetrical structure makes for two vastly different sides. The mild gradient of the western Sierra lends itself to densely wooded slopes with broad meadows, meandering rivers, and countless lakes. Conversely, the steep leeward side is much drier because it lies in the rain shadow effect of the range. It is characterized by deep, rugged canyons, sheer rock faces, and sawtooth pinnacles that seem to pierce the sky.

During the most recent Ice Age, the Earth cooled and glaciers grew in the higher elevations. As these moving masses of ice made their way down former river channels, they carved impressive U-shaped valleys and left in their wake precipitous hanging valleys, amphitheater-shaped cirques, and milky turquoise tarns.

Though the geologic forces molding the Sierra Nevada—faulting, uplift, earthquakes, erosion, volcanism, and glaciation—have varied in intensity throughout the millions of years it took to shape the range, these powerful processes remain with us, bending, building, and carving.

## HAZARDS

This section provides a cursory introduction to the potential hazards lurking in the Sierra. I recommend obtaining a copy of *The Backpacker's Field Manual* (Three Rivers Press, 2005), which provides detailed information on mastering backcountry skills, including first aid, safety, and trip planning.

### Altitude Sickness

Altitude sickness occurs when you cannot get enough oxygen from the air at high altitudes. When you go too high too fast, your body can have trouble adapting to the new altitude. Each individual's susceptibility to altitude sickness is different, however, it happens most often when people who are not used to high altitudes go quickly from lower elevations to 8,000 feet or higher. Symptoms include headache, loss of appetite, nausea, insomnia, shortness of breath, and fatigue. Considering most of the hikes in this guidebook are in the 6,500- to 11,000-foot range, understanding the symptoms of altitude sickness and how to avoid them is essential for a safe trip into the Sierra high country.

### Hypothermia

In the Sierra Nevada, weather can change rapidly, especially during the summer months, which are notorious for afternoon thunderstorms, making hypothermia a very real threat for hikers. Hypothermia is a condition in which the body's core temperature drops below normal levels. It occurs when the body loses heat at a rate faster than it can be replaced by metabolic and muscular activity. Left untreated, hypothermia can lead to death.

Wet clothing and windy weather are the primary hypothermia-inducing culprits, the combination of which can quickly strip the body of heat even when the air temperature is above freezing. Symptoms of hypothermia include: shivering, confusion, loss of coordination, slurred speech, and lethargy. As the condition progresses, a person may become unable to walk, suffer from a slow or irregular heart rate, exhibit irrational and/or incoherent behavior, and the skin may appear blue or puffy.

If you suspect someone in your party is a victim of hypothermia, seek a dry, warm place out of the elements, and remove wet clothing and replace with dry, or wrap in blankets. Have the victim drink warm liquids, ingest high-caloric foods (carbohydrates), and, if possible, get them moving to generate body heat by doing jumping jacks or running in place.

Of course, all of the above can be avoided. The best prevention is not to get wet in the first place. Dress in layers and wear a hat to easily regulate body temperature. Avoid wearing cotton, which dries slowly, and instead opt for a synthetic inner layer that wicks moisture and perspiration away from the body. Wear a wind- and waterproof outer shell that keeps your inner layers dry. Eat small amounts of high-caloric food at frequent intervals to keep your body fueled, drink plenty of water, and avoid alcohol and caffeine. If you anticipate inclement weather—or even if you don't—it doesn't hurt to carry dry clothes in a waterproof bag, just in case.

### Lightning

Mountain thunderstorms are a hazard that shouldn't be taken lightly, especially for hikers above the tree line. Even though, during the summer months, thunderstorms generally form in early to mid-afternoon in the Sierra, the reality is they are unpredictable and can move quickly into an area at any time. Hiking early so that you have descended from high-risk areas before the lightning threat is greatest and continuously monitoring the sky for changing weather conditions are important methods to reduce vulnerability.

If you are in the backcountry and hear thunder, immediately move to safer terrain, such as a dense stand of even-height trees, a significant depression, or dry ravine. Avoid peaks, ridges, wide open areas where presumably you would be the tallest object, bodies of water, lone trees or trees of uneven height, caves, rock overhangs, and electrical conductors.

By timing the interval between seeing the lightning and hearing the accompanying thunder, it is possible to estimate the distance to the lightning (five seconds equals a mile). If at risk, distance yourself from any metal objects like ice axes, crampons, hiking poles, and backpacks. If available, place an insulated object like a foam pad or a soft bag full of clothing between you and the ground. Squat, curl up in a ball, wrap your arms around your legs, and put your feet together. Make yourself as low as possible without lying prone and have the least possible amount of bodily contact with the ground. Stay in this position, sometimes called the "lightning position," until the storm passes. If you are in a group, spread out at least 50 feet apart to reduce the chance of multiple injuries. You do not have to be hit directly by lightning to be affected. Lightning can travel along the ground from a nearby strike to you, or jump from nearby objects that are struck.

If someone in your group is struck by lightning and is not breathing, you should immediately administer cardiopulmonary resuscitation (CPR) and send for help. People struck by lightning do not retain the electrical charge and are safe to touch. Use basic first aid principles to treat other injuries due to lightning, like burns or shock, and get victims to medical professionals as quickly as possible.

## Poison Oak

Western poison oak *(Toxicodendron diversilobum)* is one of the West's most notorious natural villains. This widespread deciduous shrub or climbing vine is found throughout the mountains and valleys of California, generally below 5,000 feet elevation. Because of its extremely variable growth habitat and leaf appearance, recognizing this outdoor nemesis can be difficult.

Normally, leaves are divided into three leaflets, with the middle leaflet having a much longer stalk than those of the other two, hence the adage, "leaves of three, let it be"; however, occasionally leaves are composed of five, seven, or nine leaflets. Each leaflet ranges from 1 to 4 inches in length and can have smooth, toothed, or lobed edges. Leaves are generally green and sometimes light red in early spring, bright green during the summer, and various shades of yellow, orange, and red in the fall. White flowers form in the spring and, if fertilized, develop into greenish-white or tan berries.

All parts of the poison oak plant, including roots, stems, leaves, flowers, and berries, contain the poisonous, oily substance urushiol, which causes allergic contact dermatitis in most people. Contamination can occur by direct contact with bruised or broken plants that have released their deleterious oily resin; contact with contaminated objects, such as shoes, clothing, tools, and animals; and even by inhaling smoke particles from the burned poison oak plant.

If you unintentionally traipse through a patch of the detrimental shrub, wash the affected area immediately with soap and copious amounts of cold water. Then, as soon as possible, wash again with a mild solvent such as isopropyl alcohol, followed by more cold water. If these steps are performed within the first few minutes of contact, a reaction may be prevented. Missing this small window of opportunity can lead to a blistery rash, oozing sores, and severe itching within 24 to 48 hours of exposure. If an outbreak occurs, hydrocortisone cream, antihistamines, and products like Tecnu, which removes the urushiol from the skin, can provide some relief.

## Waterborne Parasites

The water of America's backcountry has been invaded by microscopic parasites, namely *Giardia lamblia* and *Cryptosporidium,* which would like nothing better than to set up shop in your intestines and wreak havoc. Both *Giardia* and *Cryptosporidium*–"Crypto" for short–live in the intestines of infected humans or animals. They are found in soil, food, water, and on surfaces that have been contaminated with the feces from infected individuals.

Both critters cause a variety of intestinal maladies, including diarrhea, stomach cramps, gas, nausea, and vomiting. No matter how clear, cool, and free-running a stream may appear, dipping your Nalgene bottle for a swig simply isn't worth the risk of ingesting the microorganisms, bacteria, and chemical toxins lurking in the water of the world's wild places, including the Sierra.

If it's impractical to carry enough water with you for a trip, treating your backcountry water is imperative. The Centers for Disease Control and Prevention (CDC) recommends heating water to a rolling boil for at least one minute, or using either a filter that has an absolute pore size of 1 micron or smaller, or one that has been National Sanitation Foundation (NSF) rated for "cyst removal." Chemically treating water by chlorination or iodine will remove *Giardia,* however, *Cryptosporidium* is resistant to these disinfectants due to its thick outer shell. My advice: boil or filter and stay cootie free.

### Sun Exposure

Protecting our skin and eyes from the sun should be a priority every day, but even more so when we spend time at altitude. Ultraviolet (UV) radiation is greater at higher elevations, where the atmosphere is thinner and less able to filter harmful rays. Add to this the reflection of light from snow, water, and rock surfaces and the effect is intensified. Protect yourself by applying sunblock to exposed skin and wearing sunglasses that block 99–100 percent of UV radiation. Wearing a wide-brimmed hat and sun-protective clothing can also shield areas prone to overexposure.

## WILDLIFE

The Sierra Nevada are a wild and rugged range full of equally wild and rugged denizens. Observing these beautiful animals in their natural habitat can be exhilarating, but it can also be maddening. Spying a black bear feeding in a meadow can be an amazing experience; a marmot biting a hole in your backpack and raiding your gorp, not so much. My backcountry admonition: a few precautions and some common sense equals more exhilaration and less frustration.

### Bears

All bears inhabiting the Sierra Nevada are black bears *(Ursus americanus).* Sadly, though California's state flag is emblazoned with a grizzly bear, the last one was seen in the wild in California in 1924. Black bears come in shades of black, brown, and cinnamon and are generally found in the 3,000- to 7,000-foot elevation range, where food is abundant.

The likelihood of seeing a bear while day hiking is slim. Most bear encounters occur in campgrounds or at backpacker campsites where food and other scents lure them. Many drive-in campgrounds in the Sierra, and some trailhead parking areas, now provide bearproof metal lockers for securing food and other scented items—soap, sunscreen, toothpaste, lotion, lip balm, etc. If you are backpacking, safeguarding food and toiletries in trees or using bearproof canisters is imperative for both you and the bears.

Bears naturally fear humans. Those that have become habituated to our presence and food-conditioned to scavenge in campsites and trash cans for human vittles become destructive and dangerous. Sometimes the worst offenders have to be killed.

Use common sense. Never leave food unattended outside; don't take food into your tent at night; use a bear-resistant container for grocery storage or lock food in your vehicle and cover with blankets; and dispose of or store garbage immediately. Remember, proper food storage is required by federal regulations, and feeding wildlife is prohibited.

While on the trail, make noise to avoid a surprise encounter with a bear. Never approach or feed a bear, and never get between a bear and her cub or its food. If an encounter does occur, remain calm and do not run; instead, face the animal (avoid eye contact, as this is perceived as a threat), make noise, and try to appear as large as possible. If attacked, roll into a ball face down with your hands over your neck and play dead. If, despite your being passive, the bear continues its aggression, bear experts advise that you fight back.

### Mountain Lions

Mountain lions *(Felis concolor)*, also referred to as cougars or pumas, prowl the Sierra foothills and lower-elevation forests. These powerful cats are quiet, solitary, and elusive. They typically avoid people, although conflicts are increasing as California's urban sprawl encroaches on mountain lion habitat and more people venture into the backcountry.

To prevent an encounter, avoid hiking solo or when mountain lions are most active—dawn, dusk, and at night. As with all wild animals, do not feed mountain lions or approach them for any reason. If you stumble upon one, avoid the overwhelming temptation to run. Face the animal, make noise, and try to look bigger by waving your arms. Throw rocks, sticks, or anything you can get your hands on. If you have small children with you, pick them up. If attacked, do not play dead, but fight back savagely. Many people have successfully fended off an attacking mountain lion.

### Rattlesnakes

Rattlesnakes, the only poisonous snake species inhabiting California, are found throughout the lower elevations of the Sierra—typically below 6,500 feet, but most commonly below 5,000 feet. Though most of the hikes covered in this guidebook are above their preferred range, keep a vigilant eye and a keen ear nonetheless.

The western rattlesnake *(Crotalus viridis)*, the species found in the Sierra, has a wide triangular head, narrow neck, and a rattle on its tail. Their bodies are brown with a series of dark brown patches down the back. They are shy creatures that prefer to remain out of sight. Their coloring provides camouflage for their predation of small rodents; however, it also means that they blend in nicely with the trail and adjacent leaf litter, so watch where you step and place your hands. Listen for the telltale rattle or buzzing noise made when they shake their tails—a courteous warning when we get too close.

If you encounter a snake on the trail, give it a wide berth and move away slowly. Given an escape route, they will generally vacate the area and you can happily continue on.

### Rodents

Of all the creatures living in the Sierra Nevada, rodents are the most irksome, hazardous, and destructive to hikers and backpackers. They may look cute, but let's not forget that these deceptively charming mammals can carry *Hantavirus,* bubonic plague, and a host of other icky diseases.

Squirrels, mice, chipmunks, and marmots are cunning and relentless. They have one thing on their minds and one thing only—food. Don't leave your backpack or snacks unattended for a moment; these rodents are extremely fast and can scurry off with your baggie of gorp or slice a hole in your pack or tent with their razor-sharp teeth in an instant. In addition, avoid camping in areas with evidence of rodent activity, like burrows and droppings, to decrease your chance of contact with these disease-carrying varmints.

### Ticks

Ticks have the unfortunate distinction of being the number one infectious disease carrier in the United States. Though they are generally found in the chaparral and grasslands of the Sierra foothills, it doesn't hurt to keep an eye out for these miniature menaces whenever you're on the trail. Wearing light-colored clothing can make the job of spotting these bitty beasties easier. Wear long-sleeved shirts and long pants tucked into your socks or boots. Most important, use an insect repellent. Repellents containing DEET (N, N-diethyl-meta-toluamide) or picaridine (KBR 3023) typically provide the longest-lasting protection. You can also apply repellents containing permethrins to your clothing and gear, but not directly to the skin, for greater protection.

Check for ticks routinely throughout the day in heavily infested areas. If a tick has latched on, the best removal method is to firmly grasp the tick with tweezers as close to the skin as possible. Pull gently until the entire tick comes free. Avoid crushing or squeezing the tick body during removal, as this can increase the chance of disease transmission. Thoroughly cleanse the bite area with soap and water, and apply an antibiotic cream.

### Mosquitoes

Dealing with mosquitoes seems to be a rite of passage of sorts in the Sierra, especially in the spring and early summer. In the United States, these pesky disease vectors are most notable for their potential transmission of West Nile virus.

Protect yourself by wearing long pants, long-sleeved shirts, and using an insect repellent. Repellents containing DEET and picaridine are effective for mosquitoes as well as ticks. In addition, oil of lemon eucalyptus (p-menthane-3,8-diol) appears to be an effectual plant-based deterrent.

If you are bitten, an itchy round pink or red bump will develop. Wash the bite with soap and water and apply an anti-itch cream.

Scratching the bite can break the skin and lead to infection.

## BEING PREPARED

Venturing into the backcountry, whether it's for a few hours or a few days, comes with some inherent risks—risks that can be tempered with a little foresight and a lot of common sense. Ultimately, you are responsible for yourself on the trail, so be prepared.

The list below includes essential items every hiker should carry for a safe foray into the mountains. Although you may not use all these items on every hike, they can be lifesavers in an emergency.

1. Map
2. Compass
3. Water
4. Water filter
5. Raingear and extra clothing
6. Extra food
7. Food storage device
8. Firestarter and waterproof matches
9. First-aid kit
10. Knife or multipurpose tool
11. Flashlight (with extra bulbs and batteries)
12. Sunglasses and sunscreen
13. Whistle

Become self-reliant by educating yourself about the terrain you are venturing into, local weather patterns, and your equipment before ever stepping on the trail. Leave your hiking plans with someone, including where you are going and when you expect to return. Keep your group together and know your limitations.

## LEAVE NO TRACE

Leave No Trace is a program designed to educate outdoor enthusiasts about the nature of their recreational impacts and to provide techniques to prevent and minimize them.

Practicing the seven principles of Leave No Trace ensures we are all doing our part to leave natural places the way we found them: plan ahead and prepare; travel and camp on durable surfaces; dispose of waste properly; leave what you find; minimize campfire impacts; respect wildlife; and be considerate of other visitors.

## HOW TO USE THIS GUIDEBOOK

The 50 hikes included in this guidebook are divided into six regions: Gold Country, Lake Tahoe, Trans-Sierra Passes (Carson, Ebbetts, Sonora, and Tioga Passes), Eastern Sierra, Yosemite National Park, and Sequoia and Kings Canyon National Parks.

Each hike is contained within its own chapter and begins with a quick-reference information box that includes the type of hike, season, total distance, difficulty rating, elevation, location, reference maps, applicable fees and permits, and contact information.

**Type:** A hike will either be listed as a day hike, overnight, or both.

**Season:** The season provided will vary from year to year depending on weather conditions and is meant as a guide to when the trail is generally open and free of snow.

**Total distance:** Distances include the total round-trip mileage.

**Rating:** Hikes are rated easy, moderate, or strenuous based on trail length, elevation changes, and overall trail conditions and followability for the average hiker. Keep this in mind when deciding whether a hike is appropriate for your skill level.

**Elevation:** The first number of each entry is the trailhead elevation. The second set of numbers represents the total elevation gain and loss. The gain and loss data are one-way for out-and-back trips and total for point-to-point, loop, and semi-loop trips. Elevations are given in feet. To convert feet to meters, multiply by 0.3048.

**Location:** Gives you the geographic location of the hike.

**Maps:** In addition to the trail map provided in each chapter, other useful maps are listed, including the USGS 7.5-minute quadrangles, Trails Illustrated Map, and/or local jurisdiction map.

**Fees and permits:** The Sierra Nevada has multiple jurisdictions, each having its own fee structure and permit requirements. Whether you are embarking on a day hike or overnight journey, it is your responsibility to be aware of local rules and regulations. I recommend securing overnight permits well in advance, as most Sierra wilderness areas have instated peak-season trailhead quotas limiting the number of overnight users entering an area on any given day.

**Contacts:** Pertinent contact information is provided for your reference.

Following the quick-reference information box is a brief introduction to the hike, followed by directions to the trailhead from a nearby prominent locale. Finally, there is a comprehensive description of the trail and what you can expect to encounter, from its ups and downs, junctions and crossings, to significant points of interest and natural history.

Happy trails!

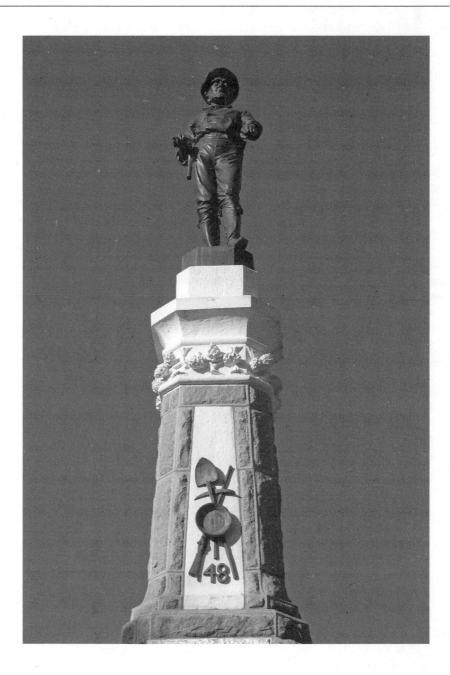

# 1

## Monroe Ridge and Monument Trail Loop

*Type: Day hike*

*Season: Year-round*

*Total distance: 3.0-mile loop*

*Rating: Easy to moderate due to some steep sections*

*Elevation: 932 feet; +620 feet/-620 feet*

*Location: Marshall Gold Discovery State Historic Park*

*Maps: USGS 7.5' Coloma (trail not shown); Marshall Gold Discovery State Historic Park map*

*Fees and permits: A permit is not required for this day hike. There is a $5 day-use fee per vehicle.*

*Contact: Marshall Gold Discovery State Historic Park (530-622-3470; www.parks.ca.gov/?page_id=484).*

This loop hike in the heart of California's Gold Country takes you through bucolic oak woodlands and visits a number of historic sites around Coloma, the former hub of the northern mining region. It was here in January 1848 that James Marshall found some flakes of gold in the American River–a portentous discovery that would forever change history. The Monroe Ridge Trail rises gradually but steadily to a ridge overlooking the Coloma Valley before descending toward the river. Explore the site of John Marshall's historic gold discovery, the replica of Sutter's Mill, and the exhibits and displays at the visitors center before joining the Monument Trail, which climbs gently along a shaded path to the lofty John Marshall Monument and completes the loop.

### GETTING THERE

From I-80 in Auburn, exit CA 49, then drive 0.1 mile south and turn left onto Lincoln Way. Proceed 0.2 mile and veer left as Lincoln Way becomes High Street. Travel 0.5 mile through downtown Auburn and cross Borland Avenue/Lincoln Way. From here, CA 49 winds 10.8 miles to Coloma. Park in the second lot on your left near the sawmill replica and pay the admission fee. Visit the Gold Discovery Museum and historic buildings to orient yourself before driving to the trailhead.

From Coloma, proceed south along CA 49. At the south end of town, CA 49 bends sharply east, but continue straight onto Cold Springs Road. Continue 0.1 mile, then turn right onto Monument Road and take this 0.3 mile to the parking area on the right.

1. Monroe Ridge and Monument Trail Loop

P Parking

N

View

0          1/2 mile

0          1/2 kilometer

## THE TRAIL

The Greek word "Eureka" has appeared on the California state seal since 1849 and means "I have found it." This motto presumably refers to the fateful discovery of gold in California's foothills. Archimedes, the ancient Greek scholar, is said to have exclaimed "Eureka!" when he discovered a method of determining the purity of gold (the Archimedes Principle). I wonder if John Marshall gave his own shout out when he scooped up a few golden nuggets from the streambed near Sutter's mill.

John Sutter, founder of Sutter's Fort, a 19th-century agricultural and trade colony—later named Sacramento—partnered with James W. Marshall, a New Jersey carpenter, to go into the lumber business. In the fall of 1847, Marshall began construction of a

sawmill along the South Fork of the American River in the peaceful Coloma Valley. A few months later, while testing the mill, Marshall discovered the tailrace, designed to carry water away from the mill, was too shallow, preventing the mill wheel from operating properly. Marshall had Native American laborers deepen the tailrace, and the loose rock and debris was washed away. On January 24, 1848, while inspecting the tailrace, Marshall spotted nuggets of gold glistening in the water. He took his discovery to Sutter, who consulted his encyclopedia and performed some tests to confirm the find. Concerned about their economic investment in the mill, they attempted to keep the discovery a secret until the mill was in operation. In the end, the secret was just too good to keep all to themselves. Within months, word had spread to San Francisco and eventually the world. The California Gold Rush was officially on.

Marshall's chance discovery sparked a mass migration of people to California in a scramble to strike it rich. The state's nonnative population soared from 14,000 in 1848 to more than 200,000 by 1852, and over the ensuing 50 years some 125 million ounces of gold were taken from California's hills.

This hike utilizes two trails to make a loop through the foothill oak woodland above Coloma. To begin, walk across Monument Road to the signed Monroe Ridge trailhead, named in memory of a pioneering African American family who settled here during the Gold Rush. Peter and Nancy Gooch arrived in Coloma as slaves in 1849, but were soon freed when California became a free state the following year. Nancy earned a living doing domestic chores for miners, and in 1861 had saved enough money to buy the freedom of her son, Andrew Monroe, who was still enslaved in Missouri. Andrew brought his family to Coloma, where they be-

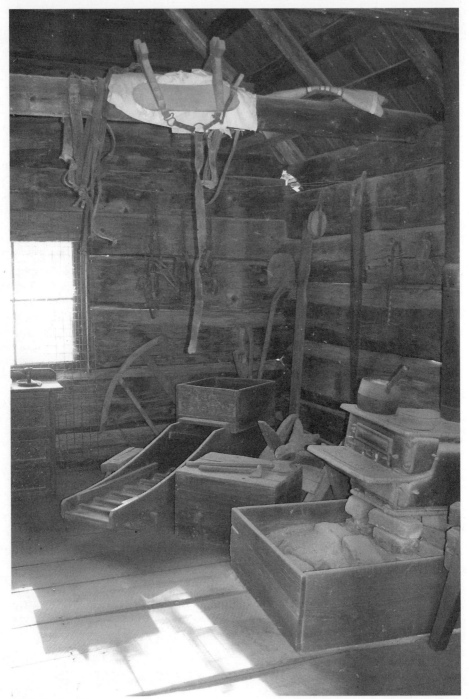

*Old miner's cabin*

came respected farmers and landholders.

Begin a 0.75-mile, 350-foot ascent through a thin canopy of digger pines and interior live oaks as you follow signs to North Beach, the picnic area at the end of this trail. If you're doing this hike in the summer, get an early start and carry plenty of water. The trail meanders in and out of shady sections and can get quite toasty. Scattered along the trail are California toyon, distinctive red-barked manzanita, fragrant California buckeye, and our favorite foothill nemesis, poison oak. At 0.65 mile, come to a spur trail on your right leading up to a vista point—definitely a misnomer as the views are mostly obscured by vegetation. Not to worry, the best view is just up ahead.

A second spur trail leads to a picnic table on your left and marks the summit, but don't stop here. Continue along the ridge as it gently descends past a fire road that veers right to a second picnic area at 1.35 miles that offers the best view of the Coloma Valley and the American River gliding below. From your vantage point, the trail begins a steep descent through a shady forest before crossing an old mining ditch at 1.9 miles. The ditches were originally used by miners to carry the vast amounts of water needed for placer mining and then later, when mining declined, for crop irrigation.

Follow the trail through the old Monroe orchard to CA 49 (the North Beach picnic area is directly across the road). Turn right and follow the highway shoulder 0.1 mile to an opening in the split rail fence with a trail marker. You can proceed through the fence and follow the dirt service road past the oak-shaded picnic area and restrooms or, if you haven't done so already, cross CA 49 and join the riverside path that visits the gold discovery site, the working replica of Sutter's Mill, and various exhibits. After exploring, cross the highway again and join the signed Monument Trail near the park museum.

If you head straight for Monument Trail, stop to check out the bedrock mortar used by Nisenan tribe to grind acorns. The bowl-shaped holes are, unfortunately, some of the last remaining evidence of their presence here. At 2.5 miles, a trail sign directs you to the Marshall Monument—California's first State Historic Monument. Following a split rail fence, ascend through vine-covered hillsides 0.5 mile farther to the end of the trail. From here a paved road leads to the imposing John Marshall Monument to your left, or proceed straight to reach the parking lot and your vehicle. The gigantic statue atop a granite pedestal marks the grave of John Marshall—his bronze finger intrepidly pointing to the spot where he found the first flecks of gold.

There are so many fascinating human stories that came out of the Gold Rush: the entrepreneurs who never lifted a shovel but made their fortunes by establishing stores, hotels, and banks to support miners who had money to spend; pickax-wielding women who toiled alongside men equally afflicted with gold fever; tales of arduous journeys over land and sea; and the devastating effect a shiny mineral had on Native American populations that once thrived here.

Ironically, neither Sutter nor Marshall ever struck it rich. Sutter's workmen abandoned their jobs to seek fortunes in the gold fields, ultimately leaving him bankrupt. When the sawmill was abandoned in 1850 due to management and legal difficulties, Marshall drifted from place to place, bitterly resenting his misfortune.

# 2

## American Canyon Trail

*Type: Day hike*

*Season: Year-round*

*Total distance: 4.8 miles round trip*

*Rating: Moderate*

*Elevation: 1,722 feet; +2 feet/-1,058 feet*

*Location: Auburn State Recreation Area (SRA)*

*Maps: USGS 7.5' Greenwood (trail not shown)*

*Fees and permits: A permit is not required for this day hike.*

*Contact: Auburn SRA (530-885-4527; www.parks.ca.gov/?page_id=502).*

This steep, but manageable, trail descends a narrow mountain canyon and passes through a variety of foothill woodland and riparian vegetation before culminating at Poverty Bar along the Middle Fork of the American River. With rugged mountain scenery, a burbling creek never far from earshot, Gold Rush–era history, and, if you hit it right, a feast of wild blackberries, this trail has a little something for everyone. Once teeming with gold-hungry prospectors, the 38,000-acre Auburn SRA, which encompasses the North and Middle Forks of the American River, is now a popular outdoor recreation area. Pack your fishing pole, swimsuit, and a picnic and do some recreating of your own.

### GETTING THERE

From I-80 in Auburn, exit at CA 49, then drive 0.1 mile south and turn left onto Lincoln Way. Proceed 0.2 mile and veer left as Lincoln Way becomes High Street. Travel 0.5 mile through downtown Auburn and cross Borland Avenue/Lincoln Way. From here, the road winds 5.7 miles through Auburn State Recreation Area to the town of Cool. Turn left onto CA 193 and drive 5.5 miles east. Turn left onto unsigned Sweetwater Trail (the road on the opposite side of CA 193 is signed Pilgrim Court). Drive 0.2 mile farther to the small trailhead parking area on your right, just before the gated entrance to Auburn Lake Trails residential development. You can also park along Sweetwater Trail in roadside pullouts farther back.

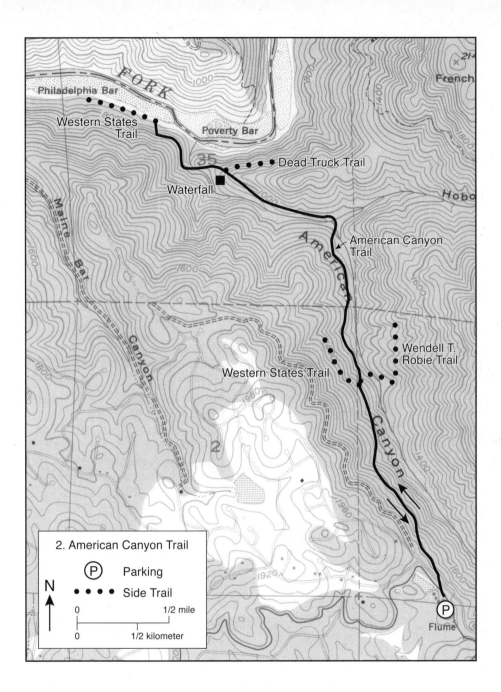

FORK

Philadelphia Bar

Western States
Trail

Poverty Bar

French

Dead Truck Trail

Waterfall

Hobo

American

American Canyon
Trail

Maine Bar

Wendell T.
Robie Trail

Canyon

Western States Trail

Canyon

2. American Canyon Trail

(P) Parking

• • • • Side Trail

N

0                    1/2 mile
0              1/2 kilometer

Flume

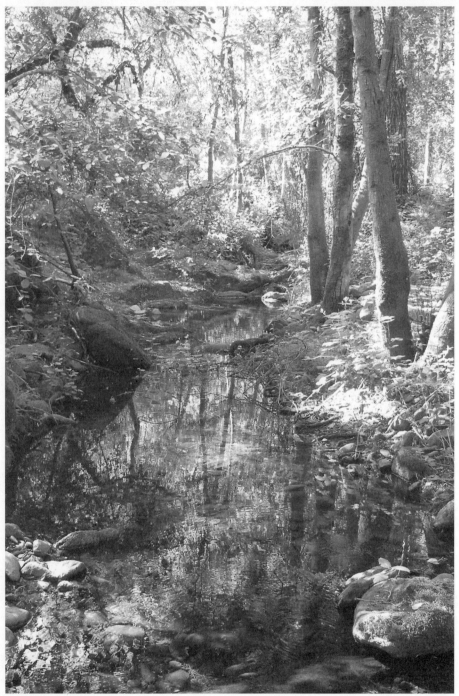

*American Canyon Creek*

## THE TRAIL

As you drive to the trailhead, notice the Auburn-Foresthill Bridge that spans the canyon some 720 feet above the confluence of the North and Middle Forks of the American River. It is the second highest bridge built by the federal Bureau of Reclamation, surpassed only by the bridge at Glen Canyon. The bridge was completed in 1973 as part of the Central Valley Project, which ultimately intended to construct the Auburn Dam. The bridge would have carried the roadway over a portion of the reservoir that would have been created by the impounded river (the considerably lower CA 49 bridge you drove over would be deep underwater).

The dam was designed to provide flood protection and water to the Sacramento Valley, but due to environmental concerns, economics, and the seismic instability of the proposed dam site, construction was halted and the project abandoned. Since it's still possible, though unlikely, that the highly contentious project could be revived, no infrastructure has been built and the Bureau of Reclamation has allowed the State of California to use a portion of the river as a recreation area.

The Auburn State Recreation Area contains 40 miles of the North and Middle Forks of the American River and is crisscrossed with over 100 miles of hiking, biking, and equestrian trails. It also includes a designated off-highway vehicle area and spectacular whitewater rafting on both forks of the river with class II, III, and IV runs. Its proximity to greater Sacramento means the park gets its share of use, but with 38,000 acres it's easy for everyone to spread out.

From the trailhead sign, start descending immediately down a well-defined dirt trail that is densely treed with a variety of oak and foothill pines. At 0.1 mile an unsigned spur trail climbs to the left. Continue straight along the wide, generally well-graded trail. Runoff has formed ruts along segments of the trail, so watch your footing.

The American Canyon Trail is no different than other Western foothill hikes listed in this book in terms of precarious denizens I think we would all prefer to avoid, namely, poison oak, rattlesnakes, ticks, and mountain lions. It goes without saying, but I'll say it anyway: Keep your guard up and be aware when entering any wilderness area.

The trail winds through several blackberry brambles as you trace along the canyon wall. The berries ripen between July and September and are just waiting to provide nourishment to passing hikers. If you are lucky enough to happen upon them before others have stripped the vines clean, by all means indulge in their wild sweetness.

At 0.7 mile, reach an intersection with the Wendell T. Robie Trail. In 1955, Robie, in a mission to prove horses could still cover 100 miles in one day, rode from Squaw Valley to Auburn along the rugged Western States Trail. He subsequently founded the Western States Trail Foundation and organized the annual Western States Trail Ride, commonly called the Tevis Cup "100 Miles One Day" ride, which remains the oldest modern-day equestrian endurance ride in the world. This is not to be confused with the Western States Trail Endurance Run, which was born in the mid-1970s when Gordy Ainsleigh joined the horses to see if he could complete the course on foot (what a stud—no pun intended). The Western States Endurance Run Foundation now hosts the annual event that draws athletes from around the globe.

Turn right and switchback down a short distance to another trail junction, where you will stay straight. The trail narrows, and the soothing sound of tumbling American Canyon Creek can be heard below. At 1.2

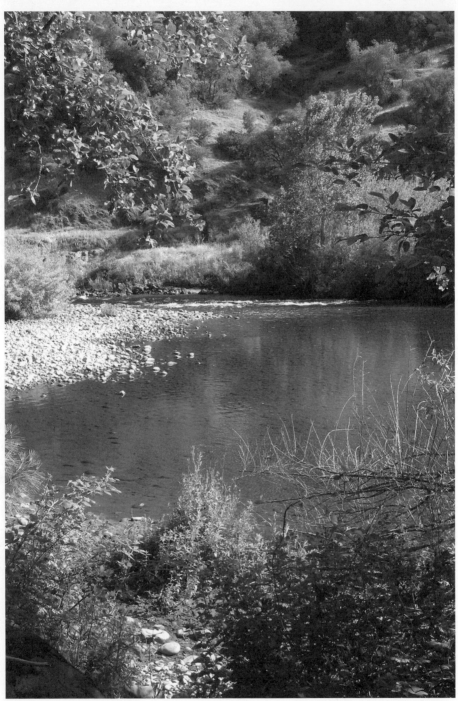

*Middle Fork American River*

miles, the trail drops down to meet American Canyon Creek, followed shortly thereafter by Hoboken Creek, a small tributary of American Canyon. Cross both using strategically placed rocks that provide dry passage much of the year. Crossing may be more difficult during the winter or after storm events when flows are high.

The trail bends sharply west after crossing Hoboken Creek, and the two creeks converge shortly thereafter. The terrain levels out and the canopy opens as you make your way to an intersection with Dead Truck Trail at 1.6 miles. Just before the junction, look for a steep, unmarked side trail branching left that leads down to American Canyon Creek Falls. The falls are only about 20 feet high, but are quite scenic as they drop through a narrow cleft into an inviting pool below.

Stay straight at the intersection with Dead Truck Trail, which rises abruptly to the right. From here the path becomes very steep and rutted as you switchback down the drier southwest-facing slope, where scrub oak, manzanita, and dry grasses dominate. Cross American Canyon Creek again at 1.75 miles using stepping stones and proceed northward as you move up and away from the creek.

As the creek drops sharply toward its confluence with the American River, there are several mini-waterfalls that are obscured by the trees. Without a safe trail to scramble down, we must be satisfied with partial views and allow our imagination to fill in the rest.

An upstream perspective of the American River as it curves beneath French Hill comes into view at 1.9 miles. Just past the viewpoint the trail drops sharply toward the river and gets narrow and overgrown. Steering clear of encroaching poison oak, come to an intersection with the Tevis Cup segment of the Western States Trail at 2.2 miles. Turn right and proceed down to the cobble-strewn southern bank of the Middle Fork.

Directly across the river on the northern bank is Poverty Bar, the location of a bustling mining outpost set up along the river after gold was discovered just upstream on the South Fork near Coloma. Thousands of prospectors panned, sluiced, or dredged every accessible river bar in the gold fever frenzy. Gold panning and rock hounding are allowed in permanent running streambeds in the Auburn SRA, so pack along your pan, but be sure to follow local rules and regulations.

The river is also a great spot to cast a line or take a refreshing dip on a warm summer afternoon. You may, however, be supremely content scouting out a shady spot along the river's edge and spreading out a picnic before retracing your steps to the trailhead.

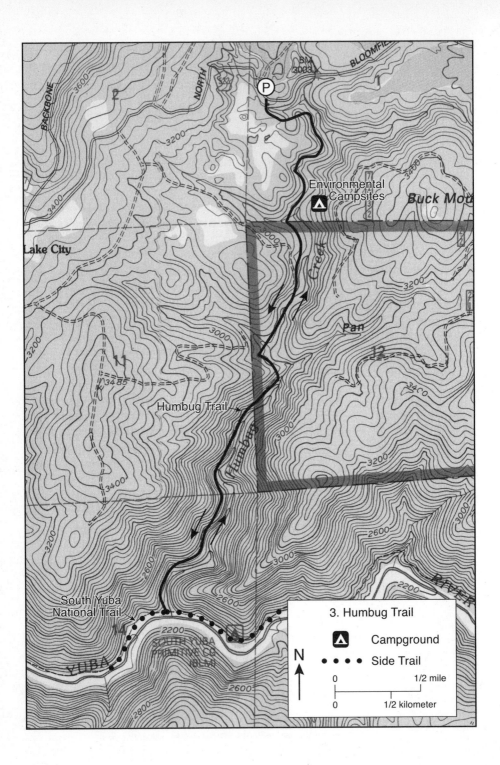

3. Humbug Trail

Campground

● ● ● Side Trail

N

| 0 | 1/2 mile |
| 0 | 1/2 kilometer |

Environmental Campsites

Buck Mou

Lake City

Humbug Trail

South Yuba National Trail

SOUTH YUBA PRIMITIVE CO (BLM)

YUBA

RIVER

Pan

BLOOMFIE

BM 3003

# 3

## Humbug Trail

Type: Day hike

Season: Year-round

Total distance: 5.4 miles round trip

Rating: Moderate

Elevation: 2,950 feet; +145 feet/-947 feet

Location: Malakoff Diggins State Historic Park

Maps: USGS 7.5' North Bloomfield (trail partially shown); USFS South Yuba River Recreation Guide

Fees and permits: A permit is not required for this day hike. There is a $6 day-use fee.

Contact: Malakoff Diggins State Historic Park (530-265-2740; www.parks.ca .gov/?page_id=494).

The bad news is this trail has a few precarious sections, is occasionally steep, and poison oak likes to invade the path. The good news is this hike into the canyon carved by Humbug Creek is replete with Gold Rush–era history and colorful springtime wildflowers, and culminates at an inviting swimming hole along the South Yuba River. The lower elevation makes the trail accessible year-round, with spring and fall being the most scenic.

### GETTING THERE
From Nevada City, drive 11 miles north on CA 49 from its intersection with CA 20 and turn right onto Tyler Foote Crossing Road. Drive 16.4 miles, following signs to Malakoff Diggins State Historic Park. The road name will change en route to Cruzon Grade Road and later Backbone Road. Before the paved road becomes gravel, turn right onto Derbec Road and follow this into the park. Stop at the visitors center to purchase a day-use pass, and then drive 1.5 miles west to the trailhead and park along the road.

### THE TRAIL
Malakoff Diggins State Historic Park is the site of what was once the world's largest hydraulic gold mine. When word got out that a prospector had discovered gold by the Yuba River, miners flooded the area. Finding nothing, they declared the site a "humbug," a pejorative name that stuck to the creek and adjacent village until several years later, when gold *really* was discovered, and

*South Yuba River*

the residents adopted the much more dignified town name of North Bloomfield.

It wasn't long before the easy-to-find surface gold played out at Malakoff and a more efficient method to extract finer particles was needed. The 1852 invention of hydraulic mining unfortunately fit the bill. Armed with giant, high-pressure nozzles called monitors, miners sprayed water onto the gold-bearing mountainside, causing the soil to give way. The mud was then channeled through sluice boxes that caught the precious gilded metal. It is estimated that during its operation from 1866 to 1884, some 41 million cubic yards of earth was excavated, yielding several million dollars worth of gold and a hefty environmental price tag.

The byproduct of this operation was an enormous amount of muddy water, rock, and debris that had to go somewhere. So, into the area streams they went. Debris dumped into the Yuba River had a devastating effect on riparian environments, raised riverbeds in the Sacramento Valley resulting in massive flooding, and hindered navigation on the Sacramento River. This went on until 1884, when, in a hallmark environmental case, *Woodruff v. The North Bloomfield Gravel Mining Company,* Judge Lorenzo Sawyer issued a permanent injunction against discharging tailings into the Yuba River, effectively bringing an end to the devastation.

Before hitting the trail, explore the visitors center, tour the historic town of North Bloomfield, and wander out to the adjacent mining pit overlook. If you're short on time, a fairly level, 3.5-mile rim trail circles the mine, or you can descend 600 feet along a 3-mile loop into the expansive pit, which looks like a scaled-down version of Utah's Bryce Canyon. Though the scene is eerily beautiful, you can't help but be saddened by the ecological damage that was caused.

From the trailhead, begin a mild descent to a wooden footbridge that crosses a seasonal tributary of Humbug Creek. The channel has a rusty tinge due to the oxidation of iron found in nearby rock deposits. Follow the rivulet downstream before the trail bends south, paralleling Humbug Creek. Douglas firs, black oaks, and dogwoods provide ample shade, and the pine-needle-strewn floor a soft tread. White star flower, wild rose, and an overabundance of poison oak line the trail (oftentimes encroaching on the path). Pass rainwater-filled shafts on your right, and at 0.7 mile a spur trail heads left to the park's "environmental campsites." Join an abandoned dirt road coming in from the right and briefly follow it downhill to its end at a seasonal creek.

After a short ascent, the path resumes its downhill trend, now more steeply. Cross a wooden catwalk near the 1.3-mile mark as Humbug Creek slips and slides between a water-honed slot in the bedrock before leaping into a pool of green water below. The creek offers up a few more watery displays as you pass several unofficial paths bound for small pools that aren't worth the effort. The river is much more inviting and isn't that much farther.

Watch your footing, as a missed step on the single-track trail could send you sliding down the declivitous ravine. Cross a rickety wooden bridge and shimmy across boulders before the grade eases somewhat. One final steep descent drops you onto the South Yuba Trail and a peaceful picnic area on a shady bench overlooking the river at 2.7 miles. Hikers wanting to cool trail-worn toes should turn left (east) and down to a bridge crossing of Humbug Creek. From there, continue 0.3 mile toward South Yuba Primitive Camp where an inviting swimming hole awaits. Linger as long as you like, keeping in mind the elevation you have to regain.

# 4

## Sierra Buttes

*Type: Day hike*

*Season: Mid-June through October*

*Total distance: 5.0 miles round trip*

*Rating: Moderate to strenuous*

*Elevation: 7,006 feet; +1,556 feet/-57 feet*

*Location: Tahoe National Forest*

*Maps: USGS 7.5' Sierra City; USFS Lakes Basin, Sierra Buttes, and Plumas-Eureka State Park*

*Fees and permits: A permit is not required for this day hike.*

*Contact: Tahoe National Forest, Yuba River Ranger District (530-288-3231; www.fs.fed.us/r5/tahoe).*

This popular climb to a fire lookout crowning the jagged Sierra Buttes will get your heart pumping. From atop the lookout at 8,587 feet, the northern Sierra panorama is seemingly endless. Pack along a good topographic map and knock yourself out identifying the peaks and valleys that emanate from this airy perch.

### GETTING THERE

From I-80 in Truckee, drive 22.5 miles north on CA 89 to Sierraville. At the stop sign, turn left onto CA 49 and drive 17.2 miles toward Bassetts. Turn right onto Gold Lake Road (near Bassett's Station) and proceed 1.3 miles to the turnoff for Sardine and Packer Lakes (County Road 621). Turn left over a narrow bridge and drive 0.3 mile to a fork, where you turn right and head toward Packer Lake. Follow paved Packer Lake Road 2.7 miles past several campgrounds to a turnoff for Packer Lake Lodge. Stay left (road designation changes to FS 93) and you'll soon pass Tamarack Lakes Trailhead, where the pavement narrows and steepens considerably as you climb toward Packer Lake Saddle. Remain on FS 93 for 0.4 mile past the saddle and veer left onto unpaved FS Road 93-2. Continue 0.1 mile to the parking area and signed trailhead. There are no facilities at the trailhead.

### THE TRAIL

The Sierra Buttes tower some 5,000 feet above Sierra City, a tiny Gold Rush–era town tucked away in the northern Sierra Nevada. The city was established as a mining town in 1850 and by the late 1800s several mines were operating on or near the buttes. In the winter of 1852, heavy snow coupled with the region's steep slopes sent a wall of snow careening down, wiping out the entire town. It was subsequently relocated to a safer site; however, avalanches continued to plague the area. Despite nature's threat, the mines were producing handsomely and the settlement flourished, reaching a population of 10,000 at its peak. The town is much quieter now with its 225 residents, but the looming specter of Sierra Buttes is still there beckoning you with the promise of stellar panoramas—it doesn't disappoint.

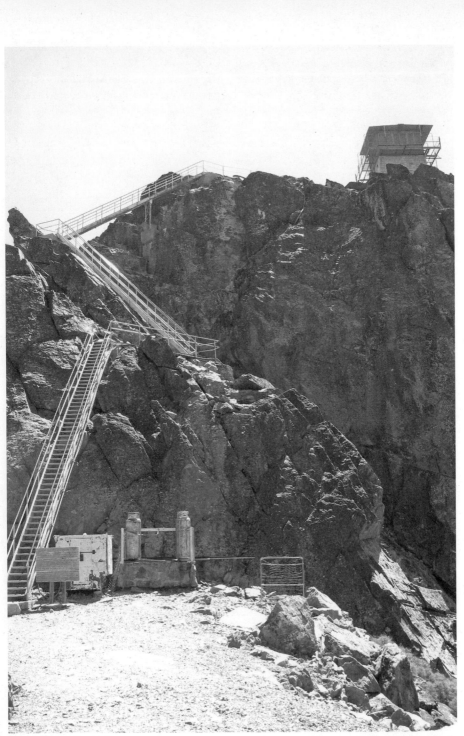

*Sierra Buttes fire lookout*

There are other routes to the top of Sierra Buttes—some longer, some shorter. This path falls somewhere pleasantly in the middle. The Sierra Buttes Trail, which briefly shares the route with the Pacific Crest Trail (PCT), wastes no time. After slipping around a gate, promptly begin a steep ascent up a wide dirt road. At 0.5 mile, abandon the road and veer right onto a single-track trail and catch your breath as you traverse a level ridgeline scattered with Indian paintbrush, arrow-leaved balsam root, and spreading phlox.

Looking closely, spot the fire lookout to the southeast, perched atop the massive mound of rock forming the buttes. Begin plodding uphill again, and at 0.9 mile reach a trail fork. Veer left, leaving the PCT, and a few yards later reach a second junction with the Tamarack Trail rising to meet you on the left. Ambitious hikers looking for a more challenging approach might consider starting from the Tamarack Lakes Trailhead (1.8 miles) or Lower Sardine Lake Trailhead (4.6 miles). The trails converge near Tamarack Lakes before ascending to this junction.

Continuing your southeast course, a moderately steep ascent ensues. The forest thickens and you weave through a field of rather large boulders before emerging onto an open ridge where you spy Young American and Sardine Lakes below, the hulking Sierra Buttes looming larger than ever.

At 1.8 miles, reach a four-wheel-drive parking area. Yes, I said four-wheel-drive parking area. By continuing about 3.75 miles past our trailhead, the fire road deposits you here, where you can easily make the 0.75-mile jaunt to the top. Granted, this would be easier on the knees, but our path is much more scenic and your lungs and legs are getting a workout to boot.

From the parking area you can either ascend via a slippery slope of switchbacks that snake through the forest, or follow the much more pleasingly inclined, though slightly longer, fire road. Sticking with the road, go around a locked gate blocking vehicular traffic and continue uphill. Soon you'll reach the junction where the steep trail joins the road. From where the two meet (easy to miss on the return trip) the trail switchbacks up the rocky road.

As you round a bend, the fire lookout appears, isolated atop a cliff of metamorphic rock whose volcanic origins date back some 350 million years. Soon thereafter you spot the precariously exposed stairway that will take you to it. Nonacrophobes can climb the stairs, installed by the Forest Service in 1964, to the lookout building. While you cannot go inside, you can walk around its vertigo-inducing, windswept balcony, where the views in every direction are stupendous.

# 5

## Round Lake Loop

*Type: Day hike*

*Season: June through October*

*Total distance: 4.0-mile loop*

*Rating: Easy*

*Elevation: 6,608 feet; +470 feet/-470 feet*

*Location: Plumas National Forest, Lakes Basin Recreation Area*

*Maps: USGS 7.5' Gold Lake; USFS Lakes Basin, Sierra Buttes, and Plumas-Eureka State Park*

*Fees and permits: A permit is not required for this day hike.*

*Contact: Plumas National Forest, Beckwourth Ranger District (530-836-2575; www.fs.fed.us/r5/plumas).*

The name of this relatively crowd-free corner of Plumas National Forest—Lakes Basin Recreation Area—should give you a pretty good indication of what you can expect to see here: lakes! This pleasant loop visits five picturesque mountain gems that tempt swimmers on hot summer days and lure anglers to their shores. The undulating trail meanders through meadows, forests, and over ridges, one scene as splendid as the next. A network of trails crisscrosses the area, making it easy to adjust the length of your journey.

### GETTING THERE

From I-80 in Truckee, drive 22.5 miles north on CA 89 to Sierraville. At the stop sign, turn left onto CA 49 and drive 17.2 miles toward Bassetts. Turn right onto Gold Lake Road (near Bassett's Station) and proceed 7.5 miles to the signed turnoff for Round Lake Trail which is just before the Plumas/Sierra county line. Turn left and proceed 150 yards to the trailhead parking area equipped with pit toilets.

### THE TRAIL

From the parking area, follow the wide path, an old mining road, southwest as it skirts behind Gold Lake Lodge. At 0.2 mile, reach a signed fork and bear left toward Round Lake. The path to the right is the return leg of our loop. Western white pines and red firs make up the forest mix while lupine, yampah, and woolly mule ears sprout from sun-drenched grassy clearings.

Breaking out of the forested confines,

you traverse a dry hillside blanketed with pinemat manzanita and at 0.8 mile spot Big Bear Lake down below. The surrounding mountainside sporadically shows itself through the trees and along open sections of trail. Continue southwest past scattered trees and shrubs and a lovely little unnamed pond at 1.2 miles. Pass through a thicket of water birch occupying the southern shore, its characteristic dark bronze bark highlighted by bright green leaves.

Hidden on the other side of the southern ridge is expansive Gold Lake, named by an expedition of Argonauts (a name chosen to describe Gold Rush immigrants after the mythic Greek tale of Jason and the Argonauts, who searched for the Golden Fleece) who were duped by Thomas Stoddard, a colorful character responsible for what came to be known as the Gold Lake Fiasco. As the story goes, Stoddard created

a flurry of excitement in 1850 when he told tales of a lake ringed with gold nuggets and a few weeks later backed up his claim with a sack full of gold. When he started out with a small expedition to rediscover the lake, nearly a thousand others followed. The group traipsed all over the mountainside visiting lakes, none of which was the one he spoke of, and it quickly became apparent that Stoddard was disoriented and confused. Some believed he was trying to hoard the find for himself and still others that it was a hoax (imagine that). The group eventually came to a large body of water, larger than what Stoddard had originally described, and he proclaimed it to be the one. Of course it wasn't, but it was dubbed Gold Lake nonetheless. Though Stoddard's fabled lake continued to lure gold seekers to the region, it was never actually found.

Leave the pond and begin a mild rocky

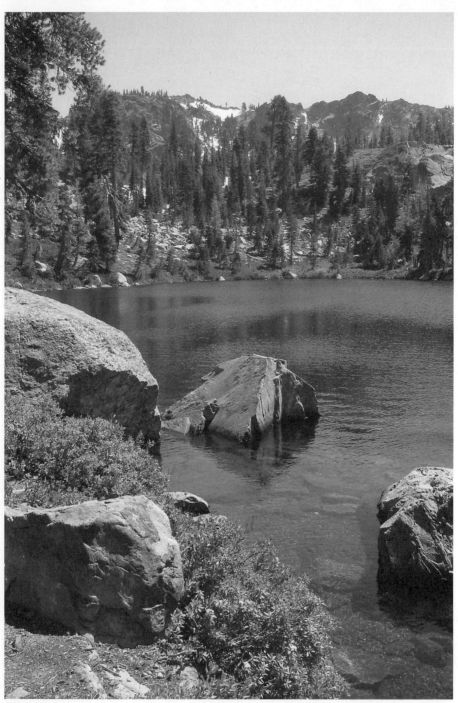

*Silver Lake*

ascent to the high point of our journey, from which you have fantastic views of the surrounding terrain. Mount Elwell, the highest point in the Lakes Basin at 7,818 feet, dominates the northwesterly view, while forested ridges and pine-ringed lakes stretch out at your feet. Descend steeply to a signed junction. Ignore a left-branching trail that ultimately meets up with the Pacific Crest Trail (PCT) and turn right toward Round Lake and the remnants of Round Lake Mine, situated on a ledge above the lake.

After exploring the scattered relics, head downhill to Round Lake's shore. Bound for the outlet, pick your way along the narrow single-track trail as it parallels the brushy southeast shoreline. The cirque lake is beautifully backdropped by a granite headwall that's studded with pines and lingering snow early in the season. Easily rock-hop over the outlet at 1.8 miles and begin a northward traverse over a low ridge that confines the clear water. Past a rather pathetic-looking pond, Silver Lake, arguably more scenic than Round Lake, comes into view. Descend and stroll along its eastern shore before crossing its outlet on steppingstones at 2.3 miles.

Not long after, reach a trail junction and turn right. The left course is bound for the summit of Mount Elwell and the PCT. The trail then makes a sweeping clockwise arc, at about the middle of which you gain a spectacular ridgetop view of Long Lake, the largest on our route, and Mount Elwell rising from its northwest shore. At 2.5 miles, reach another signed intersection and turn right on a downhill course through sun-loving pine-mat manzanita and huckleberry oak.

In quick succession pass Cub (2.7 miles), Little Bear (2.9 miles), and Big Bear Lakes (3.0 miles), all south of the trail and easily accessed via unofficial paths. All popular destinations, Little Bear and Big Bear offer the best swimming, and Big Bear, the deepest of the three, is stocked with rainbow trout.

At 3.3 miles, pass a left-branching trail leading to Long Lake Trailhead and instead veer right, soon crossing Big Bear Lake's outlet via a flattened log. Pause atop the log and look southwest for a fine tree-framed vista toward the headwall of this glacier-carved basin. A brief climb becomes a descent as you continue toward Round Lake Trailhead. Cross a seasonal stream in a grassy gully. From this low, moderately ascend toward the first trail junction and close the loop at 3.8 miles. Then, retrace your steps the final 0.2 mile back to the trailhead.

If you have the luxury of time, Plumas-Eureka State Park, site of Johnsville, an old mining settlement, is just up the road. Replete with Gold Rush–era history and beautiful mountain scenery, it is a worthy destination. There are a museum as well as several historic structures to explore, along with two splendid trails—the Eureka Peak Loop (6.0 miles) and the Grass Lake Trail, which visits a series of lakes (6.5 miles).

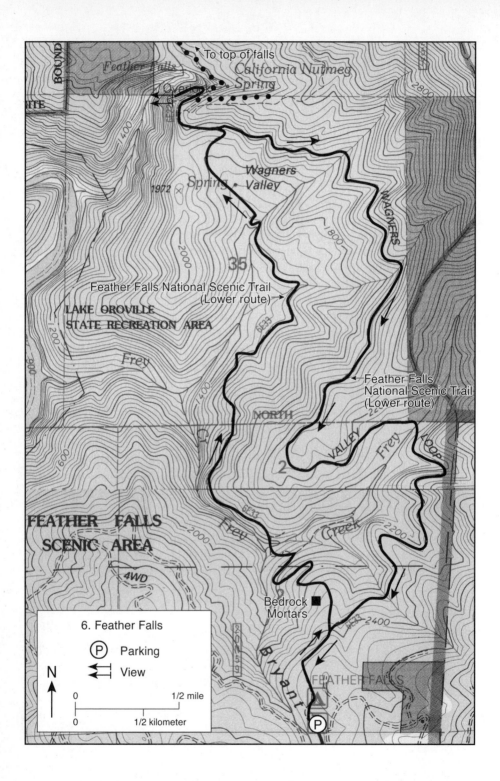

6. Feather Falls

Ⓟ Parking

◁▷ View

N

0            1/2 mile

0         1/2 kilometer

# 6

## Feather Falls

*Type: Day hike*

*Season: Year-round*

*Total distance: 8.4-mile semi-loop*

*Rating: Moderate to strenuous due to some steep sections and the overall elevation change*

*Elevation: 2,474 feet; +2,228 feet/-2,228 feet*

*Location: Plumas National Forest*

*Maps: USGS 7.5' Forbestown, Brush Creek; USFS Plumas National Forest*

*Fees and permits: A permit is not required for this day hike.*

*Contact: Plumas National Forest, Feather River Ranger District (530-534-6500; www.fs.fed.us/r5/plumas).*

This pleasant hike through the Sierra Nevada foothills leads to a spectacular overlook across from plummeting Feather Falls, the sixth highest waterfall in the continental United States, and the fourth highest in California. This hike can be done year-round, however spring affords the most dramatic water and wildflower displays, and fall is a medley of color as green summer foliage is transformed into an autumnal palette of reds, golds, and oranges. The trail, though well-shaded, can get uncomfortably hot in the summer and has some steep sections that will give your legs and lungs a workout.

### GETTING THERE

From CA 70 in Oroville, exit onto CA 162 (Oro Dam Boulevard). Proceed east 1.6 miles and turn right onto Olive Highway. Drive 6.4 miles and turn right onto Forbestown Road (a sign here directs you to Feather Falls). Continue another 6 miles and turn left onto Lumpkin Road and follow it for 10.6 miles. Turn left onto Forest Road 21N35Y just before reaching the town of Feather Falls. Continue along this paved but narrow and bumpy road for 1.5 miles to the trailhead, where you will find ample parking and pit toilets.

### THE TRAIL

Feather Falls is located within the 15,000-acre Feather Falls Scenic Area in the northern Sierra Nevada foothills. The scenic area encompasses the Middle Fork of the Feather River—one of the first eight rivers in the nation to be designated a Wild and

Scenic River—and three of its tributaries: Fall River, Little North Fork, and South Branch.

Walk to the northern end of the parking area, where an information placard marks the start of the trail. Enjoy the shade of bigleaf maple, ponderosa pine, pacific madrone, and black oaks along this fairly level segment and arrive at a trail fork at 0.4 mile. Both routes culminate at Feather Falls, so you can't make a wrong choice. The catch is that bearing left (lower route) gets you there faster (3.6 miles), but is more difficult due to a steeper gradient. Bearing right (upper route) makes the trip to the falls much more gradually, but is longer (4.5 miles). The trails join again just before the final 0.5-mile climb to the Feather Falls overlook. Enjoy both routes by taking the shorter trail down to the falls, and the longer but easier trail on the way out for a rewarding loop.

Bear left at the junction and under the mixed conifer forest begin descending Bald Rock Canyon. Receiving around 60 inches of rain per year, the area is cool and moist and plays host to a variety of plant and animal species. Spring brings a colorful bounty of wildflowers like Indian pinks, sticky monkey flower, and red ribbons. Poison oak thrives along much of the trail, so be mindful of its presence. While we're being mindful, also note that rattlesnakes, bloodthirsty mosquitoes and ticks, and mountain lions thrive here too.

Not long after the fork you come to another junction with a short cutoff trail. Bear left and climb a small hill to view bedrock mortars created by the Maidu people, who inhabited this region hundreds of years ago. The Maidu, also known as Foothill Konkow, lived in village communities and practiced a mixed gathering, hunting, and fishing economy. They were incredibly knowledgeable about the distribution and usefulness of plants in their territory. Conscious of harvest times, families would move into areas to gather seasonal foods like greens, tubers and roots, berries, nuts, and seeds, the most important being acorns. They were amassed, dried, and stored for winter use. The bowl-shaped depressions in the bedrock were used by the Konkow to grind acorns and other nuts.

Life for the Konkow changed drastically with colonization. The Gold Rush of 1849, which lured thousands of prospectors to the Feather River and surrounding hills in search of their fortune, was particularly devastating. The miners brought disease, destroyed landscapes with mining techniques, and drove the Konkow people off their land in violent confrontations.

After exploring the mortars, continue along the cutoff to rejoin the main trail. As you approach the first Frey Creek crossing at 1.0 mile, listen for the unmistakable clicking noise of bark beetles and note the appearance of willows, alders, and ferns, which are so characteristic of riparian habitats. One of our most important and most neglected natural resources, they provide food, nesting habitat, cover, and migration corridors for a multitude of birds, reptiles, mammals, invertebrates, and amphibians. Between November and March, the riparian area around Frey Creek becomes a hibernating ground for millions of ladybugs. The vegetation along the trail becomes covered with them until spring, when they take flight and return to the valley floor to feed.

Cross the creek via a wooden footbridge and continue downstream along the east bank for another 0.5 mile before arriving at an unobstructed view of Bald Rock Dome looming ominously 2,000 feet above the Middle Fork of the Feather River. Bald Rock Dome is part of a 2-mile-wide pluton of granite that formed deep below the earth's surface. As it cooled, part of its coarse-grained

*Feather Falls*

granitic rocks became very resistant to weathering, while other parts were highly susceptible to erosion. Over time, powerful erosional processes (wind, water, etc.) removed the weaker rock, exposing the granitic dome we see today. These same processes are responsible for the formation of Feather Falls. The rocks surrounding the falls are very resistant to erosion as compared with the rocks in the canyon downstream. Over millions of years as the Fall River chose its path of least resistance, the weaker rocks were worn away and Feather Falls took shape.

Continue along the shady trail past several seasonal stream crossings and rejoin the upper trail we take on the return at 3.1 miles. From this junction, the trail switchbacks up a rocky, sunny segment dominated by species of vegetation that thrive in drier areas. As you continue on, catch glimpses of the falls through the manzanita- and oak-covered hillside as you follow a steel handrail 0.2 mile farther to a trail junction. Bear left and continue 0.1 mile down to a precipitous wood observation deck directly across from the falls. From your perch watch the Fall River plunge 640 feet over a sheer granite ledge to the canyon floor in its rush to meet the Middle Fork of the Feather River and Lake Oroville.

Behind you, there is an equally impressive view of the forested slopes of Bald Rock Canyon and the river coursing below.

When you've had your fill, leave the overlook along the same trail and, if you can muster the energy, turn left at the first trail junction and hike 0.25 mile to the granite precipice atop the falls—hardly the best vantage, but a fun side trip nonetheless. Be cautious maneuvering on wet rocks around the top of the falls, as they can be slick and dangerous. Though the water is inviting, keep in mind the deadly drop. Safer swimming holes are found farther upstream and are the perfect energizer for the return trek.

Make your way back to the trail fork 0.5 mile from the overlook, but instead of returning the way you came, turn left and take the longer but less steep upper trail. This trail runs somewhat parallel to, but above, the previous trail. You will see many of the same sights and cross the same creeks and seasonal drainages, but from higher up on the canyon wall. The gentle trail gradient and shade-casting canopy make the uphill back to your car seem, well, almost effortless. When you reach the junction with the lower trail, bear left and retrace your steps back to the trailhead.

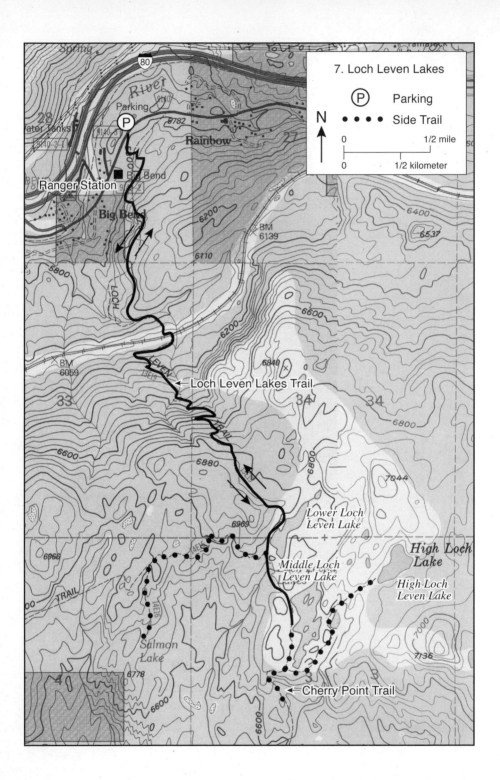

7. Loch Leven Lakes

Ⓟ  Parking

••••  Side Trail

N

0 _____ 1/2 mile

0 _____ 1/2 kilometer

Spring

River

80

Parking

Ⓟ

8782

Rainbow

28

Water Tanks

Big Bend

Ranger Station

Big Bend

6200

BM
6139

6400

6537

6110

5800

6600

LOCH

6200

BM
6059

LEVEN

13E19

← Loch Leven Lakes Trail

33

34

34

6800

TRAIL

6840

6800

6600

6880

7044

6969

Lower Loch
Leven Lake

6966

14E15

6800

High Loch
Lake

TRAIL

14E16

Middle Loch
Leven Lake

High Loch
Leven Lake

7000

Salmon
Lake

6778

7136

6600

← Cherry Point Trail

6600

# 7

## Loch Leven Lakes

*Type: Day hike*

*Season: June through October*

*Total distance: 6.0 miles round trip*

*Rating: Moderate*

*Elevation: 5,805 feet; +1,199 feet/-223 feet*

*Location: Tahoe National Forest*

*Maps: USGS 7.5' Cisco Grove, Soda Springs (route not correctly depicted); USFS Tahoe National Forest*

*Fees and permits: A permit is not required for this day hike.*

*Contact: Tahoe National Forest, Big Bend Ranger District (530-426-3609; www.fs.fed.us/r5/tahoe).*

Craving a dose of nature, but don't want to wander too far off the beaten path? This moderately challenging jaunt to Loch Leven Lakes just might be the ticket. Initially, it may not be the most pristine natural setting, as you have to contend with the hum of the all-too-near interstate, but once you slip over a ridge and deeper into the forest, all that becomes a distant memory and you are transported into more peaceful environs with a collection of fantastic glacially carved lakes to explore.

### GETTING THERE

From Truckee, drive 19 miles west on I-80 to the Big Bend/Rainbow Road exit (#168). At the end of the ramp, turn left onto Rainbow Road and proceed under the freeway. Drive 1 mile to the parking area with pit toilets. (The Big Bend Ranger Station is 0.2 mile farther.) Find the signed trailhead on the south side of the road opposite the parking area.

### THE TRAIL

From the trailhead, begin ascending a rocky, sun-drenched path that snakes through boulders and along granite slabs. Cairns (aka ducks or rock piles), the navigational beacons of the backcountry, guide you along sections where the trail is faint. The terrain is littered with huckleberry oak and dotted with occasional pines. The freeway noise can be a bit unnerving—however, press on; the roar eventually becomes a purr and later disappears altogether.

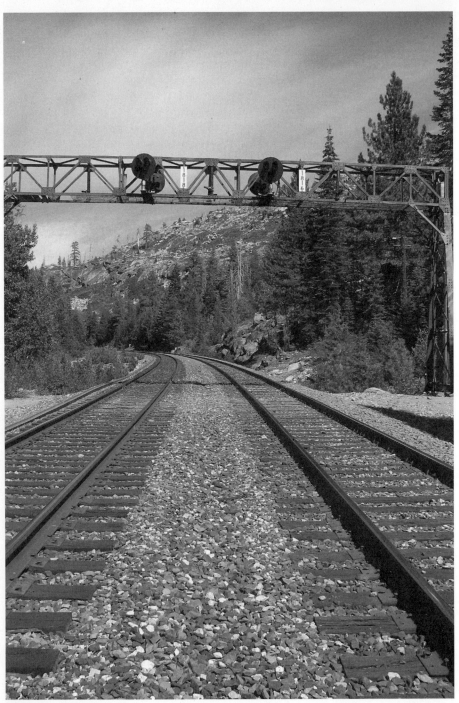

*Union Pacific Railroad*

A short descent takes you into a shady pocket size stand of lodgepole pines. Your brief forest stroll comes to an abrupt end and you ascend the boulder-strewn landscape once again. Reach a murky, grass-filled pond at 0.6 mile. Near the middle point of the pond there is a not-so-obvious trail fork. At the point where the trail descends to the shore, another path veers right and up some boulders (look for a tree root wedged between the rocks and a cairn up above). Either path is fine, as they reconvene a short while later.

Past the pond, spot the railroad cutting a path across the forested slope to the south. Begin a descent and at 1.0 mile cross a dogwood-lined creek via a wooden footbridge and follow it upstream through a somewhat overgrown area colored with leafy daisy and giant hyssop. Quickly reach a double set of railroad tracks and its accompanying signal lights.

This historically significant set of rails is on the original 1860s route of the Central Pacific Railroad—the western leg of the first transcontinental railroad. While the original rail has long since been replaced, and the roadbed upgraded and repaired, the lines remarkably run on top of the original, handmade grade. This unprecedented engineering feat opened a vital link for trade, commerce, and travel, but was also a portentous milestone of progress that hastened the closing of the American frontier and ultimately proved devastating to the country's Native American population.

Six years after the groundbreaking, laborers of the Central Pacific Railroad working from the west and the Union Pacific Railroad working from the east met at Promontory Summit, Utah. It was here in May 1869 that Leland Stanford drove the "golden spike" that symbolized the completion of the transcontinental railroad (which at the time actually connected Omaha and Sacramento).

Looking both ways, cross the tracks, and pick up the trail on the opposite side. Bending west at first, the trail eventually resumes it southward tack through a shady mixed conifer forest, and over the ensuing 1.2 miles you ascend 750 vertical feet over a rocky, root-laden path that takes some careful footwork and can be slow going at times.

Cresting a ridge, the gradient significantly eases and you meander through a thinning forest. At 2.5 miles, spot Lower Loch Leven Lake below and descend steeply to its western shore. From here, the trail parallels a bedrock ridge before coming to a right-branching trail at 2.7 miles bound for Salmon Lake. If you are spending the whole day in the area, the 0.9-mile jaunt to Salmon Lake is a worthy side trip—however, only after you've explored the more aesthetically pleasing Loch Leven Lakes and have energy to spare.

From the junction with the Salmon Lake Trail, you soon cross Lower Loch Leven Lake's outlet. Pass through a notch in a low ridge and reach Middle Loch Leven Lake at the 3-mile mark. Take a well-deserved rest atop one of the surrounding granite slabs that form the lake's margins (also perfect for sunbathing after a quick dip). This is our turnaround point, although more ambitious hikers can continue on to High Loch Leven Lake, found 0.8 mile farther at the terminus of the trail.

8. Mount Judah Loop

P   Parking

• • • •   Side Trail

N   View

0                                    1/2 mile

0                          1/2 kilometer

# 8

## Mount Judah Loop

*Type: Day hike*

*Season: July to October*

*Total distance: 5-mile semi-loop*

*Rating: Moderate*

*Elevation: 7,054 feet; +1,445 feet/-1,445 feet*

*Location: Tahoe National Forest*

*Maps: USGS 7.5' Norden; Trails Illustrated Lake Tahoe Basin No. 803*

*Fees and permits: A permit is not required for this day hike.*

*Contact: Tahoe National Forest, Truckee Ranger District (530-587-3558; www.fs.fed.us/r5/tahoe).*

Following portions of the Pacific Crest Trail, this relatively easy jaunt to the peak of Mount Judah rewards hikers with commanding views of the rugged Sierra crest north of Lake Tahoe. The trail is easily accessible from I-80, and the crowded parking area is a testament to its popularity. Though the solitude factor is low, the arresting views, pioneering history, and palette of vibrant wildflowers more than make up for its lack of seclusion. Be sure to carry a windbreaker, plenty of water, and a good map so you can match names with peaks from your panoramic perch.

### GETTING THERE

From I-80 west of Truckee, exit Donner Pass Road (Old Hwy 40) and travel west 6.7 miles toward Donner Pass (along the way you will pass Donner Memorial State Park). Just past Donner Summit Bridge, turn left (south) onto an unnamed dirt road next to Sugar Bowl Academy (look for the small Pacific Crest Trail placard). Proceed 0.1 mile to the trailhead on your left. Parking is available along the narrow road.

### THE TRAIL

This hike is set just south of Donner Pass, named for the hapless party of California-bound American migrants who became stranded here in the winter of 1846–47, just short of their destination. Filled with fabulous stories of the wonders of California and eager to make new lives for themselves, countless wagon trains made the arduous pilgrimage west. The Donner Party's journey started out just like any other, but in Wyoming, a careless decision to follow a shortcut, which turned out to be not so short, and winter's early arrival set the stage for one of the most tragic sagas of westward migration. By the time the party reached Donner Lake, there was snow covering the ground. Six miles farther along, they became snowbound at Alder Creek. In the end, nearly half the party died, and some resorted to cannibalism in an effort to survive. Just east of our hike along I-80, and well worth the visit, is Donner Memorial State Park. The base of the park's monument stands 22 feet high, the depth of the snow that trapped the ill-fated migrants.

From the trailhead, join the Pacific Crest Trail (PCT) as it heads south through a short swath of moisture-loving vegetation before steeply ascending a granitic headwall via a series of rocky switchbacks. Soon views of the Summit Valley unfold to the west. Lake Mary is directly below you, and the remnants of former Lake Van Norden, now a lush meadow, can be seen in the distance. To the south, Mount Lincoln, Mount Disney, and Crows Nest dominate the landscape with their ski-run-scarred slopes. As you continue ascending, watch for phlox spilling from the rocky crevasses and violet lupine decorating the trail.

Leave the views and boulder-strewn trail behind for the moment as you traverse the now predominantly dirt trail through a shady stand of verdant firs before emerging onto an open ski run. At 0.9 mile, reach the northern junction with the Mount Judah Loop trail. Veer left, leaving the PCT, and climb through slopes seasonally carpeted with fuzzy mule ears, Indian paintbrush, penstemon, and groundsel.

The path soon levels off, and you reach a spur trail that extends approximately 200 yards to a rocky promontory with northward views of Lake Angela and Castle Peak, the highest summit in the Donner Pass area. Return to the Mount Judah Trail and after a short distance join an old 4x4 route as you climb gently eastward to a saddle below Donner Peak (8,019 feet). A spur trail takes you to the base of the exfoliating pinnacle, and though reaching the top looks easy, you need basic rock climbing skills to scramble up the easiest summit. Though the views atop Donner Peak are vastly better than those from the rocky promontory we just left, the best views are yet to come.

From the saddle, begin switchbacking up through the thinning mixed conifer forest along the eastern slope of Mount Judah. After approximately 0.7 mile, you reach a saddle between Mount Judah's higher southern summit and its slightly lower northern summit. A short trail leads to the northern summit, but we continue to Mount Judah's true summit just ahead. Follow the exposed ridge, dotted with pink broad-stemmed onion in the early summer, to the barren apex 2.4 miles from the trailhead.

The mountain was named for Theodore Judah, architect of the transcontinental railroad and first chief engineer of the Central Pacific Railroad. Though not a part of Judah's original route, in the mid-1920s a nearly 2-mile-long tunnel was blasted beneath Mount Judah in an effort to ease the grade for locomotives making the trans-Sierra trek. From the summit, if you're lucky, you might be able to watch a train go into the tunnel underneath Mount Judah and emerge on the other side.

From the top of Mount Judah (8,243 feet), the surrounding landscape comes into full view. Donner Lake and the Martis Valley stretch eastward; Anderson Peak and Tinker Knob rise to the south; the now familiar Summit Valley stretches westward; and to

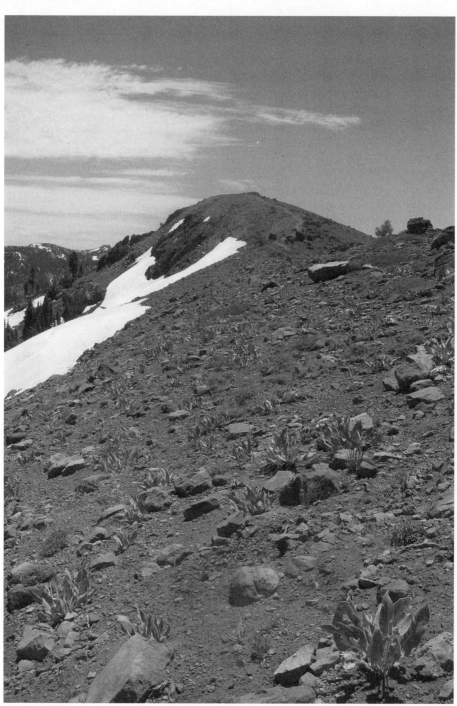

*Mount Judah*

the north, imposing Mount Lola and Red Mountain reach toward the sky.

After taking a break and soaking in the view, begin a southwestward, switchbacking descent into a forest of hemlock and, later, firs. At 3.2 miles, reach Mount Judah Loop's southerly junction with the PCT. Veer left (south) for approximately 150 yards to visit Roller Pass, a saddle between Coldstream Valley to the east and Summit Valley to the west, where the Overland Emigrant Trail crossed the Sierra. It is here that emigrants used log rollers to winch wagons up the eastern slope too steep for harnessed oxen to negotiate. Take the short path to the brink to get a better understanding of what the early pioneers faced as they traversed this roadless, rugged range.

Return to the trail junction and continue descending via the PCT. Approximately 0.8 mile past the junction, emerge from the red fir forest onto an open ski run. Cross a 4x4 road and pick up the single-track trail, arriving at the northern junction of the Mount Judah Loop Trail shortly thereafter. From here, retrace your steps back to the trailhead.

# 9

## Rubicon Trail

*Type: Day hike*

*Season: Late May through September*

*Total distance: 5.4 miles one way*

*Rating: Easy*

*Elevation: 6,333 feet; +765 feet/-511 feet*

*Location: D. L. Bliss and Emerald Bay State Parks*

*Maps: USGS 7.5' Emerald Bay; Trails Illustrated Lake Tahoe Basin No. 803*

*Fees and permits: A permit is not required for this day hike. D. L. Bliss State Park charges a $6 day-use fee (per vehicle). Parking in the Vikingsholm lot at Emerald Bay State Park is free.*

*Contact: D. L. Bliss State Park (530-525-7277; www.parks.ca.gov/default.asp?page_id=505); Emerald Bay State Park (530-541-3030; www.parks.ca.gov/default.asp?page_id=506).*

Though the majority of the 72 miles of shoreline surrounding Lake Tahoe is privately owned, you can find a little slice of heaven within D. L. Bliss and Emerald Bay State Parks, located on the southwestern shore. The Rubicon Trail traverses the adjoining parks and has some of the most splendid views of the lake's cerulean waters and pine-shrouded shoreline. The gentle trail begins near Calawee Cove in D. L. Bliss State Park and culminates at Vikingsholm, an historic Scandinavian mansion, in Emerald Bay State Park.

Since this is a point-to-point hike, you need to arrange for someone to drop you off and pick you up, have two vehicles to shuttle between trailheads, or plan to walk back to where you parked your vehicle. This is one of the easier hikes in the Tahoe Basin, and since its entirety is loaded with tantalizing sights, sounds, and smells, you can walk the trail for as long or as short as you like.

### GETTING THERE

From South Lake Tahoe, head north 10.4 miles on CA 89 from its junction with US 50 (the South Lake Tahoe Y) and turn right into D. L. Bliss State Park. Proceed 1 mile, passing the visitors center, to the entrance station where you pay a day-use fee ($6). Continue 0.6 mile along a paved, narrow road, passing alternate trailheads for Lighthouse and Rubicon Trail on your right. At the stop sign, turn right, following the signs to Rubicon Trail. The trailhead parking lot, with restrooms, is 0.6 mile farther.

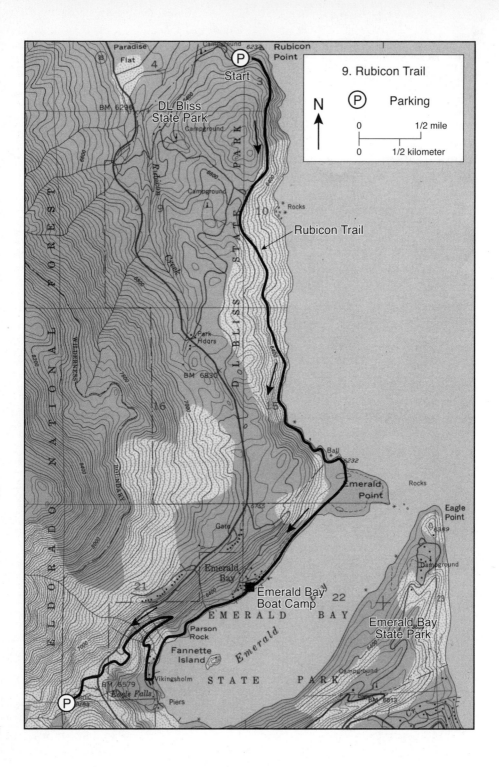

**9. Rubicon Trail**

N

Ⓟ  Parking

0            1/2 mile
0            1/2 kilometer

Paradise Flat

4

Campground

Rubicon Point

Ⓟ Start

DL Bliss State Park

BM 6296

Campground

Campground

10

Rocks

Rubicon Trail

Park Hdqrs

BM 6830

16

15

Ball

Emerald Point

Rocks

Eagle Point

Gate

Campground

21

Emerald Bay

Emerald Bay Boat Camp

22

EMERALD    BAY

23

Emerald Bay State Park

Parson Rock

Fannette Island

Emerald

STATE        PARK

Campground

Vikingsholm

BM 6579

Eagle Falls

Piers

BM 6813

Ⓟ

## THE TRAIL

Lake Tahoe straddles the border between California and Nevada and bejewels the Sierra crest with its sapphire-colored water. The Tahoe Basin, in which it lies, was formed some five million years ago during a very active mountain building period. Two parallel blocks thrust upward, one on the west (Sierra Nevada), another to the east (Carson Range). Between these, a smaller block slipped down, creating a deep, steep-sided valley, which opened to the north. The open north end allowed drainage until several volcanic eruptions filled the outlet with lava and mudflows, damming the valley. Over time, snowmelt, rain, and runoff filled the basin. Glaciers would later help shape the lake's western slopes, most notably Emerald Bay and Fallen Leaf Lake, into the landscape we see today. Although many streams flow into Lake Tahoe, the lake is drained only by the Truckee River, which flows northeast through Reno and into Nevada's Pyramid Lake, which has no outlet.

After some justifiable ogling at Tahoe's expanse of brilliant blue water, head for the signed trailhead at the far end of the parking lot. The trail follows the shoreline; however, you remain high above the water for the first half of the trip. A few steps along the trail, come to the right-branching Lighthouse Trail, which climbs a small ridge to the remains of the Rubicon Point Lighthouse. The neglected beacon, which looks more like an outhouse, was a short-lived endeavor of the early 1900s. It does, however, carry the distinction of being located at the highest elevation (6,300 feet) of any lighthouse in the United States. Stay straight here and enjoy the heavenly views as you travel a well-defined path bordered by manzanita and fragrant tobacco brush.

Continue along the backside of Rubicon Point, where you find several small unofficial trails that descend to its base. From Rubicon Point, on a calm day, you can peer a remarkable 70 feet down into Tahoe's crystal clear water.

The pine- and boulder-studded path then begins ascending to a precipitous granite bluff, where a protective chain railing has been installed. Look for an osprey nest in the top of a dead tree along this section, and if you're lucky spy the predators hunting for fish by plunging into the water and grabbing them with their sharp talons.

At approximately 0.4 mile, glimpse the old lighthouse perched on the cliff above, and after a short distance arrive at a second junction leading 0.2 mile to the lighthouse itself. Back on Rubicon Trail, continue the gentle ascent, reaching a wood-railed overlook with fantastic views of Mount Tallac and the Nevada shore. At 1 mile, an unsigned lateral takes you to the alternate roadside trailheads you drove past on the way in. Bear left and enter a viewless forest and eventually begin a 1-mile descent to Tahoe's rocky shoreline. Just past the halfway point of the descent, pass another wood-railed viewpoint. In my opinion, this sunny section of trail has some of the best vantages of the rugged western shore as it stretches toward Emerald Point.

Climb again to a tumbling streamlet shrouded with thimbleberry and American dogwood. Past the creek, the climb continues before you descend some rocky stairs and finally arrive at a small sandy beach near the northern end of Emerald Point, an ideal resting spot and a chance to take a chilly swim. From the beach, a less-used trail follows the shore around Emerald Point, eventually rejoining the main trail approximately 0.5 mile farther, on the southern end of the point. The main trail, also called the Bypass Trail, turns inland and enters a forest of incense cedar, Jeffrey pines, white fir, and

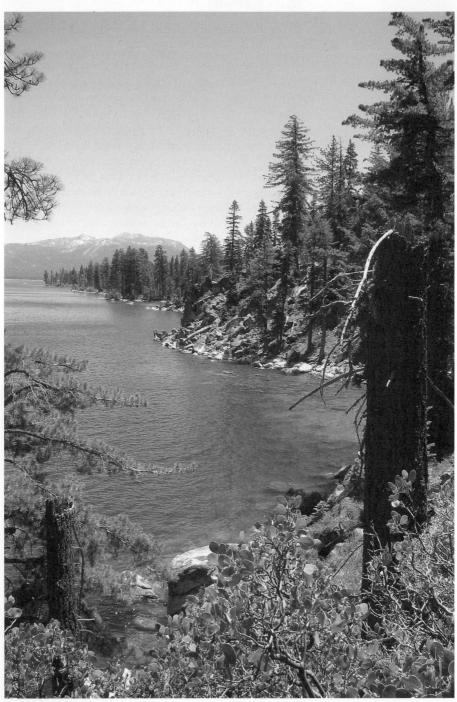

*Lake Tahoe shoreline*

sugar pines before emerging along the shore once again.

The path is mostly rocky, and several un-official trails lead down to the water's edge as you meander southwest along the level trail lined with purple lupine and bracken ferns. An obvious swath of denuded hillside at the far end of Emerald Bay marks the site of a 1955 landslide triggered during the con-struction of CA 89 across a steep, unstable slope.

The path widens as you come into Emer-ald Bay Boat Camp. At 3.6 miles, veer left on an asphalt road, passing the pier, and picking up the dirt trail on your left a short while later. Follow the trail markers through the camp-ground, crossing several raised walkways before you unfortunately trade the peaceful trail for the bustling area around Vikingsholm.

At a trail fork, go left to reach the beach, where you will find that most visitors lounge on the sand, as the water rarely gets warmer than the mid-60s even in the hottest weather. Or, stay left and proceed to Vikingsholm, a historic Scandinavian mansion and summer retreat of wealthy heiress Lora J. Knight. Completed in 1929, the house is fashioned after 11th-century castles found in the fjords of Norway. Hand-hewn timbers were used to construct the home, and granite for the foundation and walls was quarried from be-hind the house. Intricate carvings and an-tique furnishings fill rooms that overlook solitary Fannette Island and the azure wa-ters of Emerald Bay. Seasonal guided tours of Vikingsholm are available for a nominal fee (purchase tickets at the visitors center).

You can also explore Eagle Falls, an ex-cellent side trip, once you have reached Emerald Bay. To reach the trailhead, continue south along the paved path past Vikingsholm following signs to Eagle Falls Trail. Join the trail adjacent to the visitors center and pro-ceed 0.2 mile northwest along an easy path to the base of Eagle Falls. The brink of the falls is also visible from the parking area ad-jacent to CA 89.

When ready, assuming you have ar-ranged a car shuttle, head north on the paved pathway behind Vikingsholm that leads to the parking area along CA 89. The asphalt turns to dirt and you climb 360 ver-tical feet along a gravel roadbed via long switchbacks.

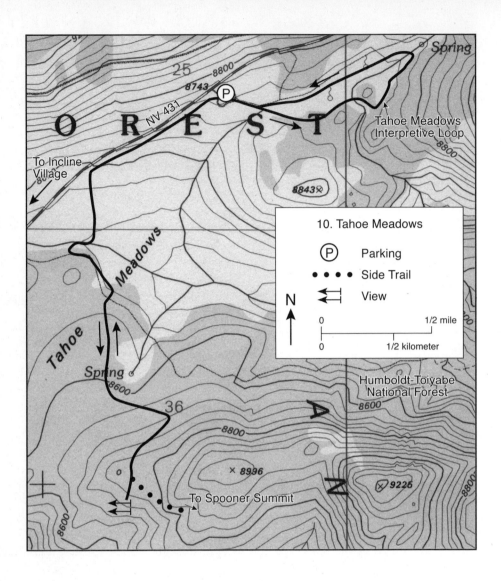

# 10

## Tahoe Meadows

*Type: Day hike*

*Season: Late June through September*

*Total distance: 1.3-mile loop/3.4 miles round trip*

*Rating: Easy/easy*

*Elevation: 8,711 feet; +74 feet/-74 feet (interpretive loop)/8,726 feet; +286 feet/- 247 feet (vista point)*

*Location: Humboldt-Toiyabe National Forest*

*Maps: USGS 7.5' Mount Rose (trail not shown); Trails Illustrated Tahoe Basin No. 803*

*Fees and permits: A permit is not required for this day hike.*

*Contact: Humboldt-Toiyabe National Forest, Carson Ranger District (775-882-2766; www.fs.fed.us/r4/htnf).*

Beneath the shadow of Mount Rose, this handicapped-accessible interpretive loop meanders around the edge of lush Tahoe Meadows. In early summer as the region emerges from its winter coat of snow, the meadow comes alive with birds, butterflies, and elegant wildflowers that add splashes of indigo, fuchsia, and lavender to the carpet of slender grasses. Placards along the trail educate you about the natural and human history of the area. Extend your visit by striking out on the Tahoe Rim Trail to an overlook high above the lake's northeast shore.

### GETTING THERE

From US 80 in Truckee, exit at CA 267 (North Shore Blvd.) and drive 12 miles south toward Kings Beach. Turn left onto CA 28 and continue 4.5 miles to Incline Village (you will cross the state line and be in Nevada). At NV 431, turn left and proceed 7.1 miles to Tahoe Meadows. Turn right at the sign and enter the paved parking area, where you will find pit toilets. Parking can be at a premium on summer weekends, so come early or during the week if possible.

### THE TRAIL

There are two trailheads served by this parking lot, the interpretive loop at the northern end and the Tahoe Rim Trail (TRT) at the southern end. Below you will find an option to extend your visit to this region by hiking to an overlook along the TRT, but first, let's start with the interpretive trail.

Leaving the parking area, you may hear

some traffic noise from the nearby highway, but it quickly dissipates and you are soon serenaded by bird songs and trickling water as you ramble past giant granite boulders and beneath towering pines. Bear right at the first of several raised footbridges as you circumnavigate the meadow in a counter-clockwise direction.

Watch for Clark's nutcrackers, mountain bluebirds, and Steller's jays foraging on the plethora of insects, nuts, and seeds found in the meadow. The forest surrounding the

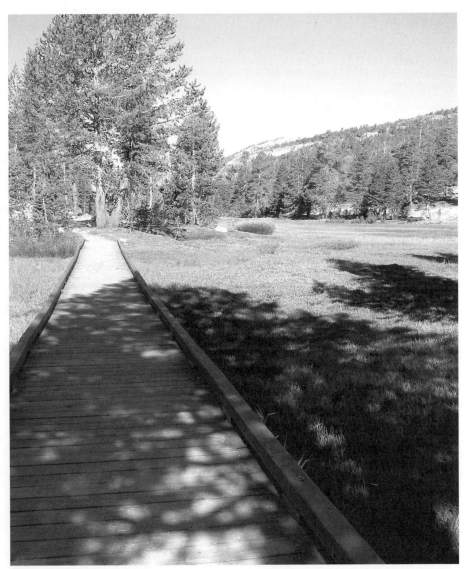

*Tahoe Meadows interpretive loop*

grassy clearing provides cover for these birds and other species that thrive here. You may even spy a red-tailed hawk circling above, its keen eyes probing the meadow floor for a scrumptious meal scurrying about.

Generally, in mid-July the meadow is brimming with delicate wildflowers with fanciful names like elephant head, alpine shooting star, water plantain buttercup, pussy paw, and monkey flower. At the northern end of the loop, cross a rivulet that drains into the meadow and come to a junction leading to a vista point. The vista is now obscured by overgrown trees, and you have much better vantages of the meadow along the main trail. Just past the vista point junction, turn left onto the TRT heading southwest, and lose your shady canopy as you stroll back to the start of the loop and the parking area.

If the interpretive loop got the blood flowing and you want to do a short climb to a picturesque viewpoint, head to the south end of the parking lot and pick up the well-signed Tahoe Rim Trail. Completed in 2001, the 164-mile TRT encircles sapphire-hued Lake Tahoe, a sparkling subalpine Sierra gem. The long-distance loop meanders through wildflower-choked meadows, traverses deep canyons and exposed ridges, passes rushing streams and pristine alpine lakes, and includes some of the most stunning panoramas around.

The TRT passes through two states, six counties, one state park, three National Forests, and three natural wilderness areas. The trail is open to bikers, hikers, and equestrians, but closed to motorized vehicles. Some sections of the trail do not allow biking, or allow it only on even-numbered days.

The TRT Tahoe Meadows Trailhead, at the south end of the parking area opposite the interpretive loop, is the southbound jumping-off point for the Tahoe Meadows to Spooner Summit section of the TRT, which is 23.1 miles long. Even though we venture only 1.7 of those miles, you get a fine sampling of the many treasures waiting along this extensive loop.

The single-track trail parallels the highway as it descends from the parking area into the lower portion of the meadow. Stay on the trail and avoid trampling the fragile vegetation. The trail bends south, away from the road, into the heart of the meadow and crosses Ophir Creek at 0.7 mile. Just past the burbling year-round stream, the path widens and you enter the mixed conifer forest that forms the distinct meadow perimeter. The intoxicating pine scent, both sweet and pungent at the same time, will no doubt envelop you. Soon you'll come to a T-intersection. Turning right takes you to an alternate roadside trailhead along NV 431. We proceed left, following the blue arrows, which mark the entire TRT.

Through this section, the subalpine forest is relatively open, with majestic firs, stout pines, and nodding hemlocks all coexisting. Stay right at the fork with Ophir Creek Trail, which takes you to Price Lakes and eventually Davis Creek County Park. Begin a gentle climb south and, 1.6 miles from the trailhead, reach a saddle where you get your first views of Lake Tahoe. A short spur trail to your right meanders out to a vista point where you can fully appreciate the scene. From 2,400 feet above the lake, the towering peaks that flank the western shore seem to jut from the serene water like a fortress wall protecting the crown jewel.

From this point, continue south along the TRT for as long as you like, but remember that what goes up must come down. Eventually you'll need to turn around and retrace your steps back to the trailhead.

# 11

## Crag Lake

*Type: Day hike or overnight*

*Season: Late June through October*

*Total distance: 10 miles round trip*

*Rating: Moderate*

*Elevation: 6,230 feet; +1,290 feet/-27 feet*

*Location: Eldorado National Forest, Desolation Wilderness*

*Maps: USGS 7.5' Meeks Bay, Homewood, Rockbound Valley; Trails Illustrated Lake Tahoe Basin No. 803*

*Fees and permits: A free permit is required for this day hike and can be obtained by self-registering at the trailhead kiosk. Overnight users must obtain a wilderness permit (fee) from Eldorado National Forest.*

*Contact: Lake Tahoe Basin Management Unit (530-543-2600; www.fs.fed.us/ r5/ltbmu); Eldorado National Forest, Pacific Ranger District (530-644-2349; www.fs.fed.us/r5/eldorado); Lake Tahoe Visitor Center (530-543-2674).*

This hike along the beginnings of the Tahoe-Yosemite Trail follows Meeks Creek upstream to a delightful string of lakes. The trail can get busy on summer weekends, but relatively speaking, it is much less crowded than other south shore trails leading into Desolation Wilderness and beyond. Though the second lake in the chain is our turn-around point, there are five more to explore before you reach Phipps Pass—any of which makes a fine destination for a longer day trip or overnight jaunt.

### GETTING THERE
From Tahoe City, head south 10.6 miles on CA 89 from its junction with CA 28. The trailhead is on the right just past Meeks Bay Resort. Parking can be found along the highway. From South Lake Tahoe, head north 16.5 miles on CA 89 from its junction with US 50 (the South Lake Tahoe Y) and find the trailhead on your left, just past Meeks Bay Campground. Fill out your permit at the information board before starting out.

### THE TRAIL
The 186-mile Tahoe-Yosemite Trail (TYT) connects Meeks Bay on the western shore of Lake Tahoe to Tuolumne Meadows in Yosemite National Park. Though it's not officially recognized and lacks the notoriety of other long-distance trails, the TYT gives those wanting to test the thru-hiker waters a shorter option than the much lengthier Pacific Crest Trail (PCT). Incidentally, about one-third of the TYT coincides with the PCT.

To begin, go around a locked gate and

11. Crag Lake

Ⓟ  Parking

••• Side Trail

N ↑

0 _____ 1/2 mile
0 _____ 1/2 kilometer

walk along a wide dirt road. As the level path takes you along the toe of a rocky, forested slope, notice the fire-scarred trees both on the hillside and in the grassy clearing to your left. Then, notice the profusion of saplings filling the meadow after the fire cleared the forest canopy—all vying for water and sunlight.

Behind them, poking above the forested slope on the opposite side of the meadow, is the knobby tip of Rubicon Peak.

Pass a small pond and immediately reach a junction at 1.3 miles. Abandon the road and bear right onto the TYT as the path narrows and begins a steady 0.5-mile climb

**Crag Lake**

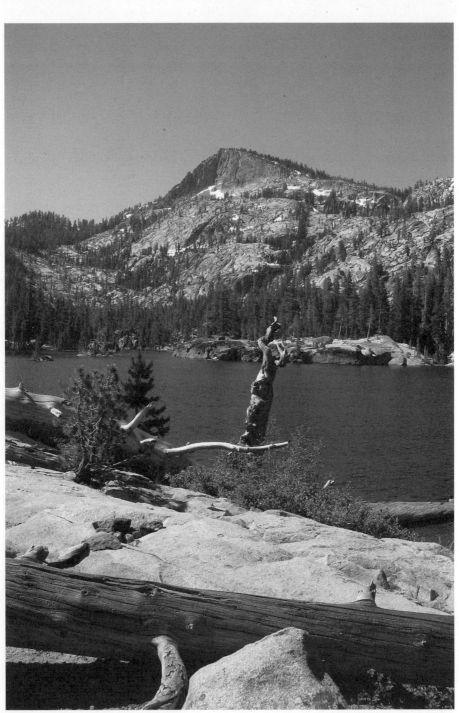

*Crag Lake*

through a forest thick with lodgepole pines, sugar pines, incense cedar, and white firs. Brewer's lupine, Indian paintbrush, and arnica can be found in the sunnier sections.

Near the crest of the climb, Meeks Creek can be heard splashing to the left. Stroll through the forest, and at 2.3 miles enter Desolation Wilderness. Paralleling the creek, the trail weaves in and out of forested flats and wetter riparian areas filled with greenery. A short 0.3 mile farther along, your stroll becomes a climb as you approach a crossing with the cavorting Meeks Creek. A sturdy wooden footbridge at 3.3 miles takes you across the shallow water, where you promptly angle east away from it. Dodging up a side canyon littered with thimbleberry, vine maple, and currant bushes, the trail makes a circuitous climb, contouring the canyon wall.

Breaking out of the forest, you traverse an open ridge, which grants views of the pine-studded granite landscape and a peek at Lake Tahoe. Rejoining the creek, you once again veer south and follow its pleasant cascades upstream. At 4.5 miles, reach the shore of Lake Genevieve and a junction with the seldom-used General's Creek Trail. Continue along the main trail toward Phipps Pass.

Lake Genevieve is a peaceful gem ringed by pines, its shallow water relatively warm for swimming. Continue south and reach larger and more scenic Crag Lake at 5 miles. A granite slab about midway down the eastern shore is a perfect spot to spread out a picnic and take in the scene. Anglers can test their skills against the resident brook, brown, and rainbow trout. If you are camping here, proceed around the lake to the southern shore for the best and most environmentally friendly sites. Remember to set up camp 100 feet from the water and trail.

Though our hike ends here, it's certainly not the end of the trail. Day hikers looking to extend their trips or backpackers can continue southeast along the TYT and visit Hidden (5.7 miles), Shadow (5.9 miles), Stony Ridge (6.3 miles), Rubicon (8.1 miles), and Grouse (8.6 miles) Lakes before the string comes to an end and you have to surmount Phipps Pass.

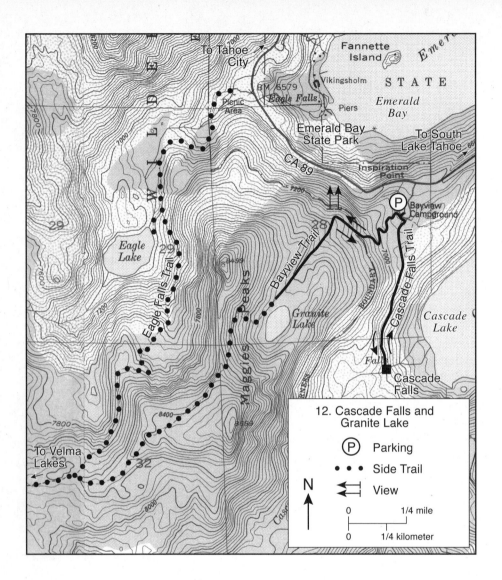

12. Cascade Falls and Granite Lake

Ⓟ    Parking

• • •    Side Trail

N    ⇄    View

| 0 | | 1/4 mile |
|---|---|---|
| 0 | | 1/4 kilometer |

# 12

## Cascade Falls and Granite Lake

*Type: Day hike*

*Season: Late June through October*

*Total distance: 1.4 miles round trip/2.2 miles round trip*

*Rating: Easy/moderate*

*Elevation: 6,920 feet; +111 feet/-211 feet (Cascade Falls)/6,920 feet; +776 feet/-33 feet (Granite Lake)*

*Location: Eldorado National Forest, Desolation Wilderness*

*Maps: USGS 7.5' Emerald Bay; Trails Illustrated Lake Tahoe Basin No. 803*

*Fees and permits: If Cascade Falls is your only destination, you need not fill out a permit, since the Cascade Falls Trail does not cross into Desolation Wilderness. Those making the trek to Granite Lake and beyond must complete a permit (free) at the trailhead kiosk.*

*Contact: Lake Tahoe Basin Management Unit (530-543-2600; www.fs.fed.us/r5/ltbmu); Eldorado National Forest, Pacific Ranger District (530-644-2349; www .fs.fed.us/r5/eldorado); Lake Tahoe Visitor Center (530-543-2674).*

The Bayview trailhead is a popular starting point for day hikers and backpackers alike. Two trails leave from here—Cascade Falls Trail and Bayview Trail—both with something unique to offer. The former visits Cascade Falls, a tumbling cataract that spills 150 feet into Cascade Lake. The path is easy to follow and offers impressive vistas of the Tahoe basin along the way. Come in the spring, as by late summer the falls are but a wee trickle. Unlike the mild gradient of the Cascade Falls Trail, Bayview Trail is a steady uphill trudge. Part of the way up, enjoy a spectacular bird's-eye view of Emerald Bay and the expansive Lake Tahoe. In the end, energize yourself with a refreshing swim in peaceful Granite Lake.

### GETTING THERE

From South Lake Tahoe, head north 7.3 miles on CA 89 from its junction with US 50 (the South Lake Tahoe Y) and turn left into Bayview Campground (just opposite Inspiration Point). Proceed 0.1 mile through the campground to the trailhead parking area.

### THE TRAIL

From the information board, proceed 25 feet up the trail to a signed fork (right for Granite Lake, left for Cascade Falls). Veer left and make the short excursion to Cascade Falls first. The wide path heads east through a forest of Jeffrey pine and white fir. Not far from the trailhead, a path from the campground joins in on the left and the route bends southward along a sandy flat.

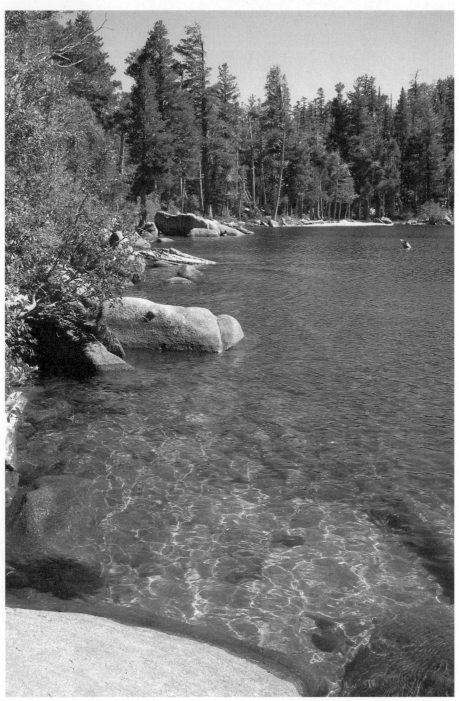

*Granite Lake*

Abandon the shady conifers and at 0.25 mile begin a short rocky ascent. Manzanita, chinquapin, and huckleberry oak now line the path. Cresting a knoll, gain your first view of the surrounding environs—spread out at your feet some 400 feet below is oblong, forest-ringed Cascade Lake, another moraine-dammed loch so typical of Tahoe's south shore. In the distance, the placid deep blue waters of Lake Tahoe give way to the towering Carson Range that borders its eastern shore.

Descend the brushy hillside, picking your way among the boulders that clutter the path. The trail then begins a mild ascent over some exposed granite slabs made slippery by a thin layer of sand. This section is short, however might result in a bit of anxiety for acrophobes and parents with young children. As you approach, the rumble of the falls grows louder, and you spot the frothy water spilling over a granite ledge. It's not the most photogenic of cataracts, and this profile view is the best you will get of the overall cascade.

Rounding a bend, gain expanded views into the canyon funneling Cascade Creek. From a signed junction at 0.6 mile, spot one of Maggies Peaks to the right, and, opposite, a pyramid-shaped mountain that occludes the craggy tip of Mount Tallac. Turn left and make your way down the boulder-lined path. The trail peters out near the brink of the falls, where you can scout out the perfect picnic spot from which to enjoy the sights and sounds.

When ready, return to the first trail junction near the information board. With your warm-up complete, you can now tackle the steep route to Granite Lake. From the trail junction, head west into a dense mixed conifer forest dominated by white firs. You'll find the soft forest floor underfoot much more pleasing than the rocky path to Cascade Falls.

The unrelenting trail zigzags up the hillside, and you eventually gain forest-framed views of Lake Tahoe. Enter Desolation Wilderness at 0.4 mile and, not long after, cross the outlet stream for Granite Lake.

At 0.6 mile, leave the trail and walk 25 feet to an overlook, where you have a sublime vista of Emerald Bay and Lake Tahoe. Peer down on solitary Fannette Island and the delta formed by Eagle Creek as it spills into the bay. With its velocity reduced, it can no longer carry its load of alluvium and rapidly deposits it at the mouth of the river.

Leaving this lovely scene, dive back into the forest and continue climbing. The gradient eases a bit as you follow Granite Lake's alder-choked outlet stream. In the spring, find an assortment of wildflowers crowding the fern, thimbleberry, and currant understory that lines the outer edges of the creek. Spot Granite Lake through the trees, but continue along the trail to an obvious side path descending to its shady northwest shore at 1.1 miles. The sparkling waters are beautifully backed by one of Maggies Peaks (the same one we admired from the Cascade Falls Trail). After that stiff climb, reward yourself with a refreshing dip in the lake's relatively warm water before returning to the trailhead.

Backpackers or ambitious day hikers can continue along the Bayview Trail, which intersects the Eagle Falls Trail 1.5 miles past Granite Lake and, eventually, the Pacific Crest Trail. Strong day hikers might consider a challenging semi-loop that visits Upper Velma, Fontanillis, and Dicks Lakes before returning along the Bayview Trail (11 miles round trip).

# 13

## Mount Tallac

*Type: Day hike*

*Season: Late June through September*

*Total distance: 9.2 miles round trip*

*Rating: Strenuous*

*Elevation: 6,440 feet; +3,295 feet/-0 feet*

*Location: Eldorado National Forest, Desolation Wilderness*

*Maps: USGS 7.5' Emerald Bay; Trails Illustrated Tahoe Basin No. 803*

*Fees and permits: A free permit is required for this day hike and can be obtained by self-registering at the trailhead kiosk.*

*Contact: Lake Tahoe Basin Management Unit (530-543-2600; www.fs.fed.us/r5/ ltbmu); Eldorado National Forest, Pacific Ranger District (530-644-2349; www .fs.fed.us/r5/eldorado); Lake Tahoe Visitor Center (530-543-2674).*

The steep, rocky, high-altitude trek to the summit of Mount Tallac is grueling, I won't deny it. At 9,735 feet, Mount Tallac is the dominant feature of the southwestern shore of Lake Tahoe. Tackling this imposing peak is a formidable challenge, but one definitely worth taking on. The trail is jam-packed with stellar views, not to mention the sublime panorama of Lake Tahoe, Fallen Leaf Lake, and Desolation Wilderness waiting for you at the top. Mount Tallac's accessibility makes it one of the most popular day hikes in the basin, so don't expect to be huffing and puffing alone. Rest assured, however, there is enough view on this hike to go around.

### GETTING THERE

From South Lake Tahoe, head north 3.9 miles on CA 89 from its junction with US 50 (the South Lake Tahoe Y) and turn left onto Mt. Tallac Road (just opposite the Baldwin Beach turnoff). Proceed 1 mile along the paved though rough and narrow road to the trailhead parking area. There are no facilities at the trailhead.

### THE TRAIL

Fill out your free permit at the information board and set out on an old gravel roadbed lined with sage and Jeffrey pines. Just past the 0.5-mile mark, the trail follows the uphill contour of a fire-scarred ridge blanketed with manzanita, where you gain your first magnificent view of the trek—a precursor of what is yet to come. To the west, Mount Tallac rises on the ridgeline beckoning you farther. To the east, Fallen Leaf Lake spreads

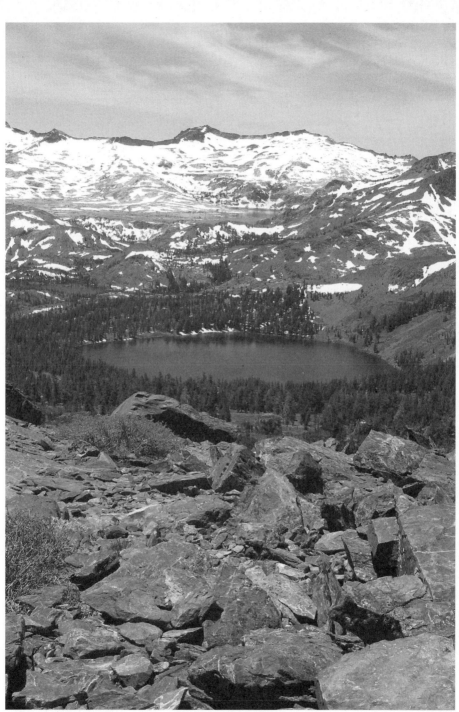

*Desolation Wilderness as viewed from Mount Tallac summit*

out before you, its watery margins bordered with a dense mass of conifers.

Glaciers once dominated this terrain. As they crept across the landscape they dug debris underneath and carried it on their surfaces and frozen in their interiors. This material was deposited along the glacier's sides, forming parallel ridges of debris called lateral moraines and terminal moraines, ridges of debris heaped at the snout or end of the glacier marking the farthest extent of the ice. In the case of Fallen Leaf Lake, the moraine along its northern shore formed a low hill, effectively creating a dam and allowing water to collect. Emerald Bay, the curious appendage at the southwest end of Lake

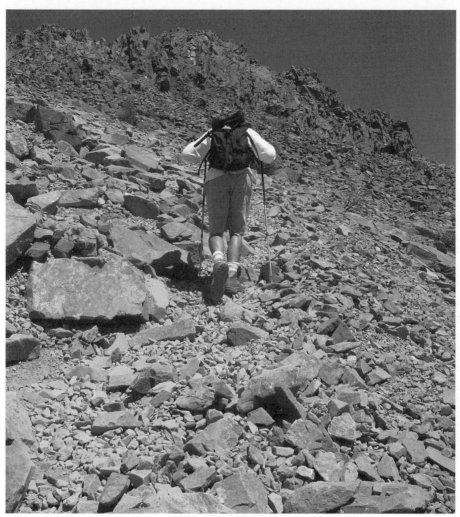

*Hiker climbing Mount Tallac*

Tahoe, was formed in much the same way, the difference being that its moraine, which should separate it from the main lake, is lower than Tahoe's current water level, allowing the two to connect.

The well-worn footpath ducks behind the ridge and descends briefly before switchbacking up and coming alongside the outlet for Fallen Leaf Lake at 1.3 miles. Pass a Des-olation Wilderness sign and soon gain the lakeshore, which is rife with hordes of voracious mosquitoes. Quickly skirt the lake, apparently named for clumps of grass that break off from the shore and float about, and trade the shady forest for an open, dry hillside carpeted with sagebrush, currant, and a smattering of wildflowers including spreading phlox and groundsel.

Step across Cathedral Creek, and at 2.1 miles ignore a steep trail bound for Fallen Leaf Lake and veer right (south). A scant 0.2 mile farther, you reach petite Cathedral Lake, whose peaceful shore tempts you to linger—but press on, there's much climbing to do. Beyond Cathedral Lake, the gradient intensifies significantly as you plod up a steep, rocky, exposed slope. The climb is long, and poor footing doesn't help the cause, so pause and admire the stunning panorama unfolding behind you—it's sure to take your mind off the uphill trudge.

With the aid of cairns, ascend past chunky boulders, along brushy slopes, and through small pine stands before reaching the base of an imposing headwall of loose talus. Zigzag up the main trail and reach the crest southeast of Mount Tallac at 3.3 miles. Because snow can be found here clinging to the rocky slopes well into summer, trailblazing, early-season hikers have cut a precarious unofficial path that tackles the scree in a more direct fashion—heading straight up it. Both eventually get to the same destination, but you will have a much easier time of it if you stick to the main trail.

From atop the headwall, enjoy the expanded westward view into the deep recesses of Desolation Wilderness. With the hard part behind you, head northwest up the more gently sloping backside of Mount Tallac. The rocky path is festooned with tufts of hardy grass, scrubby whitebark pine, and colorful wildflowers. Watch for furry marmots scurrying, lumbering around, or sunning themselves.

The steady ascent eventually leads to a signed junction at 4.3 miles with a trail that heads to Gilmore Lake. Turn right and begin the final 0.3-mile push to the summit. Regain the view of Lake Tahoe on an exposed ridge just shy of the metamorphic peak. From here, the trail grows vague, but the goal is obvious. Scramble to the top of the windswept peak and savor the vista.

Lake Tahoe dominates the scene, its deep blue water hemmed by a perfect ring of mountains. To the south, mile upon mile of rugged, majestic terrain stretches toward Carson Pass and beyond. Desolation Wilderness's stark granite landscape fills the scene over your shoulder. Spot shimmering Gilmore Lake to the southwest, followed by Susie Lake, and beyond it Lake Aloha tucked beneath the snow-capped pinnacles of Pyramid and Ralston Peaks.

When you've had your fill, begin the knee-pounding descent to the trailhead back along the same path.

# 14

## Echo Lake to Lake Aloha

*Type: Day hike or overnight*

*Season: Mid-July to October*

*Total distance: 6.8 miles round trip with water taxi (11.8 miles without water taxi)*

*Rating: Moderate*

*Elevation: 7,433 feet; +914 feet/-174 feet*

*Location: Eldorado National Forest, Desolation Wilderness*

*Maps: USGS 7.5' Echo Lake, Pyramid Peak; Trails Illustrated Lake Tahoe Basin No. 803*

*Fees and permits: A free permit is required for this day hike and can be obtained by self-registering at the trailhead kiosk. Overnight users must obtain a wilderness permit (fee) from Eldorado National Forest. The water taxi charges $10 one way with a three-person minimum.*

*Contact: Lake Tahoe Basin Management Unit (530-543-2600; www.fs.fed.us/r5/ltbmu); Eldorado National Forest, Pacific Ranger District (530-644-2349; www .fs.fed.us/r5/eldorado); Lake Tahoe Visitor Center (530-543-2674); Echo Lakes Chalet Taxi Service (530-659-7207).*

Venture into the heart of Desolation Wilderness on this busy path to sparkling, island-studded Lake Aloha. The trail's accessibility, high-elevation starting point, and convenient water taxi shortcut make it an easy way to experience the riches of the region with relatively little effort (read: expect lots of company). Nonetheless, with a boon of scenic lakes dotting the rugged landscape there is plenty of space for everyone to spread out.

### GETTING THERE

From South Lake Tahoe, head south 10 miles on US 50 from its junction with CA 89 (the South Lake Tahoe Y) and turn right onto Johnson Pass Road (about 1.25 miles west of Echo Summit). Proceed 0.5 mile and turn left onto Echo Lakes Road. Another 0.9 mile takes you to the upper parking area. From here, walk down to Echo Chalet boat dock (0.2 mile), where you can arrange for the water taxi. If you plan on walking, the trail begins across the spillway. Either way, be sure to fill out a permit at the trailhead information board.

### THE TRAIL

The section of Pacific Crest Trail (PCT) that follows the northern shoreline of Lower and Upper Echo Lake offers fine views, but quite honestly is a rather uneventful 2.5 miles. You stay well above the waterline and traipse behind cottages and cabins that line the shore. I recommend you save time and energy by boarding the water taxi that departs from the resort and deposits you at the public landing at the far western end of Upper Echo Lake.

14. Echo Lake to Lake Aloha

Ⓟ  Parking
•••  Side Trail

N ←

0        1 mile
0        1 kilometer

Ⓟ

Pacific Crest Trail

Water Taxi

E L D O R A D O

Upper Echo Lake

Start

Dock

To Glen Alpine
Trailhead

Camp Harvey West

Echo Peak

D E S O L A T I O N   W I L D E R N E S S

Haypress Meadows

Lake of the Woods

Lake Aloha

A phone near the dock provides direct access to the resort when you're ready to be picked up after your hike.

Note that Lower and Upper Echo Lakes are a glacially formed pair connected by a narrow channel, which is passable by boat only during high-water conditions (typically July 4 to Labor Day weekend). When the channel is no longer passable, passengers are dropped at the far end of Lower Echo Lake for a reduced fare.

From the boat landing on Upper Echo Lake, with a fresh set of legs, head uphill 0.1 mile to your main path, the PCT, and turn left (a sign posted on a tree ensures you won't miss this junction on the way back). The rocky trail climbs gently to a wilderness boundary sign at 0.7 mile, followed immediately by a junction with the northbound Triangle Lake Trail. This is the first of two pathways leading to Triangle Lake, this one being the shorter, steeper route. It is also the first of many trails shooting off the PCT that you should bypass if Lake Aloha is your primary destination.

Forsaking the shady woodland, enjoy over-the-shoulder views of the forested valley cradling the Echo Lakes as you climb. Intersect a spur trail heading left to a trio of picturesque gems—Tamarack, Ralston, and Cagwin—all gloriously backdropped by Ralston Peak, the highest bump on the ridgeline.

Keep to the main trail and begin a moderate climb through the gray granite landscape stippled with contorted pines as Tamarack Lake comes into view to your left. Ascend a pair of long switchbacks to a forested bench and an eastbound lateral at 1.8 miles heading toward Triangle Lake and ultimately Lily Lake. This trail originates at the Glen Alpine Trailhead south of Fallen Leaf Lake, another gateway into this stunning natural wonderland.

Stay on the PCT and continue on your northwestward course. The trail gradient eases, and a short 0.3 mile farther you skirt grassy Haypress Meadows and reach the first of two trails descending to Lake of the Woods, a popular overnight destination, evidenced by its heavily used shoreline. The 0.6-mile trail runs into the northeastern shore of this pine-ringed lake. By tracing the bank 1.5 miles south and then west, you can also visit Ropi Lake, where the trail peters out, although there are several other lakes in the area. With a good topographic map and sharp navigation skills, they are fantastically solitudinous.

Back on the PCT, reach the high point of the journey and ignore the Ralston Peak Trail (left) and later the southward intersection with a potentially waterlogged, looping trail visiting Lake Margery and Lake Lucille (right) at 2.5 miles. Farther still, pass a junction to the west bound (left) for Lake Aloha's southeast shore (take note of this junction, as it is a possible return route) and instead continue along the PCT, immediately passing the north end of the Lake Margery/Lake Lucille loop (right). From here, the trail gently descends, breaks out of the forest cover, and collides with the eastern shore of shallow Lake Aloha at 3.4 miles.

The sprawling lake occupies an enormous granite valley that was dammed to create a high-mountain reservoir. Dead tree trunks and a plethora of granite blobs dot the crystalline waters, which are backed by the imposing Crystal Range—Pyramid Peak and Mount Price dominating the ridgeline. While there is water as deep as 20 feet in places, there are many spots where you can wade across the lake. Add to this the annual drawdown, and by late summer the lake isn't nearly as spectacular. Because of this significant fluctuation in water level, visiting in late July or early August offers the best scenery and opportunity for swimming.

---

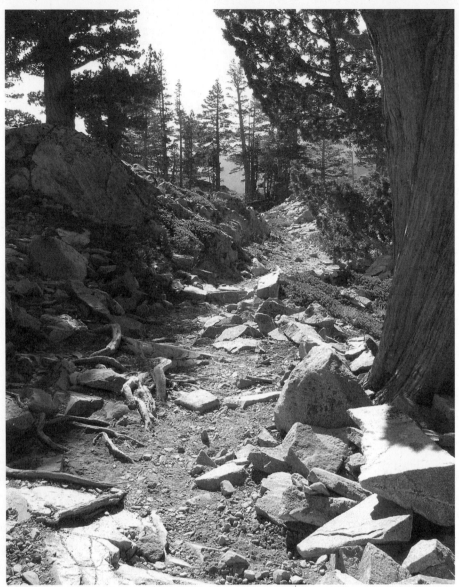

*Rocky trail to Lake Aloha*

Backpackers should turn left, where they can find the best campsites along the southeast shore. Day hikers can return via the same trail or venture 0.6 mile south alongside the east shore to a junction with the first Lake Aloha Trail, which veers northeast and rejoins the PCT after 0.5 mile. From here, turn right and make your way back to the boat landing.

# III. Trans-Sierra Passes

Woods Lake Campground

Picnic Area

Woods Lake

Lost Cabin Mine

4WD

PACK

28

8400

9000

9200

PACK

× 9460

PACK

Round Top Lake

33

9400

33

To Carson Pass

Winnemucca Lake
8980

9000

9400

To Fourth of July Lake

To Round Top

Round Top

Round Top
10381

× 10045

# 15

## Round Top Lake Loop

*Type: Day hike*

*Season: June to October*

*Total distance: 5-mile loop*

*Rating: Moderate*

*Elevation: 8,198 feet; +1,214 feet/-1,214 feet*

*Location: Eldorado National Forest, Mokelumne Wilderness*

*Maps: USGS 7.5' Caples Lake, Carson Pass; USFS Mokelumne Wilderness*

*Fees and permits: A permit is not required for this day hike. There is a $5 day-use fee (per vehicle).*

*Contact: Eldorado National Forest, Amador Ranger District (209-295-4251; www.fs.fed.us/r5/eldorado).*

This fantastic loop hike breaches the northern boundary of uncrowded Mokelumne Wilderness. Wander past hillsides exploding with seasonal wildflowers, in the shadow of brooding sawtooth ridges of volcanic rock, and take respite along the shores of two picturesque lakes. You even have the option of adding a notch to your peak-bagger's belt—if you're into that sort of thing—by climbing to the summit of Round Top (10,381 feet), the tallest peak within the Mokelumne Wilderness.

### GETTING THERE
From the junction of CA 88 and CA 89, drive 10.5 miles west on CA 88 (Carson Pass) to the turnoff for Woods Lake. Follow the narrow road 1 mile to the small trailhead parking area equipped with pit toilets. Pay the day-use fee at the kiosk adjacent the parking area, then walk south along the access road, crossing a bridge over Woods Creek, and find the trailhead on your right.

### THE TRAIL
The 105,165-acre Mokelumne Wilderness straddles parts of the Eldorado, Stanislaus, and Humboldt-Toiyabe National Forests. Its rugged terrain is characterized by dark, colorful peaks, reminders of the Sierra Nevada's volcanic past. Here you will find a pleasant mix of characteristic stark granite terrain intermingled with rich volcanic rock, creating a dramatic scene.

The well-defined trail begins by paralleling the campground access road. Quickly come to a trail fork and veer left toward

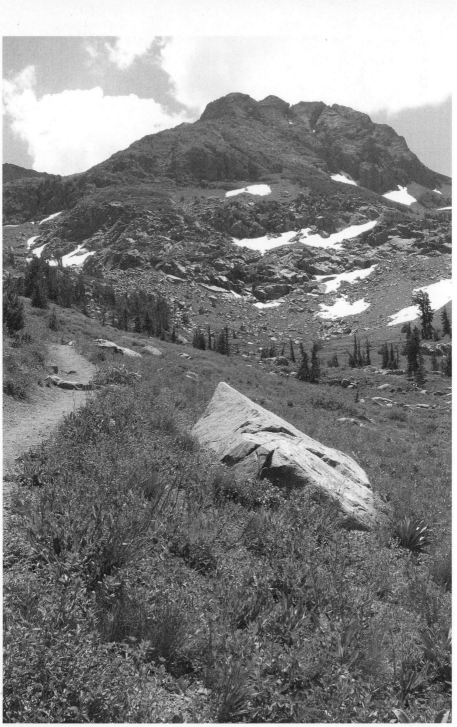

*Round Top*

Winnemucca Lake. You will be completing the loop in a clockwise direction, and the right fork represents the return leg of the journey. Cross the access road and pick up the trail on the opposite side. From here, cross a wooden footbridge spanning willow-lined Woods Creek and proceed upstream along its eastern bank. With the creek burbling on the right, make your way through a mixed forest of lodgepole and western white pines and graceful mountain hemlocks before coming to a junction at 0.4 mile. Veer left and watch for mountain pennyroyal, spirea, and triteleia sprinkled along the trail.

Begin a mild but steady uphill climb, passing an arrastra, a crushing device early Mexicans used for pulverizing ore, at 1 mile. As you continue, the thinning forest allows slivers of views of the surrounding mountainside before eventually emerging at the base of a low ridge. While the outlet creek for Winnemucca Lake serenades you from below, the trail continues south along an open hillside exploding with an assortment of wildflowers. Woolly mule's ear, lupine, paintbrush, aster, and cinquefoil carpet the slope in a magnificent display while Round Top's hulking presences fills the skyline.

Pass the boundary sign announcing entry into the Mokelumne Wilderness and enjoy the lovely cascades taking shape between the willow- and heather-lined creek sides. Several small unofficial paths lead down to the water. At 1.8 miles, reach a signed junction and Winnemucca Lake. To the east lies the rounded hump of Elephants Back and, due north of that, Red Lake Peak and Carson Pass. The pass was named after Christopher "Kit" Carson, a man indelibly linked with early Western exploration and expansion. He was a trapper, Indian agent, and soldier best known for his work as a guide to the expeditions of John C. Frémont.

From the junction, head west toward Round Top Lake. Immediately cross Winnemucca's outlet via a log that fell across the stream, and head uphill once again. Colorful columbine and heather blossoms add to the trailside bouquet. Gain over-the-shoulder views of Winnemucca Lake as you journey higher and cross several seasonal drainages. Crest a saddle between Round Top and Winnemucca Lakes, noticing the wind-battered whitebark pines that dot the landscape. The now single-track trail cuts across the grassy saddle and drops down toward Round Top Lake, beautifully backdropped by The Sisters, a pair of dark, craggy peaks.

As you approach Round Lake, a spur trail heads left (southeast) to the summit of Round Top, an old volcanic vent. This out-and-back side trip is no easy task and should be attempted only by experienced hikers. The scree-covered terrain makes travel difficult and frustrating; however, the 360-degree view from the knobby peak makes it all worth it. By climbing to the summit, you add almost 2 miles and a little over 1,000 vertical feet to your hike, putting it in the strenuous classification.

Back on the main trail, from the signed junction near Round Lake at 2.7 miles, head northwest toward Woods Lake. Views expand both north and west as you descend the rocky trail beside Round Lake's willow-congested outlet stream. Exit Mokelumne Wilderness and descend a series of short, steep switchbacks. The forest thickens and views disappear. At 3.8 miles, reach Lost Cabin Mine, marked by dilapidated buildings and rusted car frames. Though mining operations ceased many years ago, the claim is still active and there are signs posted everywhere letting you know that this is private property.

The trail's moderate descent continues

down a boulder-strewn hillside dotted with mountain hemlock. Catch glimpses of Woods Lake through the trees. Boulder-hop across Round Lake's outlet creek, and at 4.2 miles reach a junction with an old road. Bear right and follow the trail, wider now, downhill. Just before a metal gate, turn left on a narrow path heading to the trailhead parking area. Close the loop 0.4 mile later and veer left to reach the trailhead.

# 16

## Meiss Meadow to Round Lake

Type: Day hike

Season: June to October

Total distance: 10 miles round trip

Rating: Moderate

Elevation: 8,584 feet; +464 feet/-1,012 feet

Location: Eldorado National Forest, Lake Tahoe Basin Management Unit

Maps: USGS 7.5' Carson Pass, Caples Lake, Echo Lake; Trails Illustrated Lake Tahoe Basin No. 803

Fees and permits: A permit is not required for this day hike. There is a $5 day-use fee (per vehicle).

Contact: Eldorado National Forest, Amador Ranger District (209-295-4251; www.fs.fed.us/r5/eldorado); Lake Tahoe Basin Management Unit (530-543-2600; www.fs.fed.us/r5/ltbmu).

Taking advantage of the Pacific Crest Trail and Tahoe Rim Trail, this pleasant hike wanders through a broad meadow brimming with wildflowers to Round Lake, the largest body of water in the Upper Truckee River Basin. Though you can access Round Lake via trailheads at either Meiss Meadow or Big Meadow, the former, albeit a longer path, is less frequently used, which equals more solitude for you.

### GETTING THERE

From the intersection of CA 88 and CA 89, drive 8.9 miles west on CA 88 (Carson Pass) to the Meiss Meadow trailhead parking area on the north side of the road. Pay the day-use fee at the kiosk near the trailhead.

### THE TRAIL

The Pacific Crest Trail is a 2,650-mile National Scenic Trail that runs from Mexico to Canada through California, Oregon, and Washington. Though the hike to Round Lake rambles along only a small slice of this fantastic trail, each year hundreds of people attempt to thru-hike the trail's entire length in one season—an incredible physical and logistical feat, to say the least.

Departing from the northwest end of the parking area, enter an open forest of lodgepole pines, western junipers, and quaking aspens. The trail parallels the highway for a spell, making vehicle noise an unfortunate reality for the first 0.7 mile. Southward, a marvelous panorama encompassing Elephants

To Big Meadow
and CA 89

End

Round
Lake

Round
Lake

EL DORADO CO.
ALPINE CO.

Tahoe Rim Trail

Spring

Pacific
Crest
Trail

Meiss
Lake

Meiss
Meadow

Meiss
Family
Cabin

Spring

River
Trail

Pacific Crest Trail

Eldorado
National
Forest

CA 88

Lake Tahoe Basin
Management Unit

Stevens
Peak

Spring

Alpine
Mine

Alhambra
Mine

Crater
Lake

Spring

Red Lake
Peak

Vista
Point

Red Lake

Snowshoe Thompson
Kit Carson
(Historical
Monuments)

Carson
Pass

Vista
Point

Grave

Woods
Creek

BM 8130

WILDERNESS

BOUNDARY

P Parking

• • • • Side Trail

N

0            1/2 mile

0          1/2 kilometer

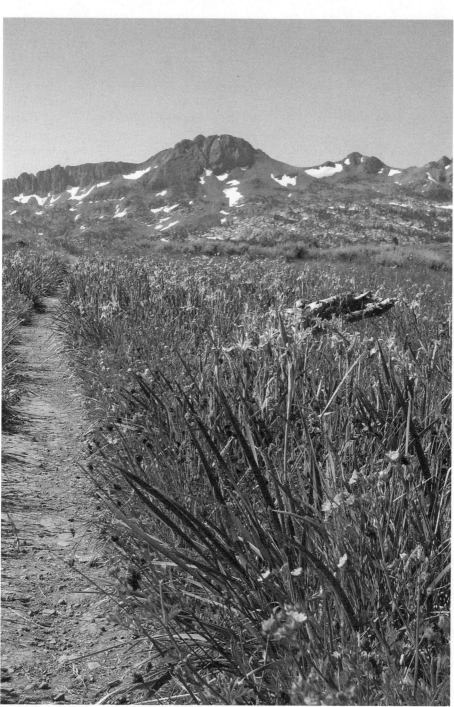
*Blue flag irises along the Pacific Crest Trail.*

Back and Round Top is on full display. Indian paintbrush, mountain pennyroyal, nude buckwheat, and lupine color the boulder- and sage-strewn hillside you traverse. Rounding a bend, Caples Lake and Covered Wagon Peak come into view over the treetops.

Soon the trail bends north and crosses a pair of seasonal drainages near the 1-mile mark. Zigzag up a dry hillside blanketed with woolly mule's ears, sage, and sulphur-flower. The views across the valley only improve from your new perspective. Pass a pond and catch your breath at 1.25 miles, where the grade eases. The single-track trail slices through a grassy saddle that is spectacularly adorned with western blue flag iris. The views from this high point along the trail are amazing. Rising behind you are the dark volcanic peaks of the Mokelumne Wilderness that harbor patches of snow well into summer, and up ahead, on a clear day, Lake Tahoe can be seen sparkling in the distance. To the east lies Red Lake Peak, believed to be the vantage point from which John C. Frémont and Charles Preuss became the first Euro-Americans to see Lake Tahoe, in February 1844.

The trail becomes rocky again and you begin a mild descent, crossing several seasonal drainages. Depending on the time of year, they can be bone dry or filled with enough water to give you a chance to hone your boulder-hopping skills. All these small, snowmelt-fed creeklets are dashing toward the deep ravine directly to the west, in which flows the fledgling Truckee River.

As you descend, keep an eye out for prairie smoke. This curious flower has fuzzy tendrils creating a twisted mass that resembles a troll doll's hair when poofed up— Mother Nature does have a sense of humor.

Easily rock-hop across the peaceful river, beyond which the trail levels as you enter the southern fringe of pastoral Meiss Meadow with Sierra penstemon, bistort, aster, California corn lily, and groundsel scattered about. Cross the Truckee River once again, and at 2.6 miles come to a small unofficial path leading left toward the Meiss cabin and barn, built in the late 1880s by a pioneering family who drove cattle here each summer for grazing. Fortunately, the Forest Service banned cattle in the area several years ago, in an effort to restore the declining meadows and fisheries.

Shortly thereafter, reach a trail fork and bear right on the Tahoe Rim Trail as it continues north toward Round Lake. The mild gradient makes for easy walking as the trail undulates through lodgepole forest and pocket-size meadows. Easily cross a rocky creek and later Round Lake's inlet. At 4 miles, begin a moderate descent to Round Lake's shore. Follow the trail along the eastern shoreline to an unofficial path (left) that departs the main trail and skirts the north side of the lake. From this junction, you have a wonderful view of Round Lake and the towering buttress of volcanic cliffs that border its east side.

Follow the unofficial path to the lake's outlet, where you can unpack a picnic and take a break before heading back the same way you came.

If you can arrange a car shuttle, another option is to walk point-to-point from Meiss Meadow to Big Meadows. Both trailheads are easily accessible from the highway, and the driving distance between the two is only about 15 miles. A car shuttle or key swap means that you don't have to backtrack, shortening the trek to a mere 7.5 miles round trip.

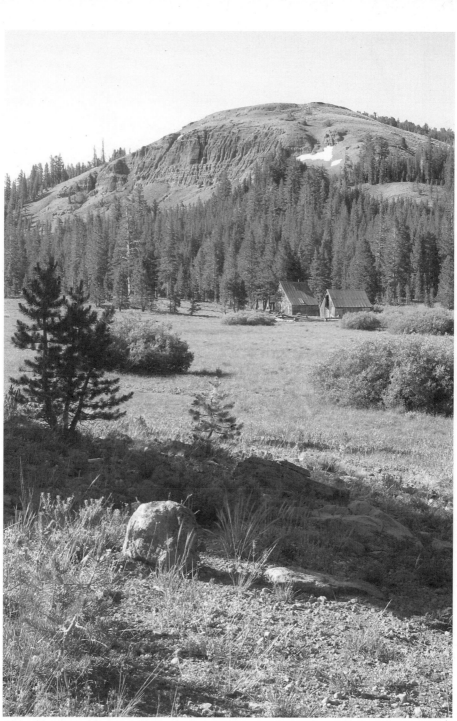

*Meiss Meadow cabin*

# 17

## Granite Lake

*Type: Day hike or overnight*

*Season: June to October*

*Total distance: 4 miles round trip*

*Rating: Easy*

*Elevation: 8,171 feet; +597 feet/-44 feet*

*Location: Eldorado National Forest, Mokelumne Wilderness*

*Maps: USGS 7.5' Carson Pass, Pacific Valley; USFS Mokelumne Wilderness*

*Fees and permits: A permit is not required for this day hike. Overnight users camping in Mokelumne Wilderness must obtain a free permit from Eldorado National Forest.*

*Contact: Eldorado National Forest, Amador Ranger District (209-295-4251; www.fs.fed.us/r5/eldorado).*

Sufficiently hidden off the main highway to deter windshield naturalists zipping by, the Blue Lakes area and its easily accessible backcountry offer a collection of lakes set amid an often-overlooked nook of Mokelumne Wilderness. This easy jaunt to Granite Lake rambles through quiet forests and wildflower-filled meadows on the way to a rock-encircled gem perfect for swimming, picnicking, or simply lounging about.

### GETTING THERE

From the intersection of CA 88 and CA 89, drive 2.4 miles west on CA 88 (Carson Pass) and turn south onto paved Blue Lakes Road. Drive 11.5 miles to a T-intersection near Lower Blue Lake. Turn right and proceed 1.5 miles to Middle Creek Campground on the narrow, mostly unpaved road. Find the trailhead (signed for Grouse Lake) on your left just past the campground.

### THE TRAIL

Washoe and Sierra Miwok peoples originally inhabited this region of the Sierras. They hunted seasonally for local game and gathered plants for food and medicine. It is also believed that they used a portion of the Mokelumne Wilderness as a major thoroughfare for social interaction and trade.

In 1848, a Mormon Battalion, recently discharged from their post fighting in the Mexican-American war, sought a route across the Sierra Nevada that avoided the infamous Truckee River Route, scene of the Donner Party tragedy a mere two years before. Traveling from Sutter's Fort to Salt Lake

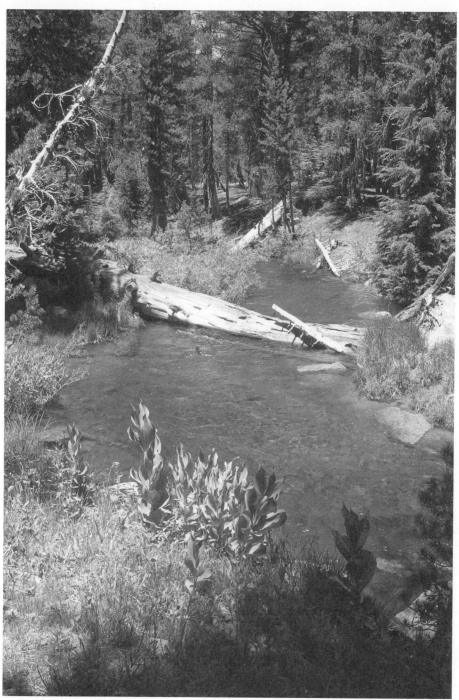

*Log crossing over Middle Creek*

City, they pioneered a trail, most likely following a Native American route, just south of present day Carson Pass. Coined the Carson River Route, this trail subsequently carried thousands of emigrants to California's fabled fields of gold.

In the 1860s, the area had its own short-lived run at gold and silver mining southwest of Blue Lakes, but by the turn of the 20th century the region saw more stockmen and shepherds grazing cattle and sheep than anything else. The passage of the Wilderness Act in 1964 secured the future of this fantastic landscape, preserving it for generations to come.

From the parking lot, head toward Upper Blue Lake and cross its wide spillway on a steel bridge. A sign directs you left onto Grouse Lake Trail, which begins by paralleling the spillway in its downhill course toward Middle Creek and eventually Lower Blue Lake. Beneath the shade of lodgepole pines and mountain hemlocks, the trail soon crosses peaceful Middle Creek via a fallen tree.

The trail then bends southwest and begins a mild ascent away from the creek. Red firs and western white pines eventually join the forest mix, while California corn lily and golden yarrow add splashes of color. At 0.7 mile, reach a crest and enjoy level walking

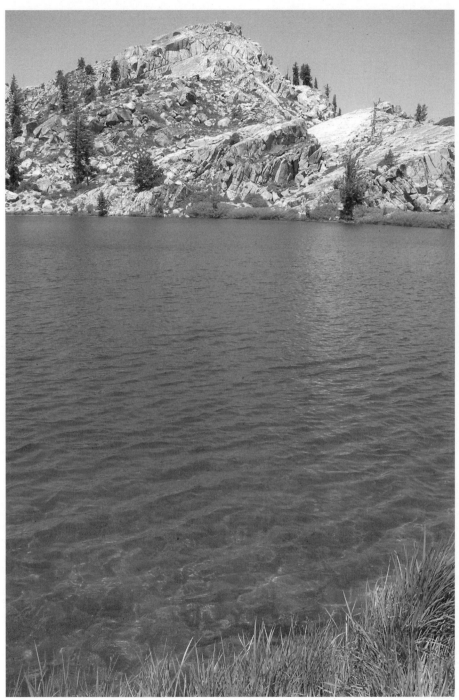
*Granite Lake*

and glimpses of the surrounding peaks through the trees before resuming the climb.

The trail weaves in and out of forested sections and open rocky hillsides, crossing the boundary for Mokelumne Wilderness near the 1-mile mark. Quickly come to a lovely little unnamed pond ringed by pines and clumps of granite. The trail is a little vague here, but, when in doubt, stick close to the southern shore and you will spot the trail as it climbs northwest away from the water.

The grade steepens for a while and the views improve slightly as you venture higher. The steady climb eases and you come to a verdant area decorated with aster, Sierra penstemon and Brewer's lupine. Leaving the wildflowers and snaking through the for-

est, the trail dries out again before cutting through a notch in a rocky knoll and dropping down to the willow-lined outlet for Granite Lake at 1.8 miles. Walk along the outlet's southern bank before cresting the south-eastern rim of the bowl confining Granite Lake's clear water.

As you would expect, the lake is encircled by a granitic barrier that is dotted with willows, heather, and scattered conifers. Campers and picnickers will find nice resting spots among the pines on the southwest shore. By continuing a short way along the trail to the western lip of the bowl, you can have sweeping views of the surrounding terrain. When ready, retrace your steps to the trailhead.

# 18

## Bull Run Lake

*Type: Day hike or overnight*

*Season: Late June through mid-October*

*Total distance: 7.4 miles round trip*

*Rating: Moderate*

*Elevation: 7,895 feet; +1,023 feet/-521 feet*

*Location: Stanislaus National Forest, Carson-Iceberg Wilderness*

*Maps: USGS 7.5' Pacific Valley, Spicer Meadow Reservoir; USFS Carson-Iceberg Wilderness*

*Fees and permits: A permit is not required for this day hike. Overnight users must obtain a free wilderness permit from Stanislaus National Forest.*

*Contact: Stanislaus National Forest, Calaveras Ranger District (209-795-1381; www.fs.fed.us/r5/stanislaus).*

Open meadows, old-growth forests, and a clear mountain lake are waiting for you on this trek into the rugged Carson-Iceberg Wilderness. Though you've got some climbing to do, the trail has a nice balance of ups and downs, and level spots too. Whether you're out for the day or overnight, Bull Run Lake is sure to please even the most discriminating hiker. Early season visitors should be prepared for several fords across snowmelt-swollen creeks.

### GETTING THERE

From its intersection with CA 89, drive 22.4 miles west on CA 4 (Ebbetts Pass) to Stanislaus Meadow, located on the south side of the road. There are no facilities here. Park in the dirt lot adjacent the highway, or if you have a high-clearance vehicle with four-wheel drive, proceed down the narrow, rutted fire road (Forest Road 8N13) 0.5 mile to a small parking area near the true trailhead.

### THE TRAIL

Ebbetts Pass is named after "Major" John Ebbetts, a California pioneer credited with the first recorded crossing in 1851. The route was infrequently used until silver was discovered east of the Sierra in the late 1850s. This prompted merchants from the Gold Rush town of Murphy to finance the present route through Ebbetts Pass to transport supplies to the miners more easily. The route eventually became part of the state highway system in the 1920s (CA 4).

This is arguably the most obscure and least traveled of all the trans-Sierra routes because of its steep grade and overabundance of hairpin turns. A large section of the highway traversing the pass is narrower than two lanes—with no dividing line—but don't let this deter you. It travels through some of the most scenic countryside around, so scenic in fact that it was designated a National Scenic Byway (incidentally, Tioga Pass also makes the list).

Start by walking downhill on a fire road that heads south from the parking area adjacent CA 4. It's not long before your path intersects the Emigrant Trail. Continue along the road, soon coming to Stanislaus Meadow, an expansive clearing that is incised by the fledgling North Fork Stanislaus

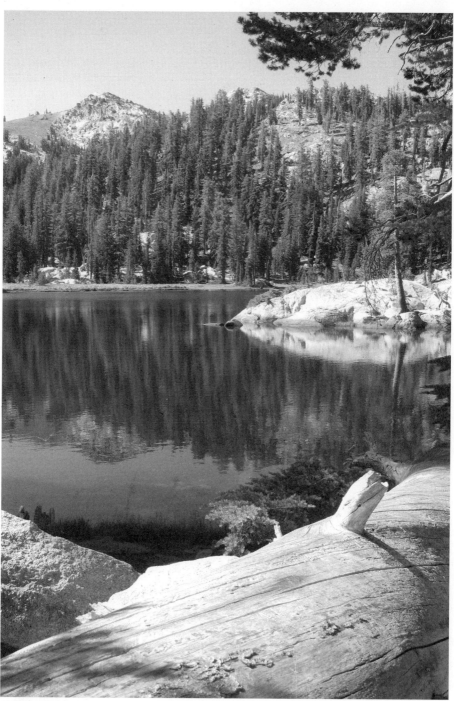

*Bull Run Lake*

River. The road follows the western fringe of the meadow before coming to the official trailhead at 0.5 mile. Those who drove along the fire road must park here.

The trail narrows past the information board as you walk amid mountain hemlocks, red firs, and lodgepole pines. The barbed wire fence to your left and the thick forest to your right are sure to keep you on track. Level walking takes you to a boundary sign for Carson-Iceberg Wilderness, beyond which you lose the barbed wire and begin a mild descent.

You are no doubt wondering about the wilderness's odd hyphenated moniker. (No, there aren't any large floating masses of ice here!) The name comes from two prominent geographic features: the Carson River, named after famed explorer Kit Carson, and a granite formation called "The Iceberg" on the southern boundary of the wilderness.

The trail loosely follows the North Fork Stanislaus River to the low point of the jaunt at 1.5 miles, where you cross several branches of the river and the outlet for Bull Run Lake. Early season hikers can expect to get their feet wet; however, late summer typically finds the river bone dry. Enjoy the lupine, California corn lily, and groundsel that fill the spaces in between the crossings. Beyond the river a mild ascent ensues, followed by level walking, which takes you to yet another ford of Bull Run's outlet at 2 miles.

The gradient steepens as you ascend an open, rocky hillside and gain views of the pine-scattered granite landscape. While the trail is not endowed with a profusion of wildflowers, they do add splashes of color here and there. Their absences make those flowers we do encounter all the more treasured.

The steady climb eases after a 0.5 mile, and you reach a junction with the Mosquito Lakes trail. Turn right and immediately boulder-hop across Heiser Lake's outlet stream.

The trail meanders through the forest, crossing a series of seasonal streams before beginning the second major climb of the hike. Follow the route as it traverses the rocky landscape and ascends along smooth granite slabs. The clearly defined path falters at times, but cairns help guide you until a more obvious trail reappears. A handful of steep switchbacks carry you up a narrow ravine. Leveling off once again, you wander past a murky pond before making the final push to the lakeshore.

Crest the top of a ridge and arrive at Bull Run Lake at 3.7 miles. The trail continues around the eastern shore but soon peters out. The crystalline lake is ringed by pines and is almost completely encircled by an imposing fortress of rock. A breach in the northern wall grants access to this most picturesque scene. In the center of the lake, a dollop of granite forms an island that is quite possibly the most perfect sunbathing spot in the entire Sierra Nevada.

Set up camp or spread out a picnic at one of the many ideal locations around the lake. When ready, return via the same path.

# 19

## Calaveras Big Trees State Park—South Grove

*Type: Day hike*

*Season: Mid May through October*

*Total distance: 5.4 mile semi-loop*

*Rating: Easy*

*Elevation: 4,431 feet; +800 feet/-800 feet*

*Location: Calaveras Big Trees State Park*

*Maps: USGS 7.5' Stanislaus, Crandall Peak (trail not shown); Calaveras Big Trees State Park Brochure Map*

*Fees and permits: A permit is not required for this day hike. There is a $6 day-use fee (per vehicle).*

*Contact: Calaveras Big Trees State Park (209-795-2334; www.parks.ca.gov/ ?page_id=551).*

Explore the remote Calaveras South Grove on this easy, well-marked trail through a pristine grove of giant sequoias, earth's largest living objects. Protected as a natural preserve, this area offers a rare opportunity to wander through an ancient undisturbed forest ecosystem in its primeval conditions. This pleasant forest walk passes several notable specimens including the Agassiz Tree—the largest tree in the park.

### GETTING THERE

From Angel's Camp, drive 22.1 miles east on CA 4 (Ebbetts Pass) to the turnoff for Calaveras Big Trees State Park. Proceed to the entrance station and pay the day-use fee. From the entrance, drive 8 miles along paved Walter W. Smith Memorial Parkway to the South Grove parking lot.

### THE TRAIL

In 1852, while Augustus T. Dowd was tracking a wounded grizzly bear, he happened upon a forest of enormous trees—what we now refer to as the Calaveras North Grove. When he told others of what he had found, no one believed him. After Dowd led a group of men to his find, word of the extraordinary giants spread rapidly, bringing a flurry of curious visitors and the exploits of enterprising individuals looking to make a buck. Coming under the purview of the State of California in 1931, Calaveras Big Trees State Park is considered the state's longest continuously operated tourist facility.

After a stop at the visitors center, make your way to the South Grove trailhead. The

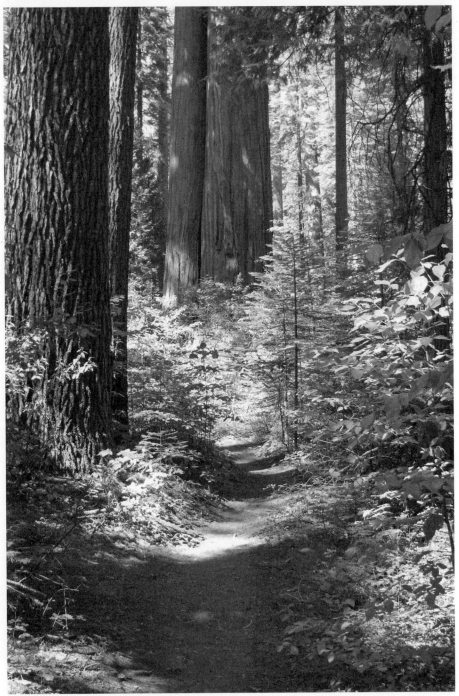

*The trail through South Grove*

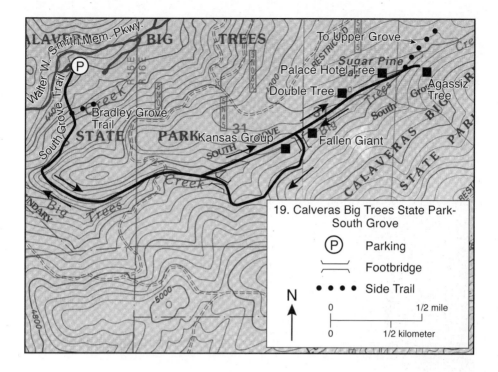

19. Calveras Big Trees State Park–South Grove

South Grove contains approximately 1,000 large sequoias, about 10 times as many as the smaller North Grove in the main area of the park. Find the path across from the restrooms and head south, soon crossing Beaver Creek, a popular summer swimming hole, via footbridge.

Although the Sierra Nevada foundation is granite, you won't see much of the salt-and-pepper flecked rock in the park, as it is almost completely covered by soil and alluvium. One exception is the channel carrying Beaver Creek. Here the soil has been eroded, revealing the underlying bedrock.

Climb away from the creek and at 0.3 mile reach a junction with the Bradley Grove Trail. This 2.5-mile loop wanders through a grove of young sequoias planted in the 1950s by South Grove caretaker Owen Bradley. A log-

ging operation left its mark on the area, but despite man's effort to destroy it, nature has restored itself in fine fashion. In the eloquent words of John Muir: "Nature is always lovely, invincible, glad, whatever is done and suffered by her creatures. All scars she heals, whether in rocks or water or sky or hearts."

With Beaver Creek splashing in the ravine to your right, gently ascend a hillside thick with a mix of conifers and mountain dogwood. In the spring, dogwood blossoms bedeck the understory in a showy display that enlivens the forest. Contrary to what you might think, the small, buttonlike center of the blossom is the actual flower. Surrounding this are large, egg-shaped white bracts, which are actually modified leaves. The leaves typically turn crimson in the autumn, painting a whole new scene.

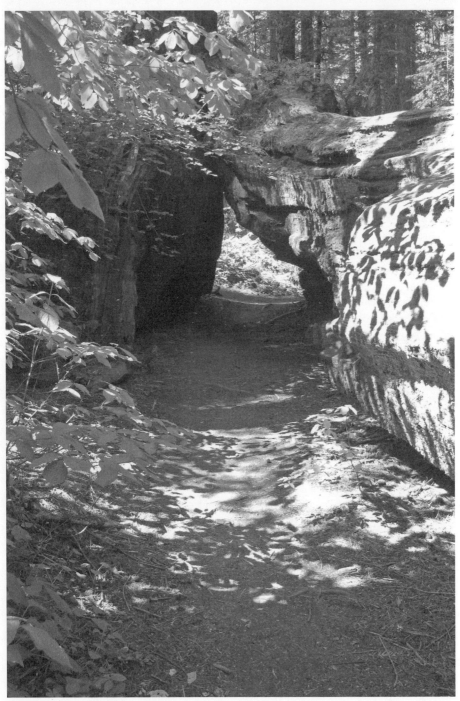

*Tunnel in fallen sequoia*

Rounding a bend, you trade the tumbling of Beaver Creek for Big Trees Creek and you follow it upstream to the western boundary of the preserve. At 1.1 miles, cross a dirt road and officially enter the South Grove. Soon you'll reach a junction and bear left. This is the beginning of the loop part of the journey.

As you travel northeast through the tranquil grove, begin to notice scattered rust-colored trunks rising about. Unlike their closely related cousin, the coast redwood, sequoia trees (also called Sierra redwoods) do not grow in pure stands. Instead they thrive in mixed coniferous forests of white fir, sugar pine, and incense cedar. In California, these stately giants are found within a narrow belt along the western slope of the Sierra, where the optimal altitude, temperature, rainfall, and soil type converge, encouraging their growth.

To your right, pass the Kansas Group, a cluster of three large sequoias, before coming to another junction at 1.75 miles. Stay straight and pass Double Tree, a pair of sequoias growing so close together they appear as one. Continue along the somewhat overgrown trail as it winds toward Palace Hotel Tree, named in the 1870s after its apparent resemblance to the courtyard carriage entrance of San Francisco's newly opened Palace Hotel (it's a stretch). At 2.5 miles, reach the end of the official trail and the Agassiz Tree, named after Louis Agassiz, the Swiss-born zoologist who became one of America's leading naturalists. This specimen is the largest sequoia in the park, at 25 feet in diameter and 250 feet tall.

Although a sign here marks the end of the trail, a faint footpath continues into the upper portion of the grove. If you are up for a little freelancing and are comfortable navigating through an unfamiliar forest, venture farther and explore The Moody Group, named for 19th-century evangelist Dwight Moody; Smith Cabin Tree, named for Alexander Jackson "Trapper" Smith, who lived in the hollowed-out behemoth in the late 1850s; and Old Goliath, which, as the story goes, came crashing down during a violent windstorm.

Return to the last junction and bear left onto the loop trail. Immediately pass through a tunnel in a fallen giant, beyond which you cross Big Trees Creek on a wooden footbridge. From here the trail meanders through the quiet forest, passing several other sequoias en route to a second footbridge over Big Trees Creek and the close of the loop trail at 4.1 miles. Turn left at the junction and retrace your steps to the trailhead.

If you're looking for a shorter option, the much more frequented North Grove has a 1.5-mile interpretive loop near the visitors center. The stump of the tree that originally caught Dowd's eye—the Discovery Tree—is located along the trail. Not long after Dowd found it, it was felled at the hands of five men over 22 days to be put on display. Other notable North Grove trees include Three Graces, Abraham Lincoln, and Old Bachelor.

CO

Sonora
Pass

BM 9643

MONO CO

CA 108

Creek

Stanislaus
National Forest

34

Deadman
9200

8965

9600

10000

35

Falls

Sardine

Pacific Crest Trail

NATIONAL

10000

10400

BOUNDARY

9500

Canyon

Emigrant
Wilderness

3

10400

10400

10000

2

Humboldt-Toiyabe
National Forest

x 11845

10800

McKay

Creek

20. Sonora Pass

P  Parking

N

0 ——————— 1/2 mile

0 ——————— 1/2 kilometer

10000

10000

10400

10400

PCT 2000

10400

INDEFINITE

10

10400

11260

11000

11

x 11000

10484  Deadman
Lake

10800

YABE

# 20

## Sonora Pass

*Type: Day hike*

*Season: Late July to October*

*Total distance: 8.6 miles round trip*

*Rating: Moderate to strenuous*

*Elevation: 9,626 feet; +1,640 feet/-502 feet*

*Location: Stanislaus National Forest, Humboldt-Toiyabe National Forest, Emigrant Wilderness*

*Maps: USGS 7.5' Sonora Pass; USFS Emigrant Wilderness*

*Fees and permits: A permit is not required for this day hike.*

*Contact: Stanislaus National Forest, Summit Ranger District (209-965-3434; www.fs.fed.us/r5/stanislaus).*

Striking south along the Pacific Crest Trail from Sonora Pass, this challenging hike climbs through moonlike terrain to a wind-swept saddle just east of Leavitt Peak. From this airy perch, you have mile upon mile of High Sierra resplendence spread out before you in spectacular display. Be sure to call ahead for trail conditions, as snow may linger well into summer, making sections of this steep trek potentially dangerous. Pack plenty of water, a windbreaker, and sun protection, as you will be well above treeline for most of the hike. Be cognizant of sudden weather changes and the reduced level of oxygen at this altitude.

### GETTING THERE

From US 395, 17 miles north of Bridgeport, turn onto CA 108 (Sonora Pass) and drive 14.6 miles west. Notice the trailhead marker on the south side of the highway as you crest Sonora Pass. There is limited parking here along the road, or you can proceed 100 yards farther and turn right into the parking/picnic area. From a dirt path on the southeast end of the parking area, walk south 0.2 mile back to the pass itself, where you cross the highway and arrive at the signed trailhead.

### THE TRAIL

At 9,626 feet, Sonora Pass is the second highest road crossing of the Sierra Nevada, with Tioga Pass, at 9,945 feet, taking the top spot. With mules, horses, and oxen, the brave Bartleson-Bidwell Party, the first organized group of emigrants to traverse the

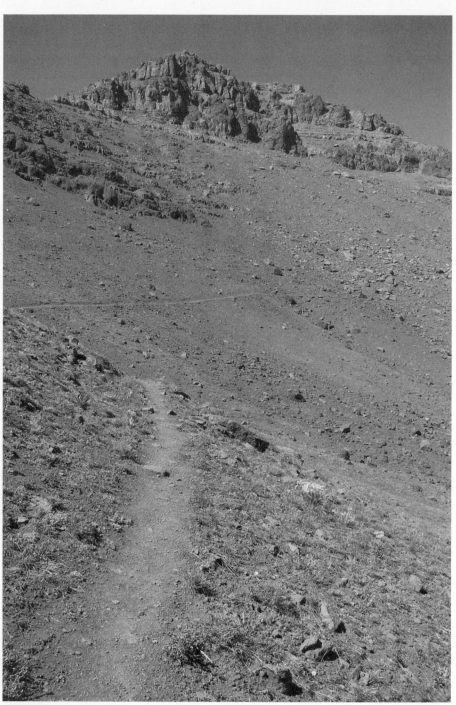

Sonora Pass

Sierra Nevada, crossed the pass in October 1841. The route was not attempted by wagon until 1852. Two years later, John "Grizzly" Adams crossed the pass and reported: "On all sides lay old axle-trees and wheels, some broken, some perfect, melancholy evidence of the last season's disasters." The present route was completed as a toll road in 1865 in an effort by Mono, Stanislaus, and Tuolumne counties to recoup some of the construction costs. The round trip from Sonora to Bridgeport, what we now drive in a matter of hours, was said to have taken a six-horse team three weeks to complete.

From the highway, immediately begin a mild ascent through a stand of lodgepole and whitebark pine. The duff-colored ground is enlivened by lavender lupine, blue flax, and woolly sunflower. The trail then dips to cross several gullies, the most notable being Sardine Creek at 0.6 mile. Watch for alpine buckwheat, woolly mule's ear, and mountain helenium as you approach the willow-lined channel.

Resume climbing and spot ruddy-colored Sonora Peak and its attendant ridgeline north across the valley. Catch your breath at a bend in the trail and admire the expanded view of hill and dale as they roll into the eastern horizon. The gradient steepens and you duck behind a hill, losing the panorama for the moment. The rocky exposed terrain negates any chance of getting off course and makes it easy to see the trail gently rising on the canyon wall ahead.

From a distance, this barren landscape appears devoid of life, but here walking through it, you can see it is rife with a hardy community of alpine plants, all well adapted to this harsh, unforgiving environment. Some plants have evolved interesting adaptations, including growing low and small to withstand high winds and stay warm. To cope with near drought conditions during the short summer growing season, many have developed specialized means to conserve and capture moisture; because manufacturing scent uses up valuable water, many plants produce relatively large flowers instead to attract pollinators.

Continue your uphill march beneath a colorful unnamed rampart of chunky volcanic rock as you circle the headwall in a clockwise direction. Spy the highway coursing below as you pass through clumps of stunted whitebark pine clinging to the hillside.

The trail doubles back on itself at 2.1 miles and heads south toward a saddle just west of our unnamed peak along the Sierra Crest. Near the bend, scramble to the ridgetop and enjoy expanded westward views of Night Cap Peak, Chipmunk Flat, and Red Peak. Back on the main trail, gain the saddle at 2.4 miles, where views improve once again to include Leavitt Peak, the tallest in a wall of 11,000-foot pinnacles forming an imposing bulwark that flanks Blue Canyon below.

The crest you now traverse is the topographical dividing line where the waters of the region part. Creeks flowing east tumble into the Great Basin, while westward flows hit the Stanislaus River and eventually spill into the Pacific Ocean.

With the major climbing behind you, the trail levels off and begins a general descent south along a steep wall and briefly penetrates the northeastern tip of Emigrant Wilderness. Watch for lingering snow along this section, which can be very treacherous. If you are early in the season, carry an ice axe just in case. At 3.6 miles, reach another saddle, where you can look down upon grimly named Deadman Lake to the south and Sardine Meadow to the north.

Past the saddle, the trail descends to more level walking and then culminates with a final steep climb to your goal—a lofty 10,800-foot notch overlooking the dusky volcanic landscape magnificently studded with a bevy of striking alpine lakes. Nearest you is Latopie Lake, followed by Koenig and Leavitt Lakes. On a clear day you can even see Mount Con- ness, Mount Lyell, and a host of other lesser peaks that form Yosemite's granite skyline.

If you aren't satisfied with the view (although that's highly unlikely) and can muster the energy, scramble to the summit of Leavitt Peak (11,569 feet). The easiest way is to continue south on the PCT and ascend along the southeast ridge.

# 21

## Sardine Falls

*Type: Day hike*

*Season: June through October*

*Total distance: 2 miles round trip*

*Rating: Easy*

*Elevation: 8,752 feet; +324 feet/-18 feet*

*Location: Humboldt-Toiyabe National Forest*

*Maps: USGS 7.5' Pickel Meadow (trail not shown); USFS Toiyabe National Forest–Bridgeport Ranger District*

*Fees and permits: A permit is not required for this day hike.*

*Contact: Humboldt-Toiyabe National Forest, Bridgeport Ranger District (760-932-7070; www.fs.fed.us/r4/htnf).*

Without a plethora of signs pointing the way or an officially maintained trail, you can expect solitude, save the grazing bovines, on this easy ramble to Sardine Falls. Secreted away in the dramatic volcanic landscape of Sonora Pass, this obscure trail isn't developed and is somewhat overgrown in spots, but that being said, it is relatively easy to follow. Wildflower enthusiasts will enjoy the wide array of blossoms found along the trail, and early season hikers should expect to get their toes wet fording a series of creeks swollen with snowmelt.

### GETTING THERE

From US 395, 17 miles north of Bridgeport, turn onto CA 108 (Sonora Pass). Drive 12.1 miles west and look for Sardine Meadows and an overgrown dirt road on the south side of the highway. If you are coming from the west, the trail is 2.5 miles east of Sonora Pass. There is no official trailhead for this hike, nor any facilities. Park along the roadside shoulder.

### THE TRAIL

The trail heads southwest from CA 108 along an overgrown dirt road that cuts through Sardine Meadow. Spy the falls southwest from the highway as you begin to walk. The expansive meadow, backdropped by dark volcanic peaks, is blanketed with mountain sagebrush and studded with lodgepole pines. As you approach Sardine Creek, sage is briefly replaced by a soft carpet of green grass. Ford the creek and con-

*Sardine Falls*

21. Sardine Falls

Ⓟ  Parking

N

0                                    1/2 mile

0                          1/2 kilometer

tinue along the level trail, enjoying brief pockets of shade cast by the towering pines.

The road narrows and you make a short, but steep, climb to the top of a low hillock sprinkled with sulphur-flower, mountain pennyroyal, and scarlet gilia. Descend into a lush area festooned with Brewer's lupine, orange sneezeweed, and Sierra angelica and soon come to a trail fork. Bear right into an overgrown mass of willows brightened by more species of wildflowers including larkspur, Oregon sidalcea, and applegate paintbrush.

Emerging from the vegetation, you ascend a dry hillside while McKay Creek tumbles to the left in a willow-filled ravine. Step across a small tributary and follow the meandering trail as it nears the debris-filled creek. Notice the water-ravaged vegetation and washed-out areas, evidence of its seasonal torrent.

The trail, overgrown once again with aspen and willows, crosses another stream while the unmistakable roar of Sardine Falls urges you on. The path gets a little vague through here, but if you generally follow the north side of the creek upstream, you will pick it up again. If McKay Creek is low, you can cross and approach the base of the falls from the south side as well.

From either vantage, you have a front row seat as the creek plunges 50 feet from a ledge of chunky volcanic rock, sending a frothy white veil of water crashing into the scree below. Enjoy the spectacle before returning via the same path.

# 22

## Bennettville Trail

Type: *Day hike*

Season: *June through October*

Total distance: *3.9 miles round trip*

Rating: *Easy*

Elevation: *9,544 feet; +359 feet/-0 feet*

Location: *Inyo National Forest*

Maps: *USGS 7.5' Tioga Pass (trail not shown); Trails Illustrated Yosemite NE– Tuolumne Meadows and Hoover Wilderness No. 308 (trail partially shown)*

Fees and permits: *A permit is not required for this day hike.*

Contact: *Inyo National Forest (760-873-2400; www.fs.fed.us/r5/inyo).*

Steeped in Sierra mining history and fantastic subalpine landscapes, this easy day hike is perfect for a summer afternoon. Just outside Yosemite National Park, explore the remains of short-lived Bennettville, a town of great expectation in 1882, and skirt a peaceful chain of lakes connected by the sinuous flow of aptly named Mine Creek.

### GETTING THERE

From US 395, 1 mile south of Lee Vining, turn onto CA 120 (Tioga Pass) toward Yosemite National Park. Drive 9.8 miles west and turn right onto Saddlebag Lake Road. Proceed 0.1 mile farther to the small parking area on the left, prior to reaching Junction Campground. Walk toward the campground and across the bridge spanning Lee Vining Creek and immediately find the trailhead on the right.

### THE TRAIL

The trail sets out briefly along the grassy west bank of Lee Vining Creek, but quickly bends away and climbs a short hill blanketed with a sparse forest of lodgepole pines. Skirting Junction Campground from above, angle toward Mine Creek and eventually meet up with it splashing below in a chasm of dark metamorphic rock. Now, following the creek upstream, look for nude buckwheat and Sierran raillardella sprouting from the rocky terrain. Come to a grassy meadow and step across a small streamlet. Continue your ramble under the shady pines, enjoying the sounds of the creek and the lovely pools and cascades it creates in

22. Bennettville Trail

P  Parking

🛆  Campground

N

0 ——————————— 1/2 mile

0 ——————————— 1/2 kilometer

its rush to rendezvous with Lee Vining Creek. At 0.9 mile, arrive at an interpretive plaque below Bennettville, a short-lived Sierra mining town.

In 1874, William Brusky, a young sheep herder, stumbled across a rusty pick, shovel, and a flattened tin can wedged in the rocks of Tioga Hill. Left by George W. Chase some 15 years prior, the tin can was etched with a location notice marking what was believed to be a rich silver vein—the "thundering big silver ledge." This fateful discovery sparked a small silver rush and gave rise to the town of Bennettville, named after Thomas Bennett,

president of the Great Sierra Consolidated Silver Mining Company.

With great expectations, the directors of the Tioga Mine ordered the latest mining technology—16,000 pounds worth to be exact. The equipment was to be transported from Lundy Canyon, some 9 miles away, up and over the rugged Sierra to the mine. Over a two-month period in late winter, a team of 12 men and a pair of mules hoisted, pulled, and dragged the equipment on sleds through blinding snowstorms and near-zero temperatures. Subsequently, the Great Sierra Wagon Road was constructed, linking

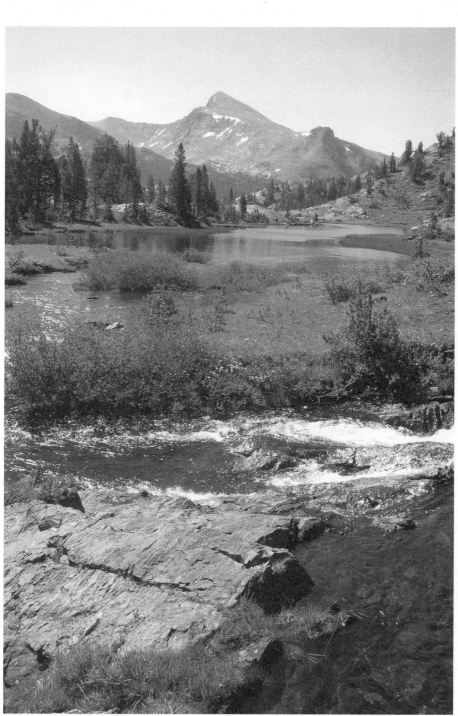

*Mine Creek and Mount Dana*

Bennettville to Sonora to the west, reducing the burden of transporting equipment and supplies into the remote mine and standing ready to carry a bonanza of silver out, hopefully.

After two years with the new machinery and upwards of 1,700 feet of tunnel dug, the propitious ledge of silver was nowhere to be found. Investors, now skeptical of the mine's profitability, backed out, effectively ceasing operations. No ore was ever mined or hauled out of Tioga Mine, and the town of Bennettville slipped slowly into obscurity as people realized the once envisioned town of 50,000 people was never going to become reality. The one positive nugget of this woeful tale is the creation of the Great Sierra Wagon Road, which eventually served as the foundation for Tioga Pass. In 1910, the eastern segment from Lee Vining to Tioga Pass was opened, linking east to west and forming the highest and arguably one of the most scenic mountain roads in all of California.

Climb a small knoll and explore the two restored wooden buildings, which stare vacantly across the canyon to a cascade of copper-colored scree, the tailings of a fruitless mine.

Shortly beyond Bennettville, come to an unsigned trail fork, veer left, and descend to a slippery log crossing over Mine Creek and then up the opposite canyon wall for 0.15 mile to the actual mine. Explore the rusty equipment scattered about and peer into the rocky orifice (now barricaded) before returning the way you came.

Back at the fork, rejoin the main trail by turning left. Round a bend where views expand northwest into the canyon to include a verdant basin and its peacefully meandering creek. Mount Conness (12,590 feet), a for-

midable challenge on Yosemite's northeastern boundary, dominates the granite skyline.

Approaching the shore of Shell Lake at 1.4 miles, gain stunning over-the-shoulder views of Mount Dana (13,057 feet), Yosemite's second highest peak. Come to a Y-junction and veer left to walk along the shore, or right to stay above it (less buggy). The two eventually reconvene at the far end of the lake. Progressing along the single-track trail, pass another unnamed lake to the left and eventually come to a boundary sign for 3,883-acre Harvey Monroe Hall Research Natural Area (RNA). This was one of the first established in California (1933) as part of a nationwide program developed to protect a network of federally administered public lands for the purpose of maintaining biological diversity, providing baseline ecological data, and encouraging research and education. Specifically, the Harvey Monroe Hall RNA has been used to study the social organization of Belding ground squirrels, the dynamics of windblown detritus in snow banks, and the community structuring of subalpine forest birds.

Forging deeper into the canyon, arrive at shallow Fantail Lake at 2.1 miles. Watch for cassiope blooming along the trail, its nodding bell-shaped flowers said to be a favorite of John Muir, who wrote: "Her blossoms . . . so beautiful as to thrill every fibre of one's being . . . No evangel among the mountain plants speaks Nature's love more plainly than cassiope. Where she dwells, the redemption of the coldest solitude is complete. The very rocks and glaciers seem to feel her presence and become imbued with her own fountain sweetness."

The trail continues around the lake, however, we retreat from this subalpine paradise and return to the trailhead.

# 23

## Twenty Lakes Basin

*Type: Day hike or overnight*

*Season: Late June through October*

*Total distance: 4.5-mile loop*

*Rating: Easy to moderate*

*Elevation: 10,071 feet; +600 feet/-600 feet*

*Location: Inyo National Forest, Hoover Wilderness*

*Maps: USGS 7.5' Tioga Pass, Dunderberg Peak; Trails Illustrated Yosemite NE– Tuolumne Meadows & Hoover Wilderness No. 308 (northern part of loop is not shown)*

*Fees and permits: A permit is not required for this day hike. Overnight users camping in Hoover Wilderness must obtain a permit (and pay a reservation fee) from Inyo National Forest. The water taxi charges $10 per person, round trip.*

*Contact: Inyo National Forest, Mono Basin Ranger Station and Visitor Center (760-647-3044 general information, 760-873-2483 permits; www.fs.fed.us/r5/inyo).*

It's hard to imagine another hike with as much austere alpine scenery as this short loop that penetrates the southern corner of Hoover Wilderness. Wander past a chain of stunning lakes, made all the more remarkable by the serrated, snow-speckled skyline that forms the backdrop of this rugged landscape. Spread out a picnic, cast a line, or just linger at any of these tranquil gems.

While such beauty has not gone unnoticed, Twenty Lakes Basin is relatively uncrowded, particularly by the standards of Yosemite, which is just a stone's throw away. By utilizing the water taxi that departs Saddlebag Lake's south shore, you can forgo the relatively uneventful trail that skirts the shoreline and save your energy for the "good stuff." If you opt to walk it, add 3 miles to your jaunt. Oh, and don't forget the bug juice.

### GETTING THERE

From US 395, 1 mile south of Lee Vining, turn onto CA 120 (Tioga Pass) toward Yosemite National Park. Drive 9.8 miles west, and turn right onto Saddlebag Lake Road. Immediately come to a fork and veer right. Proceed 2 miles on this unpaved road to a large trailhead parking area.

### THE TRAIL

From the water taxi dock, peer northwest to the far shore of Saddlebag Lake and get a glimpse of the tantalizing scenery awaiting your lug soles. After a 10-minute boat ride, arrive at the boat landing on the north shore. Follow a faint path up the rise to the main trail and turn left (you will be going in a

23. Twenty Lakes Basin

P — Parking
•••• — Side Trail
▲ — Campground

N

0 — 1/2 mile
0 — 1/2 kilometer

clockwise direction around the loop). Joining on your left is the trail traversing Saddlebag Lake's western shore (if you walked from the marina, this junction is where you will join the loop trail). Stay straight and pass the Hoover Wilderness boundary sign. In short

order, Greenstone Lake appears in the distance, and at 0.3 mile you reach its shore. If the altitude doesn't take your breath away, the sublime scenery will.

As Mount Conness, North Peak, and a host of other craggy, glacially scarred spires

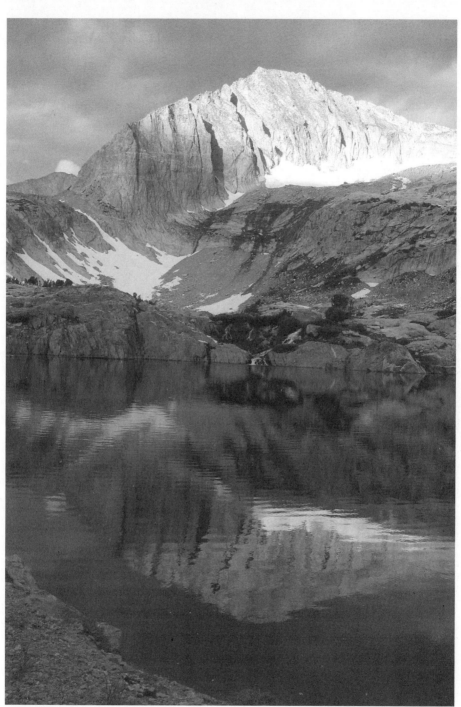

*North Peak reflecting in Steelhead Lake*

along the Sierra Crest command attention, you begin a 0.5-mile ascent past whitebark and lodgepole pines. Though the trail is rocky, the gradient is easygoing. Photographers will enjoy capturing the scenes reflected in the ponds and pools along the way. In the distance, the outlet for Conness Lakes splays somewhat erratically through chunky boulders in its downward course. The dark streaks staining the granite around the falls are caused by lichen.

Wander past sinuous marshy drainages and a variety of wildflowers that add splashes of color to the dark, metamorphic terrain. Wasco Lake appears to the left, but you will stay high above it. The level trail parallels a verdant depression and passes an unofficial trail wandering left before arriving at Steelhead Lake 1.4 miles from the boat landing. Excelsior Mountain and its rust-colored façade dominate the northern horizon, while a lovely cascade graces Steelhead's southernmost shore. Use a log to cross its outlet, Mill Creek, at 1.8 miles and begin a short but steep ascent up its rocky bank. Topping the knoll above the creek, ignore the unofficial trail that veers right and stay straight. Wander between scrubby whitebark pines, clumps of willows, and possible patches of snow as you approach island-studded Shamrock Lake.

Traverse a talus slope lining the northern shore, its jumbled pieces spilling into the chilly waters below. Descend slightly, then mount a small ridge where Lake Helen comes into view. Red heather, Labrador tea, and shrubby cinquefoil line the trail, which becomes vague as you descend a multi-tiered rock slope. Cairns help somewhat, but you may also need to do a little navigating of your own. In this open country it isn't hard,

and you can see the path below, a duff-colored streak parting a swath of grass.

Continuing on, travel across another expansive talus slope, this time around rock-bound Lake Helen. As you look back, the gray granite of the Sierra Crest stands in stark contrast to the multihued metamorphic rock under your feet.

Carefully scramble down a steep 10-foot rock ledge, and at 2.75 miles cross Lake Helen's outlet, the now familiar Mill Creek, on a pair of logs. Come to a signed T-intersection where Mill Creek exits left down Lundy Canyon, another fine destination worthy of exploration. Our described hike turns right, toward Saddlebag. The endless talus slope, wonderfully adorned with Coleville's columbine, shows no sign of stopping as you skirt the edge of Lake Helen and clamber up a narrow ravine that ushers in the outlet for Odell Lake, next on our route. Crest the scree-filled chasm and take in the view of diminutive Lake Helen and the deeply etched ebony peaks behind it.

At 3.25 miles, you approach elongated Odell Lake and walk high above its rocky shore on your way toward Lundy Pass, a windswept saddle devoid of vegetation save the hardy grasses and sporadic whitebark pines that, at this elevation, generally take the form of low, densely matted shrubs rather than trees.

A couple of unofficial trails wander left near the outlet for Hummingbird Lake, the final gem on the circuitous route. Exit the Hoover Wilderness and spy Saddlebag Lake and Mount Dana in the distance. The trail gently descends along a trickling stream, which we later cross, on our way back to the boat landing for our return trip across the water.

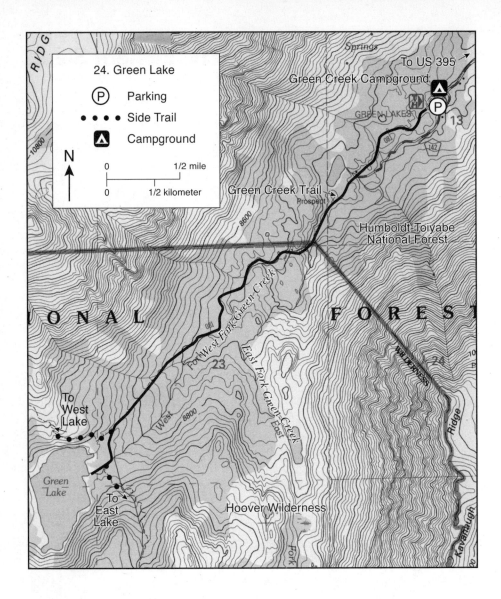

24. Green Lake

Ⓟ Parking

• • • • Side Trail

▲ Campground

N

0           1/2 mile

0         1/2 kilometer

Springs

To US 395

Green Creek Campground

▲

Ⓟ

13

GREEN LAKES

142

080

Green Creek Trail

Prospect

Humboldt-Toiyabe
National Forest

RIDGE

10800

8600

NATIONAL

FOREST

West Fork Green Creek

West Fork Green Creek

East Fork Green Creek

041

23

8800

West

WILDERNESS

Ridge

24

10

To
West
Lake

Green
Lake

To
East
Lake

East
Fork

Hoover Wilderness

Kavanaugh

# 24

## Green Lake

*Type: Day hike or overnight*

*Season: Mid-June to October*

*Total distance: 6.2 miles round trip*

*Rating: Moderate*

*Elevation: 8,003 feet; +1,004 feet/-63 feet*

*Location: Humboldt-Toiyabe National Forest, Hoover Wilderness*

*Maps: USGS 7.5' Dunderberg Peak; Trails Illustrated Yosemite National Park No. 206*

*Fees and permits: A permit is not required for this day hike. Overnight users camping in Hoover Wilderness must obtain a permit (and pay a reservation fee) from Humboldt-Toiyabe National Forest.*

*Contact: Humboldt-Toiyabe National Forest, Bridgeport Ranger District (760-932-7070; www.fs.fed.us/r4/htnf).*

Travelers along Green Creek Trail enjoy a profusion of trailside wildflowers, pass rushing streams, and wander through peaceful forests on their way to Green Lake, a scenic subalpine gem just outside the confines of Yosemite's northeast boundary. Like most other jaunts into the eastern Sierra, this hike gains a good bit of elevation in a relatively short distance. Don't worry though, the colorful peaks and pleasant vistas will keep your eyes occupied while you catch your breath. Make a day of it, or plan to overnight at Green or East Lake before returning.

### GETTING THERE

From Bridgeport, drive 4.3 miles south on US 395 to the turnoff for Green Lakes Road (FS Road 142). Allow 30 minutes to follow this unpaved road 8.6 miles to the trailhead parking area. Near the 3.4-mile mark, you come to an intersection with unsigned Dunderberg Meadow Road heading southeast. Veer sharply right and continue 5.1 miles farther to the trailhead parking area near Green Creek Campground.

### THE TRAIL

From the parking area, head southwest along a wide path through a mixed forest of lodgepole and Jeffrey pines, junipers, and aspens. Not far from the trailhead, enter a meadow filled with Richardson geranium and alpine lily. At 0.6 mile, veer right and join an old road that meanders along the north bank of willow-lined Green Creek. Heading left takes you to Green Creek Campground. Green Creek flows from its headwaters in the Hoover

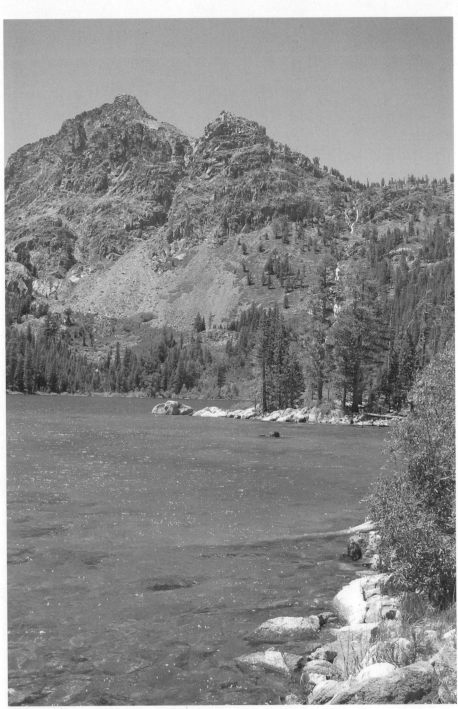

*Green Lake*

Wilderness into East Walker River, eventually spilling into Bridgeport Reservoir.

The landscape you now traverse is part of the Humboldt-Toiyabe Forest, the largest National Forest outside of Alaska, encompassing in excess of 6 million acres. Because the forest spans such a large swath of land, it includes a broad array of wildlife habitats, from arid desert to subalpine forest. Unfortunately, not unlike other regions of the globe, certain species here are in decline due to human influences and competition by nonnative species. Two local amphibians—mountain yellow-legged frog and Yosemite toad—which normally inhabit wet meadows, lakes, and streams, are struggling. The Forest Service has implemented a restoration program, but you can also help to minimize impacts to these and other species. Always practice the seven Leave No Trace principles, and if you plan on fishing, thoroughly disinfect all fishing gear if relocating to a different body of water to prevent the spread of disease. It's unlikely you will spot these critters during the hike, but if you do, consider yourself lucky.

The trail eventually narrows and you cross a small creek. A short climb and brief descent are followed by level walking. With the noisy creek still to your left, but mostly ensconced beneath thick vegetation, begin a steady ascent. The trail grade increases as you ascend a series of rocky, shadeless switchbacks. At the top of this zigzagging section, the grade mellows. Enjoy the shade now offered by a thickening canopy and cross a small creeklet at 1.8 mile, passing the entry sign for Hoover Wilderness not long after.

Look for the dark tip of Gabbro Peak poking above the greenery as you climb. Enter a wet, somewhat overgrown segment that puts on a dazzling wildflower display early in the season. Watch for cinquefoil, white-flowered bog orchid, paintbrush, and lupine.

Fall is also a magical time to visit and experience the colorful transformation of quaking aspens into their brilliant autumnal palette of yellows and oranges. The trail dries out at the top of the incline, and you have the opportunity to admire the surrounding valley over the treetops before bisecting another lush area brightly adorned with fireweed's rose-colored flowers.

Continue your ascent, enjoying the expanded view down the valley toward the Bodie Hills and of the Monument Ridge, your western flank. The drab Kavanaugh Ridge rising to the east is punctuated by ochre Dunderberg Peak, a lovely contrast. At 2.9 miles, reach a junction and turn left to reach the east shore of Green Lake. The right fork heads to West Lake, a stiff climb that tacks on another 1.5 miles (one way) and 1,000 feet of elevation.

From the junction, Green Lake is an easy 0.25 mile farther. When you run into the West Fork of Green Creek, a difficult crossing in the early season, turn right, abandoning the main trail, and follow the creek upstream. Watch for cairns to show you the way. Green Lake's water is sparkling clear and though it's a little chilly for swimming, angling for rainbow and brook trout can be fantastic. The lake is situated at the base of several colorful metamorphic pinnacles, the most notable being Gabbro Peak, which dominates the pine-dotted southern shore. Glines Canyon's forested valley stretches into the distance toward the saddle of Virginia Pass, beyond which lies Yosemite National Park. West Lake's outlet forms a thin cascade as it tumbles over chunky dark rock, accentuating the entire scene.

Backpackers will find wonderful spots to set up camp near Green Lake or can continue on to East Lake, about 1.5 mile farther. Day hikers can take a relaxing respite before returning to the trailhead.

# 25

## Virginia Lakes Basin

*Type: Day hike*

*Season: Mid-June to October*

*Total distance: 6 miles round trip*

*Rating: Moderate to strenuous*

*Elevation: 9,843 feet; +1,282 feet/-1 feet*

*Location: Humboldt-Toiyabe National Forest, Hoover Wilderness*

*Maps: USGS Dunderberg Peak; USFS Toiyabe National Forest–Bridgeport Ranger District*

*Fees and permits: A permit is not required for this day hike. Overnight users camping in Hoover Wilderness must obtain a permit (and pay a reservation fee) from Humboldt-Toiyabe National Forest.*

*Contact: Humboldt-Toiyabe National Forest, Bridgeport Ranger District (760-932-7070; www.fs.fed.us/r4/htnf).*

Beneath the watchful gaze of Dunderberg Peak and Black Mountain, glacially carved Virginia Lakes Basin is in a class by itself. This challenging hike explores a picturesque string of lakes and climbs the headwall of this vivid basin to a windswept pass where you gain arresting views of Yosemite's barren high country and a new perspective of the valley you just traversed. Though steep in sections, the trail also enjoys its share of level walking in between climbs, so you have plenty of time to recover. Pack along a windbreaker, as the pass can be breezy.

### GETTING THERE

From Bridgeport, drive 13 miles south on US 395 to Conway Summit and the turnoff for Virginia Lakes. Drive 6.1 miles southwest on Virginia Lakes Road to the trailhead parking area at road's end. Find the trailhead behind a small restroom building on the far end of the parking lot.

### THE TRAIL

The Virginia Lakes Basin has some of the most beautiful scenery in all of the Sierra Nevada. What makes it so unique is that instead of the speckled gray granite so characteristic of the High Sierras, you get deep red volcanic rock, evidence of the Sierra Nevada's tumultuous volcanic past. When you consider the whole geologic package—glaciation, volcanism, uplift—you are left with a wonderland of sparkling lakes, polychromatic mountains, and sweeping vistas.

25. Virginia Lakes Basin

Ⓟ Parking
•••• Side Trail

N ←

0 ——— 1/2 mile
0 ——— 1/2 kilometer

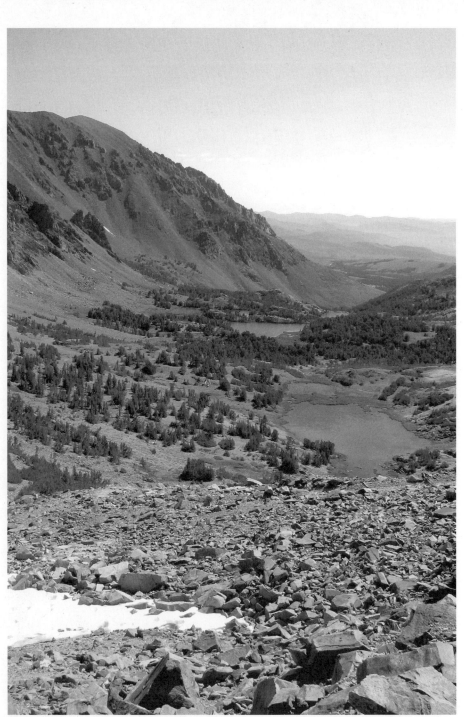

*Virginia Lakes Basin as viewed from Burro Pass*

Begin by skirting the lodgepole-lined shore of Big Virginia Lake. Not long into the hike, a spur trail from the campground joins in from the right. Pass a small pond before the trail forks at the entry sign for Hoover Wilderness. Either path is fine, as they rejoin farther down the trail; however, the left fork stays along the shore and has a milder gradient.

Leave the forest behind as you ascend an open hillside of sage, mountain snowberry, and scattered wildflowers along the northern canyon wall. Reach Blue Lake and begin a gently ascending traverse across a talus slope spanning the toe of Dunderberg Peak. Across the way, Cooney Lake's outlet stream spills from the lip of the next terrace, through a red-tinged cleft, and disappears into the trees, reappearing just before plunging into Blue Lake's deep water.

Geographically speaking, the lakes in this chain are referred to as paternoster lakes. By eroding weak rock on the valley floor, glaciers often create a series of rock steps and excavated basins, resulting in a glacial stairway. When the ice recedes, rock-bound lakes may fill the basin, often appearing like beads on a string, connected by streams flowing down the glacial trough. At the valley's head is another glacial landform called a cirque, an oftentimes steep-sided amphitheater formed at the head of an alpine valley by glacial erosion. This will all become very obvious once you reach your goal and can peer down on the landscape.

The trail grade increases as you ascend through a wet area filled with cinquefoil, aster, and arnica. The trail dries out briefly before an easy boulder hop over the outlet for unseen Moat Lake, situated high above. The streamlet is brimming with California corn lily and a profusion of lupine. Continue ascending the rooty, rocky trail and at 1 mile

pass a dilapidated log miner's cabin. As you mount the next terrace, which corrals Cooney Lake, watch for pride of the mountain blooming from rocky crevasses and enjoy the view down the valley toward Mono Basin. To the west, your goal is in sight—the low point in the saddle at the head of the valley. (Though unnamed on the USGS topographic map, the pass is unofficially referred to as Burro Pass.)

Briefly follow the shore of Cooney Lake before climbing a series of switchbacks cut into the ochre-colored terrain. Approaching the 1.5-mile mark, use steppingstones to cross the creek that spills from a cluster of lakes collectively called Frog Lakes. Enjoy level walking as you meander through the trio and make another easy crossing of the stream linking them together. The largest of the Frog Lakes (the last one you come to) makes a pleasant picnic spot.

The ascent gently resumes, a warm-up for the steeper climb ahead, and you wind through clumps of weather-battered whitebark pine and a smattering of mountain hemlock. At 2.1 miles, rise above the first lake in the chain, a grassy, unnamed tarn situated at the foot of brooding Black Mountain and the headwall you are about to tackle. Later switchbacks slice through the scree-covered hillside, taking you higher. Watch your footing along the rocky path and look for red heather and Davidson's penstemon sprouting from the rocks. The views down canyon are nothing short of amazing and will hopefully keep your mind off the steady trudge.

Reach the broad bench of Burro Pass (11,125 feet) at 3 miles. Follow the trail a few yards beyond the actual crest and take in the stunning multicolored scene. To the west, the mountains and peaks of Yosemite's rugged northeast corner pitch and roll into the horizon. Stark and barren but fantastically beautiful, this is a panorama you won't soon forget. The vista to the east is no less impressive. From your lofty saddle, the Virginia Lakes Basin is on full display, its lake-filled terraces stretching toward the dry expanse of Mono Basin. If the elevation on this hike doesn't take your breath away, the vistas will.

When you're done admiring the scene, return to Frog Lake for a picnic out of the wind before descending back to the trailhead.

# 26

## Mono Lake

*Type: Day hike*

*Season: May through October*

*Total distance: 2-mile loop (Panum Crater)/0.75-mile loop (South Tufa)*

*Rating: Easy/easy*

*Elevation: 6,842 feet; +357 feet/-357 feet (Panum Crater)/6,413 feet; +31 feet/-31 feet (South Tufa)*

*Location: Mono Basin National Forest Scenic Area, Inyo National Forest*

*Maps: USGS 7.5' Lee Vining (trail not shown); USFS Inyo National Forest*

*Fees and permits: A permit is not required for these day hikes. There is a day-use fee of $3 per person charged at the South Tufa area (children 15 and under are free).*

*Contact: Mono Lake Tufa State Reserve (760-647-6331; www.parks.ca.gov/?page_id=514).*

While not technically "in" the Sierra Nevada, Mono Lake lies in the Great Basin along the eastern margin of this massive range. The exposed high desert terrain makes it easy to explore the surrounding volcanic landscape and the unusual tufa towers of the ancient landlocked lake. Two hikes are detailed here. If you find yourself limited on time and can choose only one, definitely head for the South Tufa area. There is no shade along either trail, and during summer, the region can be extremely hot, so an early morning start is best.

### GETTING THERE

From the Mono Lake Visitor Center just north of Lee Vining, drive 5.8 miles south on US 395 and turn left onto CA 120 east toward Benton. Drive 3 miles and turn left onto the signed turnoff for Panum Crater. Follow the narrow, unpaved road 0.8 mile to the parking area with no facilities. To get to the South Tufa Area from US 395, drive 4.7 miles along CA 120 east toward Benton (passing the turnoff for Panum Crater) and turn left onto the signed turnoff for Mono Lake South Tufa. Pass the unpaved road leading to Navy Beach at 0.1 mile and proceed straight. Continue along the now unpaved road 0.8 mile to the large parking area with pit toilets.

### THE TRAIL

The Mono Basin visitors center is a great place to start your visit, and includes a variety of exhibits explaining the natural and human history of the area.

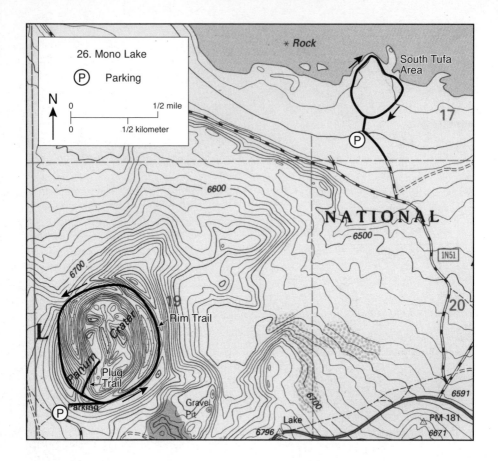

The first hike explores Panum Crater, one of the northernmost plug-dome volcanoes in a chain stretching from Long Valley Caldera near Mammoth Lakes some 30 miles to the south.

The Mono Craters, as the chain is collectively called, represent the youngest mountain range in North America, having erupted into existence within the last 40,000 years. (Panum Crater is the youngest, having erupted around 650 years ago.) After the eruption, cooled lava created a domelike structure that now "plugs" the volcanic vent beneath the dormant—not extinct—crater.

From the parking area, ascend a wide, pumice-laden trail lined with bitterbrush and desert peach to the rim of the crater. From here you can see the rocky plugged dome (you'll walk inside later). Follow the Rim Trail in a counterclockwise direction (the open terrain makes it difficult to get lost). As you make your way around the rim, enjoy splendid views of the eastern Sierra Nevada, notice the Mono Craters extending south, and garner a bird's-eye view of Mono Lake. The entire trail is rather sandy and there are a couple of steep sections, but for the most part it's easy going.

Watch for butter-colored blazing star and sulphur-flower along the trail, adding splashes of color to the otherwise drab desert palette. You might also spot obsidian, a shiny black rock that has extremely sharp edges when broken, making it a favorite of Native Americans for spear and arrow points. Circumnavigate the rim after 1.5 miles and then head toward the center of the crater via the Plug Trail, which climbs 0.25 mile to the top of the dome. Follow all trail signs and avoid cutting or collecting.

The shore of Mono Lake and the South Tufa area is our next stop. The 60-square-mile lake is one of the oldest lakes in North America (more than one million years old).

Because the lake has no outlet, water's only means of escape is through evaporation, a process that leaves behind a profuse amount of dissolved salt, making the lake two and a half times as salty and eighty times as alkaline as seawater. Once referred to as a dead sea, Mono Lake is actually a productive ecosystem, albeit a fragile one, that supports a variety of bird species including grebes, phalaropes, and gulls.

Our walk begins near several information boards that detail the flora and fauna that have adapted and thrive in this saline-rich environment. The paved trail heads north through a Russian thistle- and sage-covered landscape. Interpretive signs guide you

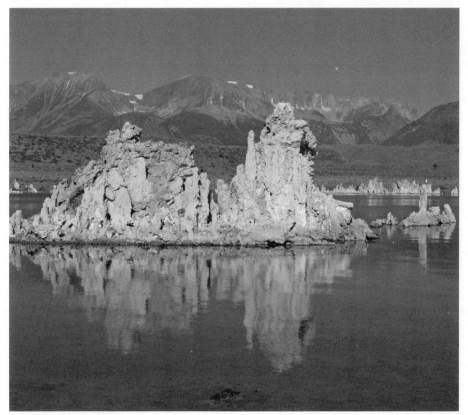

*Tufa towers at Mono Lake*

along the way. Take note of the lake level signs signifying the lake's historic elevation. In 1941 the City of Los Angeles began diverting four of the five major streams that empty into Mono Lake, causing the lake to drop more than 40 feet. Concerns over the lake's fragile ecosystem, health risks associated with airborne alkali dust, and aesthetics led to a long-running political and judicial battle that finally ended in 1994 when the State Water Resources Control Board issued an order protecting the lake and its tributary streams.

Approaching the lake, the path turns into a boardwalk and you begin to see the peculiar tufa formations sprouting about. Tufa is formed when underwater springs rich in calcium mix with lake water rich in carbonates, resulting in a chemical reaction that creates calcium carbonate, or limestone. Over time, the limestone accumulates, forming the towers and spires that decorate Mono Lake's shoreline. On a calm day, photographers will enjoy the chance to capture the otherworldly reflection of tufa towers and the distant Sierra Nevada Mountains in Mono Lake's brackish water.

The boardwalk ends at the beach, where you will undoubtedly notice the carpet of black alkali flies near the water's edge and perhaps clouds of tiny brine shrimp swimming in the water. Both serve as the main course for more than eighty species of migratory birds that depend on the lake for food and refuge.

Turn right at the end of the boardwalk and follow the shore 0.15 mile to a trail sign and a narrow single-track trail that leads to a second beach. The trail then meets a junction heading east toward Navy Beach which, if you have time, creates a longer loop. We stay straight and return to the parking area.

# 27

## San Joaquin Ridge

*Type: Day hike*

*Season: Mid-June to mid-October*

*Total distance: 4.5 miles round trip*

*Rating: Moderate*

*Elevation: 9,255 feet; +1,044 feet/-51 feet*

*Location: Inyo National Forest*

*Maps: USGS Mammoth Mountain; Trails Illustrated Mammoth Lakes Mono Divide No. 809*

*Fees and permits: A permit is not required for this day hike.*

*Contact: Inyo National Forest, Mammoth Ranger Station (760-924-5500; www.fs .fed.us/r5/inyo).*

This hike traverses a high-altitude ridgeline that serves as the boundary between the Ansel Adams Wilderness and Inyo National Forest. The trail climbs steadily along a wide four-wheel-drive road toward Deadman Pass and our goal, a lofty unnamed knoll (10,248 feet) along the summit ridge. Along the way, enjoy breathtaking vistas of the Ritter Range jutting to the west and the docile White Mountains rising on the eastern horizon. If the climb is too rigorous, simply walk for as long or as short as you like, and the views all along the trail won't disappoint. The limited canopy (which gradually dwindles the higher you climb and eventually become nonexistent) can make this jaunt rather warm in the afternoon, so get an early start and pack along plenty of water and sunblock.

### GETTING THERE

From Bishop, drive 39 miles north on US 395. Exit CA 203 and drive west 3.8 miles toward Mammoth Lakes/Devils Postpile. Turn right onto Minaret Road (still designated CA 203) and continue 5.4 miles to Minaret Summit, passing Mammoth Mountain along the way. Turn right just before the entrance station to Devils Postpile and follow the paved road 0.3 mile to the small trailhead parking area.

### THE TRAIL

Start at the stone overlook that has a helpful display to familiarize you with the jagged peaks of the Ritter Range that dominate your field of view. Mount Ritter, the most prominent peak, rises 13,157 feet on this

imposing skyline of granite. Immediately north of Ritter is Banner Peak, and immediately south of both is a cluster of serrated peaks collectively known as The Minarets, named for their resemblance to the spires on Muslim temples (minaret means "pillar" or "tower" in Arabic). Their sawtooth appearance is a result of the expansion of ice that has formed in the cracks of the rock. The seasonal repetition of freezing and thawing fragments the granite, chiseling the mountains' jagged appearance.

From the far end of the parking area, behind the restrooms, join a footpath that descends briefly northeast to a four-wheel-drive road. Veer left onto the road as it heads due north through a diffuse mixed conifer forest. Take note of where you joined the road—sans signs pointing the way, it's easy to miss on the return trip. Not long after you merge with the road, a narrower trail branches left. Continue along the wider road and emerge onto a dry hillside covered with sage and mountain snowberry and speckled with Brewer's lupine, nude buckwheat, woolly mule's ears, and mountain pennyroyal. Without trees blocking the view, you can peer both east and west as you make your way uphill.

At 0.4 mile, you get a short breather as the grade eases, but don't get too comfortable.

*The Ritter Range*

The level stretch covered in sun-bleached pumice and occasional sprouting sulphur-flower is short-lived, and the climb resumes less than 0.5 mile later. The higher you climb, the sparser the trees and ground cover become. Lose the view briefly as you enter a swath of pines and a miniature field of aster.

Past the occlusive vegetation, on the now shadeless path, don't forget to turn around and take in the view of Mammoth Mountain at your back. Its slopes, devoid of snow, are rife with unseen mountain bikers sprinting down its ski-run-scarred face. A fork at 1.3 mile calls for a decision. Stay left and slowly advance along the steepening ridge. As you attain the crest of this challenging hump, the grade eases and your views expand south and east to include Lake Crowley and the White Mountains.

At 1.6 miles, stay left at another junction and once again head steeply uphill. Gnarled and weather-battered whitebark pines dot the hillside. These hardy pines can eke out an existence in the most unforgiving environments. You will also spot sporadic wildflowers such as ranger's buttons, lupine, and Sierra penstemon. Spot your goal up ahead, the views taking your mind off the trudge still remaining.

Though it may seem illogical, the ridge beneath your feet is where High Sierra waters divide. From west to east, the Sierras take the form of a non-equilateral triangle—the altitude gradually increases as you travel east toward the crest, beyond which the altitude swiftly decreases, resulting in the abrupt eastern Sierra escarpment. Precipitation falling on the western slope of this ridge feeds the San Joaquin River, eventually emptying into the Pacific Ocean. Precipitation dropping on the eastern slope flows into the Owens River, which ultimately provides water to parched southern California, little of it reaching the ocean.

Attain the knoll at 2.25 miles and bask in the 360-degree panorama. Views north expand toward Deadman Pass, the Two Teats, and countless distant peaks poking toward the sky. To the west, the forested valley gives way to barren granite pinnacles and shady crevasses that harbor lingering snow. The tempered topography of the White Mountains and the Great Basin stretches east and Mammoth Mountain, and behind it Mammoth Crest, bulges to the south.

Experienced hikers can continue another 3.5 miles along the challenging ridge to San Joaquin Mountain (11,600 feet). For now, be content to savor the views before returning to your vehicle.

# 28

## Devils Postpile to Rainbow Falls

*Type: Day hike*

*Season: Mid-June to mid-October*

*Total distance: 3.5 miles one way*

*Rating: Easy*

*Elevation: 7,564 feet; +455 feet/-347 feet*

*Location: Devils Postpile National Monument, Ansel Adams Wilderness, Inyo National Forest*

*Maps: USGS Mammoth Mountain, Crystal Crag; Trails Illustrated Mammoth Lakes Mono Divide No. 809*

*Fees and permits: A permit is not required for this day hike. From mid-June into September, day-use visitors to Devils Postpile must ride a shuttle bus. Purchase tickets and board buses at Mammoth Mountain ($7 for adults, $4 for children ages 3 to 15, and free for kids under 2).*

*Contact: Devils Postpile National Monument (760-934-2289; www.nps .gov/depo).*

Explore a fantastic columnar basalt formation and watch the Middle Fork of the San Joaquin River plunge over a volcanic cliff on this easy hike through Devils Postpile National Monument. By disembarking the shuttle bus at stop 6 (Devils Postpile) and boarding at stop 9 (Rainbow Falls Trailhead) you can do this hike one way and only retrace your steps for about 0.5 mile.

### GETTING THERE

From Bishop, drive 39 miles north on US 395. Exit CA 203 and drive west 3.8 miles toward Mammoth Lakes/Devils Postpile. Turn right onto Minaret Road (still designated CA 203) and continue 4.2 miles to Mammoth Mountain. Park here and buy tickets for the shuttle bus.

### THE TRAIL

Find the trailhead on the south side of the ranger station at the Devils Postpile shuttle stop (#6). The wide trail begins by bisecting verdant Soda Springs Meadow. The Middle Fork San Joaquin River flows lazily to your right. Enter a lodgepole forest and after a gentle climb, come to a trail fork at 0.2 mile. Veer left and continue your ascent toward Devils Postpile. Nearing the postpile, come to the northern junction of a loop trail that climbs to the top of this unusual geologic formation. Stay straight and explore the postpile from below before backtracking to this junction and venturing atop the columns.

Devils Postpile is one of the finest examples of columnar basalt in the world. About

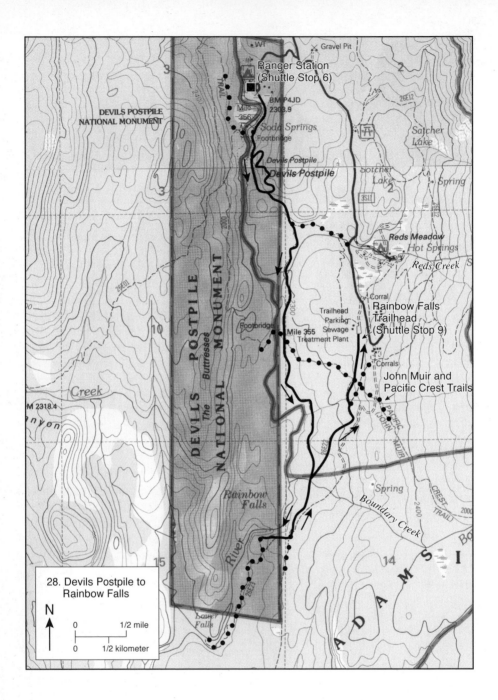

Ranger Station
(Shuttle Stop 6)

BM P4JD
2303.9

Soda Springs
Footbridge

Devils Postpile

Devils Postpile

Satcher
Lake

Sotcher
Lake

Spring

Reds Meadow

Hot Springs

Reds Creek

Corral

Trailhead
Parking

Sewage

Treatment Plant

Mile 355

Footbridge

Rainbow Falls
Trailhead
(Shuttle Stop 9)

Corrals

John Muir and
Pacific Crest Trails

PACIFIC

JOHN MUIR

Spring

Boundary Creek

CREST TRAIL

Rainbow
Falls

River

Lower
Falls

DEVILS POSTPILE    NATIONAL MONUMENT

The Buttresses

Creek

Canyon

BM 2318.4

ADAMS

28. Devils Postpile to
Rainbow Falls

N

0        1/2 mile

0        1/2 kilometer

100,000 years ago, lava erupted some 2 miles upstream from the current location of the monument. As lava flowed down the valley, it presumably ran into a natural obstruction, causing it to pool (up to 400 feet in some places). The lava, which was remarkably uniform in its mineral composition, then began to cool at a very slow rate. As the molten lava cooled, it contracted and cracked, forming hexagonal columns. Later, a glacial event exposed the columns and polished the top of the formation, which looks like tile flooring.

In the early 1900s, pressure from local mining interests who wanted to blast the postpile and dam the river won out briefly, and the monument, originally part of Yosemite National Park, lost its park status. Luckily, before any devastation took place, conservationists pushing for federal protection prevailed, and in 1911 the 798-acre monument was created.

Today, the dark basalt columns range from 40 to 60 feet high. Most are vertical but some are irregular and contorted. The formation appears as a giant chain of volcanic rock dominoes frozen in mid-topple—the warped northern fringe in the process of collapsing, the southern end erect and poised. Many of the columns, felled by natural processes such earthquakes and erosion, lie in a fragmented heap at the base of the postpile.

Past the monument, the trail moves away from the river and climbs again. You eventually meet up with the southern junction of the loop trail to the top of the postpile near the 0.5-mile mark. (If you climb to the top of the postpile and complete the loop, this is where you will rejoin the main trail.) From here, the trail generally descends through a lodgepole pine and red fir forest.

Although it is geographically located on the western slope of the Sierra Nevada, the monument's proximity to the eastern escarpment puts it at the nexus of several climatic regions, resulting in a rich and unusual mix of species. Flora includes both the wetter western species (red fir, mountain hemlock, alder, and gooseberry) and drier eastern species (quaking aspen, Sierra juniper, sagebrush, and Jeffrey pine).

At 0.75 mile, reach the junction with the Reds Meadow Trail. Stay straight and shortly thereafter navigate an easy log crossing of Reds Creek. Our trail, which generally follows the eastern boundary of the park, continues in a southward direction, meeting up with the river once again. Carefully walk to the edge of the ravine to spy it coursing below.

Pass an intersection with the John Muir Trail at 1.25 miles. You have undoubtedly noticed the thinning forest and the plethora of downed and fire-scarred trees since leaving the postpile, all the unfortunate result of the lightning-ignited Rainbow Fire in 1992, which destroyed the thickly forested slopes near the monument, taking away the shady canopy and leaving only singed stumps in its wake.

Enjoy mostly level walking with some mellow ups and downs on the now shadeless and sandy path as you approach the junction with the Rainbow Falls Trail. Take note of this intersection, as you will turn right here on the return trip to reach the Rainbow Falls Trailhead.

Cross Boundary Creek via a wooden footbridge and you'll soon pass a sign announcing your entry into Ansel Adams Wilderness. Veer right at the junction with Fish Creek Trail and descend a log-lined stairway to an overlook directly across from the falls. From a cliff of volcanic rock, watch the wide San Joaquin River plummet 101 feet into a pool of green water at the base of a dark, vertical-walled canyon. When the

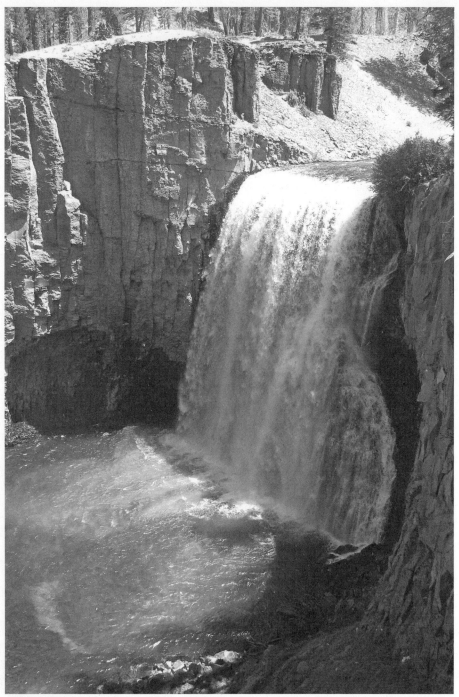

*Rainbow Falls*

sun is just right, you can watch rainbows dance in the billowing mist.

From the viewpoint, you have the option of continuing along the east bank of the river to Lower Falls, about 0.7 mile farther, and a stairway that leads down to river level (this mileage is not considered in the total given above). When you are done admiring the falls, retrace your steps to the Rainbow Falls Trail junction, where you take the right fork and head uphill 0.75 mile to the trailhead. The gradient is easy and there are several shady spots to rest. Along the way you will pass a junction leading to Reds Meadow Resort, and later the Pacific Crest Trail will cross your path. From the trailhead sign, proceed 100 yards up the unpaved road to the shuttle stop.

# 29

## Little Lakes Valley to Gem Lakes

*Type: Day hike or overnight*

*Season: June through October*

*Total distance: 7.1 miles round trip*

*Rating: Moderate*

*Elevation: 10,264 feet; +760 feet/-73 feet*

*Location: Inyo National Forest, John Muir Wilderness*

*Maps: USGS Mount Morgan, Mount Abbot; Trails Illustrated Mammoth Lakes Mono Divide No. 809*

*Fees and permits: A permit is not required for this day hike. Overnight users camping in John Muir Wilderness must obtain a permit (and pay a reservation fee) from Inyo National Forest.*

*Contact: Inyo National Forest, White Mountain Ranger Station (760-873-2500 general information, 760-873-2483 permits; www.fs.fed.us/r5/inyo).*

Little Lakes Valley is one of the most scenic areas in the entire eastern Sierra. With a paved roadway ready to deposit you at the over 10,000-foot altitude trailhead, it's the easiest way to experience High Sierra splendor with the least amount of effort. This ease of arrival is both a blessing and a curse, and you should be prepared to share the trail with everyone from young families to 70-somethings, but don't let that stop you. This trail meanders past a delightful chain of lakes into a wonderland of exposed granite, and with the mellow gradient and variety of turnaround options this out-and-back hike is one to add to your must-do list.

### GETTING THERE

From Mammoth, drive 14.8 miles south on US 395 and turn right (southwest) onto Rock Creek Road (near Tom's Place). The roadway is two-lane and paved for 8.8 miles. Past the pack station, the road becomes a single lane with turnouts for the final 1.6 miles to road's end at Mosquito Flat, where you will find the trailhead parking area.

### THE TRAIL

The starting elevation of this hike is undoubtedly higher than most of us are accustomed to, so take precautions to avoid the effects of altitude sickness by drinking plenty of fluids and taking it slow.

From the southern end of the parking area, past the restroom, begin by gently ascending the west bank of willow-lined Rock Creek. The sandy trail is brightly trimmed with lupine, cinquefoil, larkspur, and Indian

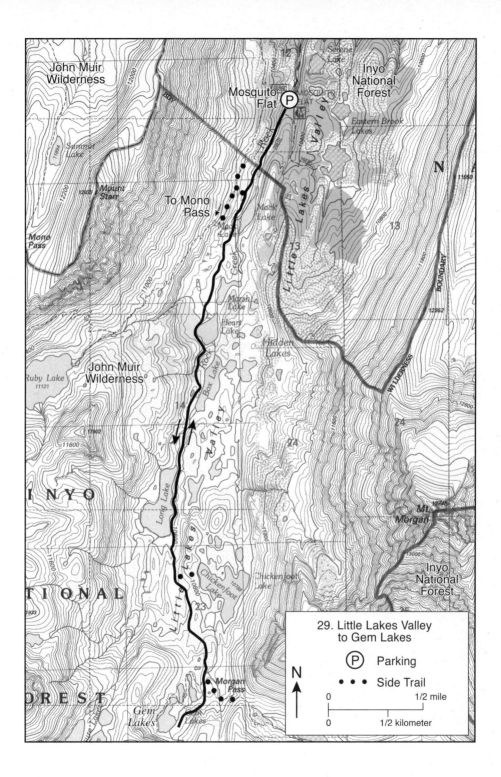

John Muir
Wilderness

Inyo
National
Forest

Serene
Lake

Mosquito
Flat

Eastern Brook
Lakes

Summit
Lake

Mount
Starr

To Mono
Pass

Mack
Lake

Mono
Pass

VALLEY

Creek

Marsh
Lake

Heart
Lake

Hidden
Lakes

John Muir
Wilderness

Ruby Lake
11121

Box Lake

Valley

WILDERNESS

BOUNDARY

INYO

Long Lake

Little Lakes

Chickenfoot
Lake

Chickenfoot Lake

Mt.
Morgan

TIONAL

Inyo
National
Forest

REST

Morgan
Pass

Gem
Lakes

Little Lakes

29. Little Lakes Valley
to Gem Lakes

(P)   Parking

• • •   Side Trail

N

0             1/2 mile

0          1/2 kilometer

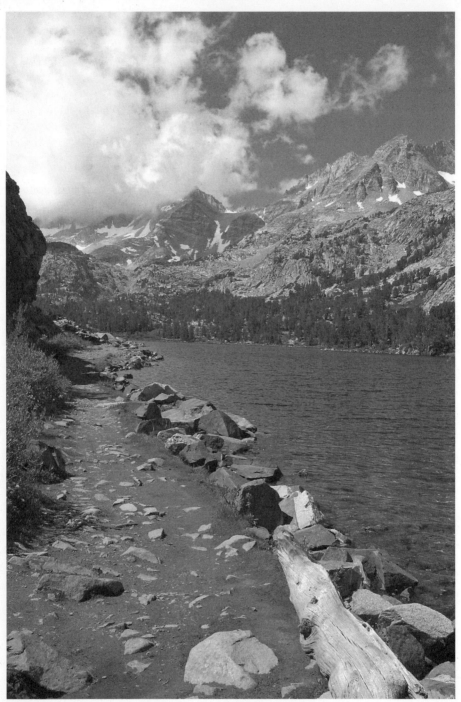

*Long Lake*

paintbrush. A short distance from the trail-head, pass a sign indicating entry into the John Muir Wilderness and climb a series of widely spaced rock steps.

Take the left fork at the Mono Pass trail junction and continue toward Morgan Pass. Cresting a short climb, gain a magnificent view of Little Lakes Valley and a host of 13,000-foot snow-clad peaks standing sentinel at its helm—Mount Mills (13,451 feet), Mount Abbot (13,704 feet), Mount Dade (13,400 feet), and Bear Creek Spire (13,713 feet). Along much of the trail, the lodgepole and whitebark pine forest is open, allowing full appreciation of the ever-changing vistas as you delve deeper into this glacially carved valley.

The trail descends into a small meadow and crosses the inlet for Mack Lake, which is somewhat shrouded to the left. This process repeats a few times—gentle climb, fabulous view, descend to flower-filled meadow. Pass a footpath heading east to Marsh Lake and, at 1.2 mile, an easy boulder hop—and later a wooden footbridge—take you across an inlet to Heart Lake. Skirt the western shore of this popular fishing hole, admiring the small cascade on the opposite side where Rock Creek spills in.

Leave Heart Lake and begin another brief ascent, which crests high above Box Lake. Its sparkling blue-green water is like a mirror reflecting the pines, granite, and sky that encircle it.

Rejoin the western bank of Rock Creek and use steppingstones to cross it at 1.8 miles. Look for Coleville's columbine sprouting from the cracks and crevasses in a talus slope to the left. Opposite, Rock Creek, pacified for the moment, meanders through a grass-filled meadow. Traverse a somewhat shady section and arrive at Long Lake's boulder-strewn shore just past the 2-mile mark. Bear Creek Spire and Mount Abbot dominate the southern horizon. The trail is hemmed by a sheer cliff to the left and Long Lake's clear, trout-filled waters to the right. At the far end of the lake there is a broad grassy area, ideal for spreading out a picnic or casting a line.

Past Long Lake, the largest lake of the chain, the trail gradient increases as you climb to a junction with Chickenfoot Lake, which lies in the shadow of Mount Morgan (13,748 feet). Oddly enough, the lake looks like a chicken's foot on the topographic map. The lake is 0.2 mile from the main trail, and backpackers will enjoy excellent camping near its shore. Forgoing this side trip, continue up the rocky path which rolls up and down through the narrowing valley and its imposing granitic terrain. Cross the outlet for Gem Lakes at 3.25 miles, and immediately bear right at the Morgan Pass junction to head toward Gem Lakes.

Morgan Pass, at just over 11,000 feet, is a relatively easy conquest at this point. Vertically ascend 225 feet over 0.35 mile and you're there. From the rocky saddle, you have fantastic views down Little Lakes Valley and of the Morgan Lakes extending southeast.

For now, follow the verdant single-track trail along the outlet's southern bank. The level trail is dotted with red heather, water-loving willows, and swamp onion. Gem Lakes is comprised of a trio of peaceful alpine ponds. Passing the two smaller ones first, notice Mount Dade's hulking presence in the background. The trail culminates at the largest lake, which is framed by steep, striated granite walls and a monstrous talus slope. Trout are found in all three lakes, and if you've packed a rod, now's the chance to test your mettle against the resident wild brookies, which are delightfully hungry. Campsites near Gem Lakes are limited due to the marshy, rocky nature of the terrain.

Linger as long as you like before back-tracking along the same trail and enjoying the scenery all over again in reverse.

# 30

## Blue Lake

*Type: Day hike or overnight*

*Season: Late June to mid-October*

*Total distance: 6.3 miles round trip*

*Rating: Moderate to strenuous*

*Elevation: 9,080 feet; +1,383 feet/-76 feet*

*Location: Inyo National Forest, John Muir Wilderness*

*Maps: USGS Mount Thompson; Trails Illustrated Mammoth Lakes Mono Divide No. 809*

*Fees and permits: A permit is not required for this day hike. Overnight users camping in John Muir Wilderness must obtain a permit (and pay a reservation fee) from Inyo National Forest.*

*Contact: Inyo National Forest, White Mountain Ranger Station (760-873-2500 general information, 760-873-2483; permits, www.fs.fed.us/r5/inyo).*

This moderately challenging hike near the Sierra Crest is chock full of fantastic vistas and austere alpine scenery. Throw in a few splashing cataracts, superb trout fishing, and a fine picnic spot, and you've got the makings for a perfect day in the backcountry.

### GETTING THERE

From US 395 in Bishop, head west on CA 168 toward Lake Sabrina and South Lake. At 15 miles, the road to South Lake veers left. You stay straight and continue toward Lake Sabrina and the trailhead 3.7 miles farther. The road narrows past the Sabrina Campground. Early birds can find parking in the small roadside turnouts nearest the trailhead; otherwise park in the designated hiker parking area near the intersection with North Lake Road (0.4 mile northeast of the actual trailhead). Walk along the road and find the trailhead on the left-hand side.

### THE TRAIL

Long before Samuel Addison Bishop drove herds of cattle into the Owens Valley in 1861 to support miners and business owners in the booming city of Aurora, Nevada (now a ghost town) some 80 miles to the north, the area was inhabited by resourceful Paiute people. Like other Native Americans of the Sierra Nevada, the Paiute were nomadic. As seasons changed, they moved throughout the region harvesting pine nuts and other vegetation, fishing, and hunting game such as deer and desert bighorn sheep.

The winter of 1861–62 was especially severe for the Paiute, and traditional food

WILDERNESS

Parking
Area

To
Bishop

Inyo National
Forest

36

Boat
Ramp

Sabrina

Lake

ELEVATION
9128

32

11642

WILDERNESS

Spring

BOUNDARY

SECOND

To George
Lake

Spring

6

10200

+ 10588

Little George
Lake

To
Midnight
Lake

Blue Lake

John Muir
Wilderness

To
Donkey
Lake

8

### 30. Blue Lake

<table>
<tr><td>Ⓟ</td><td>Parking</td></tr>
<tr><td>•••</td><td>Side Trail</td></tr>
</table>

N

0          1/4 mile

0          1/4 kilometer

sources became scarce. When the recently transplanted cattle began foraging on vegetation they depended on for survival, it seemed only natural to the Paiute that the cattle could be killed for their own use. This sparked a period of fierce fighting, which ultimately ended a little over two years later with the surrender of hundreds of Paiute. The Owens Valley Paiute Shoshone Cultural Center-Museum in downtown Bishop is a great place to gain a better understanding of their culture and traditions before hitting the trail.

Begin by heading uphill above the dam confining the trout-filled waters of Lake Sab-rina. As quaking aspens are tickled by the breeze, look for mountain pennyroyal, Indian paintbrush, and fireweed burgeoning in the cracks between boulders. The first mile of this hike is relatively level as it traverses high above the eastern shore of the lake. Initially, you meander through lush areas decorated with brightly colored wildflowers, but soon leave that behind for dry slopes littered with sage, mountain mahogany, and bush chinquapin. Enjoy fantastic views of the Sabrina basin and at 0,8 mile, cross the boundary for John Muir Wilderness.

Just past the 1-mile mark, climb a series of switchbacks and pass a junction heading

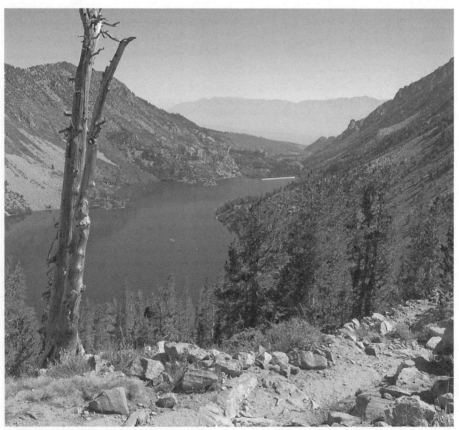

*Lake Sabrina and the distant White Mountains*

*Eastern Sierra*

steeply east toward George Lake, then up and over the Table Mountains to Tyee Lakes. Continue straight and boulder-hop across the outlet for George Lake, and not long after spot a lovely sheet of water sliding down a rock face to the left and cross another small stream it creates. Navigate a series of switchbacks, and at 1.7 miles catch your breath and take in the view from a rocky overlook. The lake, flanked by talus- and sage-covered slopes, appears as glass, unbroken except for the ripples cast by fishing boats as they troll the sapphire waters in search of Alpers trout, rainbows, and big browns.

Under the sporadic shade of lodgepole pines, a granite stairway takes you higher. A thin ribbon of water slices down the opposite canyon wall, the outlet for a collection of unseen alpine lakes. At 2.3 miles, views expand to include a ridge of imposing peaks stretching out along the western skyline. Follow the boulder-lined trail over an exposed granite slab and descend ever so briefly back into the forest.

Climb another series of rock stairs before emerging at the base of a dry streambed with a handy set of switchbacks festooned with two varieties of showy columbine. The most common and most widely distributed of the native western columbines has five red elongated petals that stretch backward toward the sky while the forward portions are yellow.

Coleville's columbine has large yellow to white flowers. Where the two are found in close proximity, they tend to hybridize.

As you ascend the jumble of rocks and close in on your goal, don't forget to turn around and take in the views. Also notice the dikes (vertical) and sills (horizontal) streaking through the granite walls. These white lines are formed by igneous intrusions that create rock masses after molten material has been forced between rock layers and subsequently cools.

Crest the dry ravine, pass a muddy pond to your right, and spy Blue Lake through the trees. Level walking brings you to Blue Lake's outlet stream at 3 miles. Cross the wide outlet using rocks and logs and continue along the western shore for 0.15 mile to a granite rise. From here you have a fine view of the lake's clear waters peacefully nestled beneath the snow-clad peaks of the rugged Thompson Range. If you've packed along a pole, keep heading south along the trail where you will gain shoreline access.

Backpackers will find excellent campsites near Blue Lake or a host of other picturesque lakes farther along the trail with clever names like Dingleberry, Drunken Sailor, and Hungry Packer. With the hard climbing behind you, the trail past Blue Lake has an easy gradient, and the scenery improves with every step.

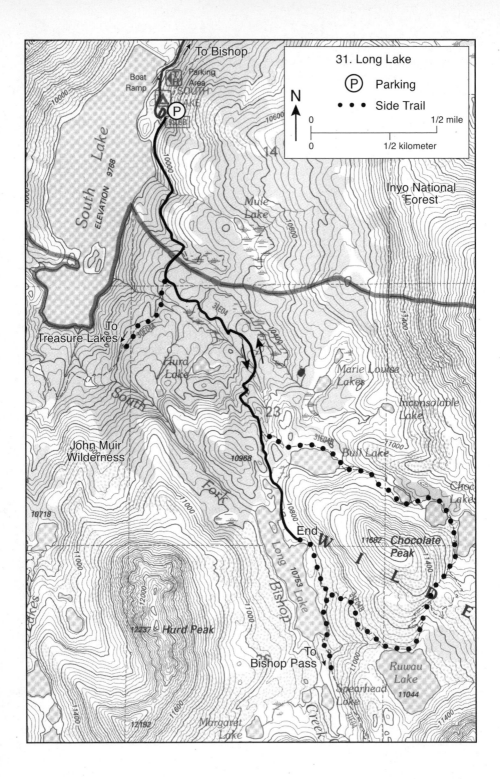

To Bishop

Boat Ramp

Parking Area

SOUTH LAKE

P

Parking

Side Trail

N

0      1/2 mile

0      1/2 kilometer

10000

South Lake

ELEVATION 9768

14

Mule Lake

10600

10600

10000

Inyo National Forest

11400

To Treasure Lakes

31E04A

31E04

10400

Hurd Lake

Marie Louise Lakes

Inconsolable Lake

11000

South

23

Bull Lake

31E04B

11000

Choc Lake

John Muir Wilderness

10968

Fork

11682

Chocolate Peak

11400

10718

1000

10800

End

W

I

L

D

E

11400

Bishop

Long Lake

10753

11000

10968

11000

12000

Hurd Peak

12237

Ruwau Lake

11044

To Bishop Pass

11000

Spearhead Lake

11600

Creek

11400

11400

12192

Margaret Lake

# 31

## Long Lake

*Type: Day hike or overnight*

*Season: Late June to mid-October*

*Total distance: 4.2 miles round trip*

*Rating: Moderate*

*Elevation: 9,833 feet; +955 feet/-43 feet*

*Location: Inyo National Forest, John Muir Wilderness*

*Maps: USGS Mount Thompson; Trails Illustrated Mammoth Lakes Mono Divide No. 809*

*Fees and permits: A permit is not required for this day hike. Overnight users camping in John Muir Wilderness must obtain a permit (and pay a reservation fee) from Inyo National Forest.*

*Contact: Inyo National Forest, White Mountain Ranger Station (760-873-2500 general information, 760-873-2483 permits; www.fs.fed.us/r5/inyo/).*

Mere minutes from Bishop, you can trade the arid Owens Valley for a more pleasant world of rushing streams, pine forests, and deep-blue lakes. The well-used South Lake trailhead offers a multitude of desirable destinations for day hikes or extended overnights. Photographers, anglers, and nature lovers alike will find something to love about this fine Eastern Sierra jaunt bursting with resplendent alpine scenery and a collection of picturesque lakes.

### GETTING THERE

From US 395 in Bishop, head west on CA 168 toward Lake Sabrina and South Lake. At 15 miles, turn left onto South Lake Road. Continue another 7 miles to road's end and the ample trailhead parking area with pit toilets.

### THE TRAIL

This hike begins near South Lake, one of the many manmade lakes created in the early 1900s as a means of corralling Sierra runoff and producing hydroelectric power. The lake is well stocked with brown, brook, and rainbow trout, making it a popular destination with anglers.

From the parking area, head south into a willowy meadow and immediately cross two wood plank footbridges. Look for ranger's buttons, fireweed, and Sierra lily along this brief section. Mere minutes from the trailhead, a postcard panorama of South Lake's forest-ringed shores and the Sierra Crest rising in the distance fill your view. Hurd

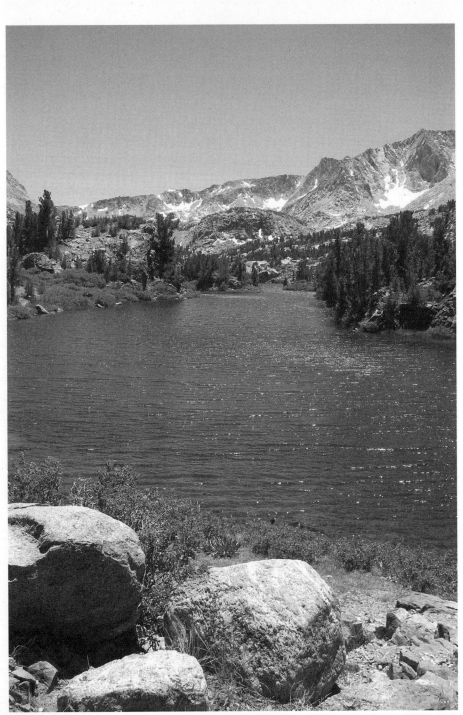

*Long Lake*

Peak, Mount Gilbert, and Mount Thompson all vie for your attention. Continue along the aspen-lined trail as it climbs above the eastern shore. Intermingled amid the aspens is a hodgepodge of sun-loving species, including mountain mahogany, sage, and their wildflower brethren—nude buckwheat, mountain pennyroyal, and fiery red penstemon.

At 0.5 mile, curve away from the lake and ascend a narrow ravine sprinkled with shooting star and columbine. Underneath the shade of lodgepole pines, switchback up the rocky trail and enter the John Muir Wilderness. The trail alternates between somewhat level walking and moderate climbs. Arrive at a junction with a trail heading to Treasure Lakes at 0.8 mile. Proceed left toward Bishop Pass and cross a shallow creek via a wooden footbridge. Below and to your right the creek drains into a grassy meadow. Shortly, the hulking mass of Hurd Peak is front and center and we arrive at another junction this time heading to Mary Louise Lakes. Keep right and continue ascending to another willow-filled glen crossing it via wooden footbridge at 1.4 miles.

Negotiate a series of short switchbacks a glimpse pine-encircled Hurd Lake below. At 1.8 miles, come to the southern end of a semi-loop trail that circumnavigates Choco-late Peak, passing Bull, Chocolate, and Ruwau Lakes in the process. This spur eventually rejoins the main trail toward the southern end of Long Lake. Maintain your course toward Bishop Pass as you make the final push toward your goal. Reach the crest after traversing yet another willow-laden section of trail and get a good look at Chocolate Peak—its anomalous brown hue a vivid contrast to the surrounding sea of gray granite.

Begin a gentle descent, reaching the north shore of Long Lake at 2.1 miles. The elongated lake, cradled between Chocolate and Hurd Peaks, is riverine looking as it snakes into the distance. In the background, Bishop Pass and Mount Goode frolic on an enormous granite teeter-totter—Bishop Pass, the low point on the horizon, holding the contraption down, allowing weary hikers passage to points beyond.

There is a healthy population of rainbow, brook, and brown trout swimming in Long Lake's cool water and an equally healthy number of anglers attempting to catch them. The trail continues along the lake's edge for a little over 0.5 mile, so continue as long as you like before turning around. Campers can stake out a spot here or continue on toward Saddlerock Lake, which sits in repose at the foot of Mount Goode.

32. Big Pine Lakes Basin
to Second Lake

# 32

## Big Pine Lakes Basin to Second Lake

*Type: Day hike or overnight*

*Season: June through September*

*Total distance: 9 miles round trip*

*Rating: Moderate to strenuous*

*Elevation: 7,820 feet; +2,314 feet/-22 feet*

*Location: Inyo National Forest, John Muir Wilderness*

*Maps: USGS 7.5' Coyote Flat, Split Mountain; USFS John Muir Wilderness*

*Fees and permits: A permit is not required for this day hike. Overnight users camping in John Muir Wilderness must obtain a permit (and pay a reservation fee) from Inyo National Forest.*

*Contact: Inyo National Forest, White Mountain Ranger Station (760-873-2500 general information, 760-873-2483 permits; www.fs.fed.us/r5/inyo).*

First, Second, and Third Lakes, although mundanely named, are anything but ordinary. In a range famous for deep-blue colored waters, this stunning trio of glacially fed lakes, their brilliant turquoise water backdropped by pine-studded shores and granite spires, is sure to grab your attention. The climb is rather unrelenting as you follow Big Pine Creek upstream to these unique High Sierra gems. A good part of the trail traverses a shadeless sagebrush landscape, so carry plenty of water and sun protection.

### GETTING THERE

From Bishop, drive 15 miles south on US 395 to Big Pine and turn right (west) onto Crocker Street, which eventually becomes Glacier Lodge Road. Signs on US 395 direct you toward Big Pine Creek Recreation Area. Follow the paved road 10.6 miles to road's end where you will find the day-use parking area with pit toilets. If the lot is full, return to the backpacker parking area farther back along the road near the pack station.

### THE TRAIL

Walk around a closed gate and begin by strolling up an old roadbed as birch- and willow-enshrouded Big Pine Creek tumbles to your left. Wander past some private cabins and follow the painted trail signs (no doubt put in place by residents tired of hikers accidentally traipsing onto their property) and cross raucous Big Pine Creek on a wooden footbridge at 0.3 mile.

Reach a junction, turn right up the North Fork Trail, and ascend the sagebrush- and mountain mahogany-covered hillside via a series of switchbacks. The South Fork Trail heads to Brainerd and Finger Lakes, which lie tucked beneath the Middle Palisade Group, a collection of peaks that attract technical climbers.

Beyond the switchbacks, rejoin the old road and turn right. Shortly thereafter, re-cross the creek on another sturdy foot-bridge. From here you can follow the Lower Trail (the old road) upstream along the creek or walk across the road and head briefly up-hill to connect with the Upper Trail, which begins at the backpacker parking area. Ei-ther way is fine; however, the Lower Trail is slightly longer. We choose the shorter path and head uphill. After a steep—but brief—climb, join the Upper Trail by veering left. The sandy trail steadily ascends the north-eastern canyon wall. Watch for mountain pennyroyal, sulphur-flower, and the occa-sional cacti interspersed among the sage-brush and scrub. By getting an early start, you can walk in the shade cast by the canyon wall before the sun gets high enough to drench it with sunlight.

Continue to a four-way intersection with Baker Trail (bending sharply right) and the Lower Trail (joining us on the left). Your cur-rent goal is the top of Second Falls, which is visible in the distance. Mount a series of rocky switchbacks and pass the John Muir Wilderness boundary sign near the top of the falls at 1.8 miles. Climb a rock staircase ad-jacent the noisy creek before leaving the scattered shade of Jeffrey and lodgepole pines to cross a field of bushy manzanita.

Enter a peaceful meadow filled with ranger's buttons, Sierra lily, Indian paint-brush, and monkshood and arrive at the Big Pine Creek Wilderness Ranger Camp cabin at 2.6 miles. The rustic stone domicile was originally built in the 1920s by silent film star Lon Chaney, best known for his roles as creepy, deformed monsters like Quasimodo and the Phantom of the Opera.

The trail continues its ascent, alternating between dry segments and wildflower-filled meadows. Round a bend at 3.3 miles and behold Temple Crag (12,975 feet). Don't be surprised to encounter helmet- and rope-toting climbers along the trail, many of whom plan on scaling this sheer rock face (I think I'll just watch). Farther along the trail, the view expands down canyon to include Mount Sill (14,163 feet), Thunderbolt Peak (14,003 feet), Mount Winchell (13,893 feet), and Mount Agassiz (13,893 feet).

The trail levels somewhat until you step across the willow-lined outlet for Black Lake and ascend a series of stone steps and ensuing switchbacks. Later, recross the stream, this time wider now, with the aid of steppingstones. At 4.1 miles, reach the Black Lake Trail junction. Backpackers or strong hikers prepared for a long day can veer right and complete a loop that travels past Black, Fourth, Third, Second, and First Lakes, ultimately returning to this junction (this semi-loop is 13 miles round trip from the trailhead).

Take the left fork and continue toward the unimaginatively named Lakes 1–7, crossing Black Lake's outlet for the final time. Glimpse First Lake's stunning aquamarine water through the trees and pass an excellent campsite in a small depression beneath the trail. This is an excellent base camp for back-packers planning to further explore Big Pine Canyon.

First through Third Lakes are fed by streams formed by the melting Palisade Gla-cier. Their characteristic turquoise color comes from light being dispersed by finely ground glacial silt suspended in the water. The Palisade Glacier holds the distinction of being the largest glacier in the Sierra and the southernmost in the United States.

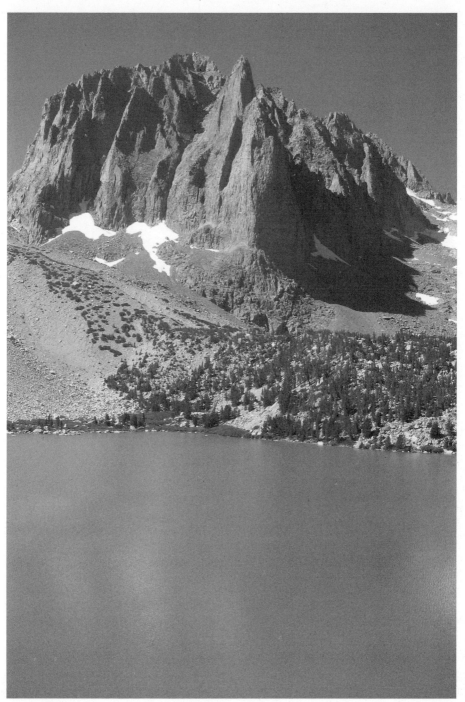

*Second Lake*

Continue 0.25 mile farther to Second Lake. Look for a small footpath between some boulders leading to a rocky perch high above the lake. Second Lake is definitely the most scenic of the trio, and from the overlook you will understand why. The lake sits in a deep granite bowl, Temple Crag's steeples towering above the southern shore. To the west, Third Lake's milky water tumbles through a rocky cleft, forming a lovely cascade.

Take time to explore the shore as far as you wish, keeping in mind that you eventually have to return to your starting point. If time allows, venture 0.7 mile farther to Third Lake. Being first in line for the glacier's runoff, it has the milkiest appearance.

# 33

## Lone Pine Lake

*Type: Day hike*

*Season: June through October*

*Total distance: 5.5 miles round trip*

*Rating: Moderate to strenuous*

*Elevation: 8,296 feet; +1,852 feet/-195 feet*

*Location: Inyo National Forest, John Muir Wilderness*

*Maps: USGS Mount Langley, Mount Whitney; USFS John Muir Wilderness*

*Fees and permits: A permit is not required for this day hike. Day hikers going beyond Lone Pine Lake and overnight users entering the Mount Whitney Zone must obtain a permit (for a fee) from Inyo National Forest. There are strict quotas and a specific application process for this trailhead.*

*Contact: Inyo National Forest, Mount Whitney Ranger Station (760-876-6200 general information, 760-873-2483 permits; www.fs.fed.us/r5/inyo).*

At 14,496 feet, Mount Whitney is the highest mountain in the continental United States. As you can imagine, with that lofty distinction, the trail to its summit is one of the most heavily traveled in all of the Sierra Nevada—so much so that the USFS has instituted a strict quota system and random lottery process as a means of divvying out permits. Day hikers can experience a slice of this magnificent trail without a permit by staying outside the Mount Whitney Zone and turning around at Lone Pine Lake, a photogenic destination and perfect picnic spot in its own right. Granted, solitude is not one of the virtues of this wildly popular trail, but the phenomenal scenery more than makes up for it.

### GETTING THERE

From US 395 in Lone Pine, turn west onto Whitney Portal Road and drive 13 miles to road's end. The trailhead is located on the north side of the roadway near the store. Park in the lot closest to the trailhead if possible; if not, backtrack to one of the other lots farther down the road.

### THE TRAIL

In 1860, under the direction of Josiah Dwight Whitney, the California Geological Survey was created. Its establishment directly correlated to California's exploding population due to the Gold Rush and the need for reliable maps and geologic data. In 1864, a small survey team, including Clarence King, one of the High Sierras' most famous explorers, entered the region

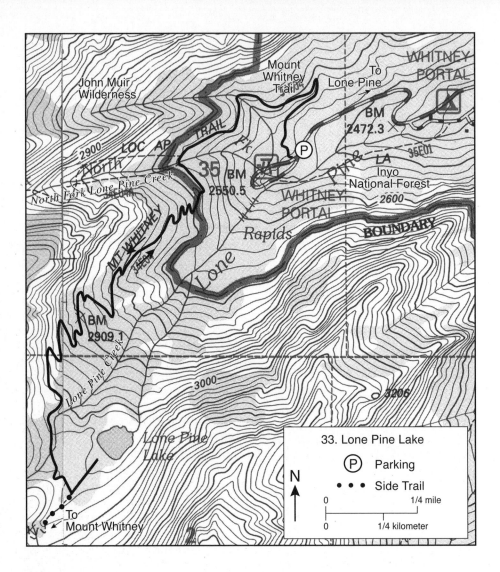

and discovered a cluster of high peaks, naming the tallest in honor of Whitney.

King attempted to climb Mount Whitney twice during their trip but was unsuccessful. He later returned, in 1871, to summit what he believed to be Mount Whitney, but which was in actuality Mount Langley farther south. By the time the error was discovered two years later, the first ascent had already been made in 1873 by three local fishermen. King eventually made the fourth ascent. John Muir, who made his first ascent in 1873 as well, was the first person to climb Mount Whitney from the east via what is today known as the Mountaineers Route.

None of these early explorers could have possibly imagined that 136 years later this mountain would attract peak baggers from

*Mount Whitney*

all corners of the globe, and that they would be required to reserve a spot months in advance for the chance to set foot on its craggy summit.

Though this hike culminates at Lone Pine Lake, a good distance from the summit, we get a taste of the many sights and sounds the trail has to offer. From the signed Mount Whitney Trailhead, just east of the store, immediately begin ascending through a mixed conifer forest. The trail initially heads in a northeastward direction before sharply bending back on itself and heading west along the northern canyon wall. The forest thins, giving way to chinquapin-, mountain mahogany-, and manzanita-covered slopes. This section of trail can be especially hot on summer afternoons, so an early start is recommended. An early start also gives you the chance to witness the sun fill the valley with warm light as it makes its daily round.

At 0.5 mile, enter a lush thicket of alder and ferns and boulder-hop across an unnamed creek. Off to your left, locked in its rocky confines, spy Lone Pine Creek putting on a display as it crashes down the valley. Not long after, cross wider North Fork Lone Pine Creek via a combination of rocks and logs. At 0.9 mile, enter John Muir Wilderness and begin switchbacking up, and up, and up.

Looking eastward, you have fine views of the Alabama Hills, the floor of the Owens Valley, and the distant White Mountains, all neatly framed by Whitney Portal Canyon's sheer granite walls. Cross willow-choked Lone Pine Creek at 2.5 miles by traversing a series of wooden logs expertly assembled to avoid soggy toes. Come to the junction with a spur trail descending left to Lone Pine Lake a short distance farther.

From the shore, granite-hemmed Lone Pine Lake appears to be dangling at the edge of the world—a natural infinity pool of sorts. Walk around its edge to the natural dam that confines it and peer up at Lone Pine Peak towering to the south while Thor Peak and Wotans Throne loom to the north. In the distance, with Mount Whitney just out of sight, serrated peaks invite us farther but alas without a permit we must return to the trailhead.

Permit-carrying travelers can continue along the main trail to Mirror Lake, Trail Camp, and finally the apex of Mount Whitney. If you've set your sights on the summit, do your research on the application process and know the rules. The hike to the top is 11 miles one way and gains upwards of 3,700 feet from its starting point at Whitney Portal. This is a nontechnical climb, and any person in good physical condition can complete the hike. There are super-hikers who ascend in one day, starting in the wee hours of the morning by flashlight and hoofing it all day, but I don't recommend it. For the best possible experience and to better your chances of reaching the summit, I suggest acclimating at Whitney Portal for one night before commencing, and then taking two to three days to summit and descend (day one, overnight at Trail Camp; day two, climb to summit and return to Trail Camp; day three, descend to Whitney Portal).

# V. Yosemite National Park

34. Wapama Falls

Ⓟ  Parking

• • •  Side Trail

⟝⟞  Footbridge

N

0 _____ 1/2 mile

0 _____ 1/2 kilometer

Falls

5400

5200

5469

Wapama
Falls

To
Rancheria
Falls

Footbridges

Footbridge

Tueeulala
Falls

4200

BDY

WILDERNESS

To Tiltill
Valley

BM
4050

×9

Mile
119

10  RESERV

HETCHY

3797

4200

HETCH

Kolana
Rock

×57

5400

BM 3814

O'Shaughnessy
Dam

BM 3813

4000

5000

Yosemite
National Park

Ⓟ

WT

Quarry

HETCH HETCHY

4600

6600

3956

× 3709

16

To CA 120

# 34

## Wapama Falls

*Type: Day hike*

*Season: April through October*

*Total distance: 5 miles round trip*

*Rating: Easy*

*Elevation: 3,805 feet; +581 feet/-515 feet*

*Location: Yosemite National Park*

*Maps: USGS 7.5' Lake Eleanor; Trails Illustrated Yosemite NW–Hetch Hetchy Reservoir No. 307*

*Fees and permits: A permit is not required for this day hike. Passenger vehicles entering the park are charged a $20 admission fee, which is good for seven days.*

*Contact: Yosemite National Park (209-372-0200 general information; www.nps.gov/yose).*

While much of the Sierra Nevada remains blanketed in snow, this low-elevation hike in Yosemite's peaceful northwest corner is a perfect primer for those itching to lace up their lug soles. The gentle trail to thunderous Wapama Falls follows the northern shore of 8-mile-long Hetch Hetchy Reservoir, passes Tueeulala Falls, and offers spectacular views of the valley along the way. The region is best experienced in the spring when flows are abundant and temperatures are mild. Summer tends to be quite warm, often reaching 90–100 degrees Fahrenheit, and although autumnal temperatures are pleasant, the valley's waterfalls aren't nearly as impressive as they are in spring.

### GETTING THERE

From the Big Oak Flat Entrance, exit the park and drive 1 mile west on CA 120, following signs for Hetch Hetchy Reservoir. Turn right on narrow Evergreen Road and travel 7.4 miles. (No vehicles over 25 feet long or 8 feet wide are allowed in the Hetch Hetchy area.) At Camp Mather, turn right on Hetch Hetchy Road and proceed 1 mile, where you will reenter the park at the Hetch Hetchy Entrance. Hetch Hetchy Reservoir and the day-use parking lot are 8 miles farther. The road to Hetch Hetchy is open 7 AM to 8 PM daily.

### THE TRAIL

John Muir (1838–1914), a man indelibly linked to Yosemite and the Sierra Nevada, was one of America's most influential naturalists and conservationists. Although Muir is most widely known for his involvement in the creation of Yosemite and other national parks, affording him the patriarchal moniker "father of our national parks," one of his most challenging battles involved the proposed damming of Hetch Hetchy Valley, said to rival Yosemite Valley itself, in an effort to supply water to the City of San Francisco.

In 1901, Muir led the Sierra Club, a group he formed in 1892, and a coalition of civic and conservation organizations in a campaign to protect the Hetch Hetchy Valley from being flooded. His lengthy and contentious battle unfortunately failed. In 1913, Congress passed the Raker Act, granting the City of San Francisco the right to dam the Hetch Hetchy Valley as a reservoir.

One of Muir's famous quotes underscores his passion for this beautiful valley: "Hetch Hetchy is a grand landscape garden, one of nature's rarest and most precious mountain temples. As in Yosemite, the sublime rocks of its walls seem to glow with life . . . while birds, bees, and butterflies help the river and waterfalls to stir all the air into music. . . . These temple destroyers, devotees of ravaging commercialism, seem to have a perfect contempt for Nature, and, instead of lifting their eyes to the God of the mountains, lift them to the Almighty Dollar. . . . Dam Hetch Hetchy! As well dam for water-tanks the people's cathedrals and churches, for no holier temple has ever been consecrated by the heart of man."

*Hetch Hetchy Reservoir*

Muir's battle wasn't all for naught. It ultimately resulted in a greater awareness and widespread conviction that our national parks are sacrosanct. Subsequent attempts to dam our national parks have been stopped because of Muir's earlier environmental campaign. Incidentally, the restoration of Hetch Hetchy still remains at the forefront of the Sierra Club's agenda.

From the parking area, walk across O'Shaughnessy Dam, named for the chief engineer, pausing atop the 312-foot-high structure to take in the view of the Poopenaut Valley and Tuolumne River to the west. To the east lies Hetch Hetchy Reservoir. The sheer face of Kolana Rock, an active breeding area for peregrine falcons, stands sentinel along the southern shore. Along the north shore, Tueeulala and Wapama Falls tumble into the reservoir, and Hetch Hetchy Dome reposes in the distance.

Once across the dam, walk through a 500-foot-long granite tunnel to a trail sign at 0.3 mile. This section of trail, an old roadbed, lies above and parallel to the northern shore of the reservoir. Lined with manzanita, gray pines, California black oak, and California bay trees, the trail is mostly exposed although there are intermittent sections of shade. Carry plenty of water and sun protection, and be aware that poison oak and rattlesnakes exist in this area of the park.

At 1 mile, you reach a left-branching trail to Tiltill Valley. Bear right, following the sign to Wapama Falls. The trail narrows past the junction and gently rises and falls as you make your way through small meadows sprinkled with purple brodiaea, monkey flower, and farewell-to-spring. As butterflies flutter about and you make several seasonal stream crossings, watch for California newts

making their slow spring migration to ponds for mating season. If you encounter them along the trail, as we did, be sure to give them plenty of space.

Leaving the meadows, come to a polished granite slab where the trail becomes vague for about 150 feet. Just keep heading east and easily pick up the trail. At 1.5 miles, arrive at the base of seasonal Tueeulala Falls. Though Tueeulala and Wapama Falls are both fed by Falls Creek, Wapama siphons the majority of water, and the feeder creek to Tueeulala is usually bone dry by July. In spring, when flows are heavy, Tueeulala Falls plunge gracefully into the valley from 1,000 feet above.

Crossing a footbridge at the base of the falls, continue along the trail where views around Kolana Rock unfold and the boisterous spray of Wapama Falls rises into the air in the distance. The trail gets increasingly rocky as you approach, and at 2.5 miles you come to the first of a series of wooden footbridges that span the base of the falls. During peak spring flows, water can cover the bridges, making passage dangerous. For the most part, though, if you aren't afraid of getting wet, crossing is well worth the drenching.

Viewing the falls from all angles as the frothy water of Falls Creek spills over the cliff edge, crashing down on the boulder-strewn landscape below, and experiencing the power of this vigorous cataract is refreshing and exhilarating. If you want to cross, but can do without the deluge, pack along a poncho and some water sandals. When you've had your fill, return via the same trail.

Those looking for a more challenging hike can continue past Wapama Falls to Rancheria Falls (13 miles round trip).

# 35

## Panorama Trail

*Type: Day hike*

*Season: Late May to October*

*Total distance: 8.2 miles one way*

*Rating: Moderate to strenuous*

*Elevation: 7,135 feet; +900 feet/-4,000 feet*

*Location: Yosemite National Park*

*Maps: USGS 7.5' Half Dome; Trails Illustrated Yosemite SW–Yosemite Valley & Wawona No. 306*

*Fees and permits: A permit is not required for this day hike. Passenger vehicles entering the park are charged a $20 admission fee, which is good for seven days. One-way bus tickets to Glacier Point cost $20 for adults, $18 for seniors, $12 for children, and nothing for kids under 5.*

*Contact: Yosemite National Park (209-372-0200 general information; 209-372-1240 bus reservations; www.nps.gov/yose).*

Panorama Trail isn't named Panorama Trail for nothing. From your starting point perch atop Glacier Point, the Yosemite Valley unfolds before you, a life size relief map at your feet. Glacier Point is one of the most easily accessed vantage points in the entire Sierra Nevada, as evidenced by the hordes of summertime visitors filling the parking lot. Leave the masses behind and descend 3,100 vertical feet along a well-graded, well-marked trail, where the jaw-dropping views only get better as each bend in the trail offers a new perspective on the glacially carved grandeur below. Though the hike is mostly downhill, there is a moderate climb after crossing Illilouette Creek before the trail continues its descent to Happy Isles.

### GETTING THERE

This point-to-point hike requires a little coordination. Arrange to have someone drop you off at Glacier Point and meet you in the Valley or, even better, purchase a one-way bus ticket to Glacier Point through the Yosemite tour desk. Reservations are required, and you should make them far in advance, as seating is limited. The bus leaves Yosemite Lodge daily and takes a little over an hour to get to Glacier Point. I recommend leaving early so you have all day to ooh and aah as you make your way into the Valley. At the end of the hike, ride the free Yosemite Valley shuttle back to your vehicle. If you are driving, from Chinquapin (10 miles south of Yosemite Village on CA 41) follow the signs to Glacier Point. Drive 16 miles along Glacier Point Road (open seasonally) to its

35. Panorama Trail

Parking ⓟ

Side Trail •••••••

N

0     1/2 mile

0     1/2 kilometer

terminus, where you will find restrooms, water, and a gift shop.

## THE TRAIL

Glacier Point was once the stage for the after-dark "firefall" spectacle—a bonfire of red fir bark shoved over the cliff's edge. To spectators gathered below, the veil of burning embers appeared as a flaming waterfall plunging into Yosemite Valley. The practice was halted in 1968 when the National Park Service began deemphasizing manmade attractions within the park. Who needs manmade attractions when you're in Yosemite?

Once atop Glacier Point, take the short walk to the viewpoint before commencing this hike. The commanding view of the Valley floor and the High Sierra landscape in the distance won't soon be forgotten.

The signed trailhead is located at the eastern end of the Glacier Point parking area near the amphitheater. Mere seconds after stepping onto the trail, reach a junction with the Pohono Trail. Stay left and follow the sign to Illilouette Falls.

The exposed trail gently switchbacks downhill through the open, fire-scarred landscape where manzanita and deerweed proliferate. These low-lying shrubs thrive after fire has devastated an area, quickly covering exposed slopes and reducing erosion.

As you descend through sparse stands of mixed pines and charred stumps, you get a fantastic view of Liberty Cap standing sentinel over Nevada and Vernal Falls, while Half Dome looms defiantly, back turned on the whole scene.

Look closely and you can spot the trail zigzagging below along Panorama Cliff. Come to a trail fork at 1.5 miles leading to Mono Meadow. Stay left and continue toward Illilouette Falls, which comes into view not long thereafter. A short spur trail leads to an overlook directly across from the falls

that isn't for the faint of heart. Carefully maneuver to the edge for a view of the entire falls as they spill 370 feet from a narrow opening in the canyon wall. Continue along the trail to the bank of Illilouette Creek, a perfect spot to take a break before heading uphill for the first time.

At 2.2 miles, cross the Illilouette Creek footbridge just upstream from the falls and begin ascending 765 feet through a forest of red fir, lodgepole, and Jeffrey pine. After a short distance, Upper Yosemite Falls and later Lower Yosemite Falls come into view across the Valley. Yosemite Creek plunges over the edge of what geographers call a hanging valley to create these impressive falls. While the huge mass of ice that sculpted the main Yosemite Valley was at work, smaller glaciers filled the Valley's feeder streams and tributaries. These smaller glaciers weren't able to carve as deeply as the large Valley glacier, so when the ice finally retreated, tributary valleys were left "hanging" precariously above the Valley floor. For those visual learners out there (myself included) this vantage suddenly makes it all crystal clear.

Come to a junction at 4.1 miles leading to Ottoway Lake, among other backcountry destinations. Stay straight on the main trail to Yosemite Valley where the downhill begins in earnest again. In the spring, as you pass through the shaded boulder-strewn landscape, watch for the unmistakable red snow plant emerging from the duff-covered forest floor, its fiery leaves a stark contrast to the earth tones surrounding you.

At 5.1 miles, the Panorama Trail intersects the John Muir Trail. From here you can either turn left (west) and proceed 2.3 miles to the base of Vernal Falls along the John Muir Trail, or turn right (east) and proceed 0.2 mile to the top of Nevada Falls and eventually descend via Mist Trail. Even if your pref-

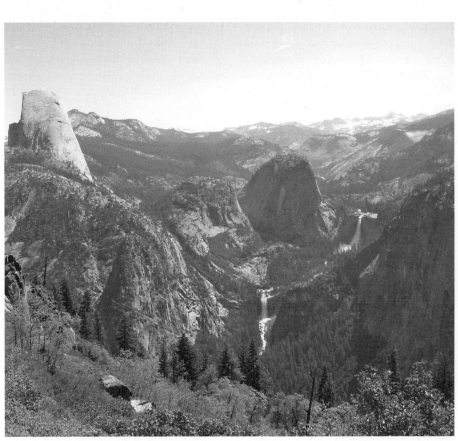

*Yosemite's stunning granite landscape*

erence is to take the John Muir Trail, continuing on to Nevada Falls is definitely worth the extra mileage. The trail opens onto a broad flat expanse of granite atop the falls that funnels the swift Merced River and sends it plummeting 594 feet into the abyss. It's a perfect spot to rest your legs and have a snack, but keep a vigilant eye for fearless critters looking for an easy meal.

Don't expect solitude, as this is a popular rest stop for hikers making the trek from the Valley to the top of Nevada Falls and points beyond. Expect a significant amount of company from here on out.

After absorbing the sights and sounds, you can either turn back and head down the longer but less steep John Muir Trail, or cross the footbridge spanning the Merced River and continue 0.2 mile to the Mist Trail junction. There are pit toilets here, but expect a line. Turn left at the junction to head down extremely popular Mist Trail. Continuing straight takes you to Little Yosemite Valley.

Carefully make your way down the steep granite stairway alongside thundering Nevada Falls, being mindful of ascending hikers. Follow the trail along the frothy Merced River until you reach the edge of Nevada Falls' downstream neighbor—317-foot high Vernal Falls. At this point, I recommend slipping into rain gear before embarking down the next soggy 0.5 mile of trail, especially during spring and early summer, when billowing spray and mist can be a real drencher. Follow the procession of people through a rock opening and down a wet granite staircase to the western junction with the John Muir Trail.

If your knees and ankles are too fatigued, avoid Mist Trail and instead take the John Muir Trail. It affords outstanding views of Nevada Falls just past the Panorama Trail junction, but you won't see Vernal Falls until you reach the footbridge at the base of the falls 2.3 miles beyond. A convenient 0.4-mile cutoff trail at Clark Point leads to just above Vernal Falls, providing a connection between the John Muir and Mist Trails and allowing you to experience both trails if you choose.

At 7.2 miles (via Mist Trail), cross the Merced River again via a footbridge and enjoy the paved walkway back to the Happy Isles trailhead, where you can catch the free Yosemite Valley shuttle back to your vehicle.

# 36

## Half Dome

*Type: Day hike or overnight*

*Season: The cables are usually up by mid-June and removed in October*

*Total distance: 14 miles round trip via Mist Trail; 16.4 miles round trip via John Muir Trail*

*Rating: Very strenuous*

*Elevation: 4,053 feet; +4,953 feet/-216 feet*

*Location: Yosemite National Park*

*Maps: USGS 7.5' Half Dome; Trails Illustrated Yosemite SW–Yosemite Valley & Wawona No. 306*

*Fees and permits: A permit is not required for this day hike. A wilderness permit (with reservation fee) is required for all overnight trips into Yosemite's backcountry. A trailhead quota system is in effect, so if you plan on camping, reserve as early as possible. Space is limited and disappears quickly. Passenger vehicles entering the park are charged a $20 admission fee, which is good for seven days.*

*Contact: Yosemite National Park (209-372-0200 general information; 209-372-0740 wilderness permits; www.nps .gov/yose).*

If Yosemite has an icon, Half Dome is it. Climbing to the top of this monolith is an amazing experience, but it's not for everyone. It's a grueling journey, and you should expect to share the trail with hordes of other hikers trudging to the summit alongside you. The final push to the top is especially demanding. If any part of two metal cables, 400 feet of sheer rock face, and no safety net sounds overly unnerving, then sit this one out. Otherwise, be prepared to experience some of the most resplendent scenery Yosemite Valley has to offer and add an impressive peak to your bag. A few musthaves for this trip: ample water (or a water filter), a poncho, a pair of work gloves, and a good attitude.

### GETTING THERE

From the Arch Rock Entrance Station on CA 140, drive 12 miles east into Yosemite Valley. Just past Curry Village, turn right into the backpacker parking area. From here, walk along a paved pathway 0.6 mile farther east to the Happy Isles Trailhead. Alternatively, board the free Yosemite Valley Shuttle from any location in the park and get off at Happy Isles (Stop 16).

### THE TRAIL

During the summer, hundreds of people a day make the trek to Half Dome. The overwhelming majority do it as a day hike, but I think an overnight is the way to go (if you can secure a permit). You can take your time and savor every step of this epic journey. A good option is to camp at Little Yosemite

Valley (3.2 miles from the summit), but an even better one is to set up camp on the forested saddle just below Half Dome's northeast shoulder (a little less than a mile from the summit). This does mean you'll have to schlep your backpack that much farther, but once the last day hikers have disappeared, you will have the place gloriously to yourself. The best part is that you can wake up early the next morning and make the final push to the summit, sans crowd, just in time to watch the sunrise.

Begin by following the rowdy Merced River upstream on a dirt path that soon gives way to a pleasantly paved pathway. At 0.8 mile, cross a sturdy wooden footbridge spanning the river. Vernal Falls is putting on a fantastic display to your left. Now on the south bank, the trail reverts to dirt. Bear left, soon reaching the John Muir Trail (JMT)–Mist Trail junction. Both paths lead to the top of Nevada Falls, the difference being that the JMT ascends via a series of well-engineered switchbacks, making it longer, while the Mist Trail is more direct, climbing a massive rock staircase alongside Vernal and Nevada Falls. The staircase is steep, wet, and slick (a rain poncho will keep you from getting completely drenched by the billowing mist). The choice is yours. Since both trails are incredibly scenic and you don't want to miss either one, I advise ascending Mist Trail while your legs and mind are fresh and descending via the JMT.

From where the JMT and Mist Trail reunite (2.4 miles from the trailhead), continue following the Merced River upstream on the wide, sandy trail. Come to a Y-junction just before Little Yosemite Valley. Either path is fine as they eventually rejoin, however, the left fork climbs up and over the eastern ridge of Liberty Cap, while the right fork is blissfully flat. Level trail is something that, as you have no doubt realized, is in short supply on this trek and should be savored. Bearing right also gives you the chance to replenish your water supply from the Merced River, your last reliable source, and to use the convenient solar toilet near the overused Little Yosemite Valley campground (3.8 miles from the trailhead). As with all backcountry water sources, be sure to treat before drinking.

Head north out of the campground and rejoin the JMT by veering right and heading steeply uphill along Sunrise Creek. Continue 1.2 miles to a junction, where the JMT veers right (east) on its long-distance trek to the top of Mount Whitney. You go left onto the Half Dome Trail for the final 2 miles to the summit. The trail bends west and crests a saddle along the northeast shoulder of Half Dome. Though there is no designated campground, you can set up camp as long as you follow park rules and regulations. Dispersed wilderness camping is allowed 2 miles beyond Little Yosemite Valley campground, at or beyond Moraine Dome or beyond the junction of the Half Dome and John Muir Trails. Camping is not permitted on top of Half Dome. This is a good time to note that if thunderstorms are threatening, you should scrap your summit attempt. The top of this exposed dome is the last place you want to be if lightning strikes.

With blue skies overhead, zigzag up a rocky slope. The gradient progressively steepens as you creep higher, the incredible views taking your mind off the arduous climb. The switchbacks soon end and you drop down to the base of the infamous cable route. There is usually a pile of gloves at the base of the cables, but I am a firm believer in self-sufficiency, so play it safe and pack a pair of your own. Don your gloves and haul yourself up the final 400 vertical feet. This is where the good attitude comes in. The slow procession of people can be frustrating, and passing isn't exactly an option. Take your

*Half Dome*

time and be patient—you will get there. Temper the off-the-charts crowd factor by overnighting as I recommended earlier.

From the broad summit of Half Dome (8,836 feet), the views are phenomenal. Looking west, several of Yosemite Valley's notable features are on display: Glacier Point, the Merced River, and El Capitan. Behind you, Quarter Domes, Clouds Rest, and the distant Cathedral Range fill the horizon, creating a sublime scene. This sanctuary of forested valleys, granite domes, and plummeting waterfalls seems to radiate from this single point, making you feel as though you are at the center of something magical—well, you are!

When ready, carefully descend the cables and retrace your steps. When you make it back to the JMT–Mist Trail junction, stay straight on the JMT and continue toward Nevada Falls. The top of the falls is a fantastic spot to take a break. Scout out a nice boulder and drop your pack, but watch out for fearless varmints ready to abscond with your grub. Bid farewell to the falls and continue your descent, passing a junction with the Panorama Trail (left) that heads to Glacier Point and later a junction at Clark Point (right) that cuts across to Mist Trail. Follow the endless series of switchbacks downhill, eventually meeting up again with the paved walkway you started on.

Snow Flat

Y O

To Tenaya Lake

Tenaya Lake Campground

To Yosemite Valley

BM 8123

N A T I O N

CA 120

BM 8325

BM 8294

BOUNDARY TRAIL

WILDERNESS

PACK

Olmsted Point

Y O S E M I T E

Tenaya Creek

Sunrise Lakes

9166

9258

Creek

9242

To Sunrise High Sierra Camp

Yosemite National Park

Hidden Lake

Mountain

### 37. Clouds Rest

Ⓟ Parking

•••• Side Trail

N

0 — 1/2 mile
0 — 1/2 kilometer

To Merced Lake

Sunrise

Clouds Rest
9926

# 37

## Clouds Rest

*Type: Day hike*

*Season: June to October*

*Total distance: 14.4 miles round trip*

*Rating: Strenuous*

*Elevation: 8,170 feet; +2,355 feet/-696 feet*

*Location: Yosemite National Park*

*Maps: USGS 7.5' Tenaya Lake; Trails Illustrated Yosemite National Park No. 206*

*Fees and permits: A permit is not required for this day hike. Passenger vehicles entering the park are charged a $20 admission fee, which is good for seven days.*

*Contact: Yosemite National Park (209-372-0200; www.nps.gov/yose).*

If you've got a day at your disposal, this demanding trek to Clouds Rest (9,926 feet) is definitely one to add to your list. As its lofty name implies, Clouds Rest is where the clouds go to rest—well, not really, but it sure feels that way from atop this rocky perch, where 360-degree views are yours for the taking. Because Clouds Rest lacks the notoriety of Half Dome (although I'm not sure why), you won't have to do as much elbowing along the way. Acrophobes may want to sit this one out, as the final stretch to the summit is a little hairy. Get an early start and don't attempt the climb if a storm is threatening. Ambitious hikers might even consider an early morning moonlight hike to reach the top before dawn—watching the sun's rays illuminate the valley from this airy summit is a magical experience.

### GETTING THERE

From the Tioga Pass entrance station along CA 120, drive 15.6 miles west to the Sunrise Trailhead (shuttle stop #10). There is limited parking in the lot, so make use of the wide roadside shoulder.

### THE TRAIL

Two major trails emanate from this trailhead, so don't get confused. You want to follow the signs toward Sunrise High Sierra Camp (HSC), which means you start out on a paved pathway that meanders through a thick forest of lodgepole pines on its way toward Tenaya Creek. Just when you're wishfully envisioning a paved walkway all the way to the top, you trade the pavement for dirt and make a long, but simple boulder hop across shallow Tenaya Creek (a tricky crossing during times of high water).

Veer right at a junction on the opposite bank. The trail is pleasantly flat for the first mile and a half as you stroll alongside the peaceful creek and past flowering meadows filled with California corn lily, arrowleaf butterweed, and alpine lily. The trail descends slightly to cross Mildred Lake's outlet creek, beyond which you ascend a short hill. Navigate a dry cobble-strewn creekbed as red firs and mountain hemlocks join the forest mix and mountain spirea's hot pink flower clusters decorate the trail.

The trail gradient increases and you head up a rocky slope of seemingly unending switchbacks that rise 1,000 vertical feet. Climbing higher, enjoy views of the pine-scattered granite landscape punctuated by dramatic Mount Hoffman and Tuolumne Peak to the north.

Just when you thought you should have taken the elevator instead of the stairs, reach the ridgetop at 2.5 miles and a trail leading left toward Sunrise High Sierra Camp. Stay straight and unfortunately zigzag steeply down the drier, south-facing slope, forfeiting some of the precious elevation you just fought so valiantly for.

Lose the view toward the bottom where the trail levels and you pass through a verdant meadow, stepping over a couple of small streamlets as you go. Climb above the meadow and across a jumbled pile of boulders at the base of Sunrise Mountain. Sun-seeking aspens poke through the rocky crevices, coloring the chunks of pale granite with clumps of green. Reenter the forest and entertain Yosemite's characteristic boulder-strewn landscape before coming to a verdant pocket and the shore of a small unnamed lake.

The now sandy trail wanders through a densely forested section before intersecting a small creek, which you easily cross. Begin a mild ascent and reach a trail fork at 4.7 miles heading toward Merced Lake. Stay straight and continue the steady uphill trudge. Off to your left, catch glimpses of Bunnell Point, Cascade Cliffs, and Mount Starr King between gaps in the trees.

Cresting the climb, enjoy relatively level walking as you traverse a broad ridgeline before dipping down along its right shoulder to a low saddle at the base of Clouds Rest. From here the grade significantly increases as you close in on your goal. Steep switchbacks carry you uphill, affording spectacular views back toward Tenaya Lake sitting serenely in a bowl of granite. As you approach the summit, the rocks begin to change and appear layered like a stack of pancakes.

Clouds Rest is a perfect example of an arête, a thin, almost knifelike ridge of rock typically formed when two glaciers erode parallel U-shaped valleys. The word arête is actually French for edge.

The trail isn't particularly clear, but the goal is obvious. If there is any doubt, a sign identifying the Clouds Rest Foot Trail points you in the right direction. Carefully make your way up and along a narrow spine of disjointed rocks. This final push to the summit can be unnerving due to the steep drop-offs on either side of the ridge. Just take it slow and reach the broad summit in no time and savor the well-earned, 360-degree panorama.

Lording some 5,900 feet over Yosemite Valley, suspended between two granite chasms, the view from Clouds Rest is nothing short of amazing. Yosemite Valley's forested floor and the hunched backside of Half Dome dominate your southern vista. Sharp eyes will spot the famous cable trail draped along its shoulder. Peer down Merced and Tenaya Canyons and behold the

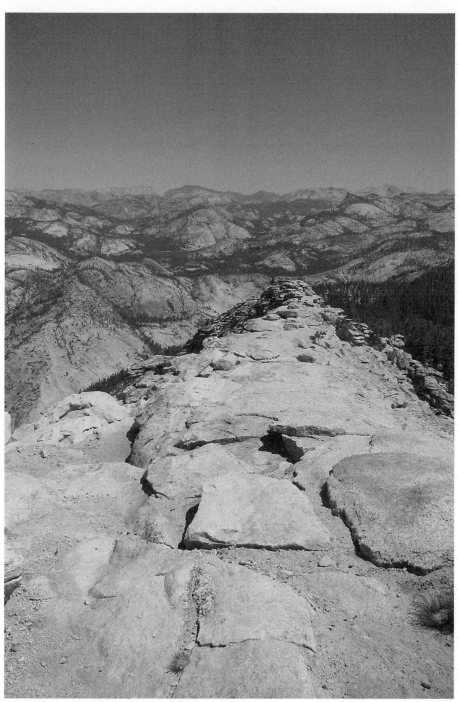

*Trail along narrow arête near the summit of Clouds Rest*

fantastic landscape of domes, spires, and sheer granite faces that undulate into the limitless horizon.

Perhaps John Muir was perched atop Clouds Rest when he wrote: "Glaciers, back in their cold solitudes, work apart from men, exerting their tremendous energies in silence and darkness. Outspread, spirit-like, they brood above the predestined landscapes, work on unwearied through immeasurable ages, until, in the fullness of time, the mountains and valleys are brought forth, channels furrowed for the rivers, basins made for the lakes and meadows, and long, deep arms of the sea, soils spread for the forests and the fields—then they shrink and vanish like summer clouds."

When you're ready, silent reverie complete, begin the long descent back to the trailhead.

# 38

## Cathedral Lakes

*Type: Day hike*

*Season: Mid-June to early October*

*Total distance: 6.5 miles round trip to Lower Cathedral Lake (add 1.2 miles round trip if you tack on a visit to Upper Cathedral Lake)*

*Rating: Moderate*

*Elevation: 8,577 feet; +1,010 feet/-294 feet*

*Location: Yosemite National Park*

*Maps: USGS 7.5' Tenaya Lake; Trails Illustrated Yosemite NE–Tuolumne Meadows & Hoover Wilderness No. 308*

*Fees and permits: A permit is not required for this day hike. Passenger vehicles entering the park are charged a $20 admission fee, which is good for seven days.*

*Contact: Yosemite National Park (209-372-0200; www.nps.gov/yose).*

This hike along a portion of the John Muir Trail visits a pair of liquid gems tucked amid the Yosemite backcountry. Easy access and splendid scenery make this a popular destination and almost guarantee you won't be alone. Nonetheless, this pleasant day hike is a worthy venture. Though camping is allowed at the Cathedral Lakes, I recommend doing this as a day hike due to the sheer numbers of people passing through the area—not the most ideal overnight backcountry experience.

### GETTING THERE

From the Tioga Pass Entrance Station along CA 120, drive 8.7 miles west to the Cathedral Lakes Trailhead located on the south side of the road. Park along the shoulder. The trailhead has sparkling clean portable toilets (at least when I visited). For a bit of luxury, however, stop off at the Tuolumne Meadows Visitors Center just minutes east, where you can peruse the exhibits and use a "real" bathroom before hitting the trail.

### THE TRAIL

The John Muir Trail (JMT) is one of the Sierras' eminent long-distance trails. It is 211 miles long and stretches from Yosemite Valley south to Mount Whitney (mostly in conjunction with the much longer Pacific Crest Trail). The segment this hike follows serves as the primary footpath between Tuolumne Meadows and Yosemite Valley.

A few steps from the trailhead, come to a four-way junction—left heads toward Tuolumne Meadows Campground, right to-

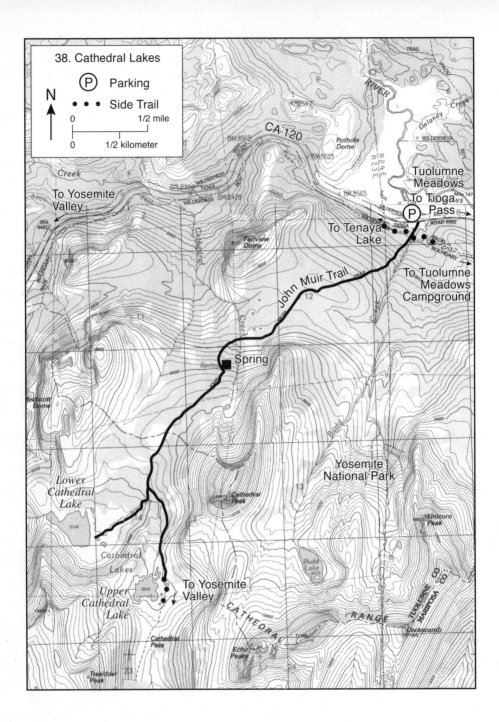

ward Tenaya Lake. Stay straight and begin a steady uphill trudge through a thick forest of lodgepole pines and red firs. Budd Creek tumbles to your left for a time.

After a rather uneventful 0.75 mile, the trail levels off and gets sandy in spots, most likely due to heavy usage by pack trains ferrying supplies to Sunrise High Sierra Camp. The trail wanders between alternating patches of dry forest and wet meadow. At 1.25 miles, the forest opens and you run smack into the domelike northern buttress of Cathedral Peak. For now, the peak's jagged pinnacles are concealed from view behind this imposing wall of granite. To the north, obscured by trees, is Fairview Dome. Nodding hemlocks join the forest mix and near the 1.5-mile mark you step over a small offshoot of Cathedral Creek, and not long after cross the main channel via a log.

Past the creek, level walking comes to an abrupt end and you begin ascending via a series of switchbacks. As the creek playfully splashes to the left, follow it upstream to its origin—an effluent spring that seeps from the ground. Looking north, views of Fairview Dome improve, its rounded cap framed by erect red firs. At 2.1 miles, the trail tops out onto a broad saddle (the high point of the journey). Enjoy level walking for a spell before leaving the dry ridgetop and descending toward the junction for Lower Cathedral

*Lower Cathedral Lake and Tresidder Peak*

Lake. Mendicott Dome is visible to the right while Cathedral Peak, the pulpit in Nature's temple of granite, rises to the left.

Cathedral Peak is a geographic anomaly in this landscape of smooth, glacially rounded rock. It is believed that when glaciers covered the area, the peak's uppermost tip remained above—and therefore out of—the sculpting path of the moving mass of ice. The peak has many different personalities, depending on your perspective.

Reach the junction for Lower Cathedral Lake at 2.7 mile and veer right. The trail narrows and you step across the outlet creek flowing from Upper Cathedral Lake. Continue on a general descent along the creek's southern bank, admiring California corn lily and arrowleaf butterweed as you go. Follow a boulder-lined path over a rock slab and break out of the forest and into a broad meadow lushly carpeted with verdant grasses.

From here, a host of narrow footpaths cut across the meadow—none of them straight. When the flowing creek hits the flat meadow it splays in several directions, creating a web of snaking channels. Early in the season, this area can be quite muddy so expect to get a little dirty and maybe even get your toes wet as you must make a couple of giant leaps over the sinuous creek. (Mother, may I?) In

any event, do your best to follow an existing footpath rather than blazing your own trail and carving the landscape up any further.

From the lengthy granite lip corralling Lower Cathedral Lake, the views are splendid. Southwest, prominent Tresidder Peak juts above the sparkling blue water. Across the lake, Mount Hoffman and Polly Dome appear above the tree tops, and behind you, the spiky spires of Cathedral Peak pierce the sky. From the lake's outlet on the far western end (an approximately 0.5-mile walk), you can gaze across Tenaya Canyon, taking in the expanded southwestward vistas. Some will be quite content spending the day here admiring the scene and exploring the shoreline.

For my favorite thing to do, though—take a refreshing dip and recline on a sun-warmed slab of granite—there's no better place.

If time allows, return to the junction with the JMT and turn right to proceed to Upper Cathedral Lake 0.6 mile farther. The trail loosely follows the lake's outlet stream. When you arrive at a small pond (no, this isn't the lake) turn right along a narrow unofficial path to a granite bench, beyond which lies smaller, but no less scenic, granite-hemmed Upper Cathedral Lake.

Spend as much time as you like before retracing your steps to the trailhead.

# 39

## Waterwheel Falls

*Type: Overnight*

*Season: June through October*

*Total distance: 16.4 miles round trip*

*Rating: Moderate to strenuous*

*Elevation: 8,584 feet; +592 feet/-2,375 feet*

*Location: Yosemite National Park*

*Maps: USGS 7.5' Tioga Pass, Falls Ridge; Trails Illustrated Yosemite NE–Tuolumne Meadows & Hoover Wilderness No. 308*

*Fees and permits: A wilderness permit (with reservation fee) is required for all overnight trips into Yosemite's backcountry. A trailhead quota system is in effect, so if you plan on camping reserve as early as possible. Passenger vehicles entering the park are charged a $20 admission fee, which is good for seven days.*

*Contact: Yosemite National Park (209-372-0200 general information; 209-372-0740 wilderness permits; www.nps.gov/yose).*

If you're looking for waterfalls, this trail's got them; five major ones in fact, not to mention a multitude of delightful unnamed pools and cascades in between the big drops to keep you oohing and aahing the whole way. Last, but certainly not least, in this procession of cataracts is Waterwheel Falls. Keep in mind that the descent comes first on this hike, quite steeply toward the end, and you climb on the way back out. Strong hikers can make the trek in a day, but it's much more enjoyable to do as an overnight.

### GETTING THERE

From the Tioga Pass Entrance Station along CA 120, drive 7 miles west to the Lembert Dome parking area on the north side of the road (also signed for Soda Springs, Dog Lake, and Glen Aulin). Turn right onto the gravel road and park on the left-hand side, where space allows. The trail begins past a gate blocking vehicular traffic 0.3 mile from the turnoff where the road bends right toward the stables.

### THE TRAIL

Begin by walking 0.5 mile along a wide dirt road (actually part of the Pacific Crest Trail) as it skirts the northern fringe of Tuolumne Meadows to the official trailhead. Follow the signs to Glen Aulin as you pass several interpretive plaques. Soda Springs and historic Parson's Lodge are nearby and worth quick exploration before forging on.

Leaving the road, the path narrows. Although it is sandy, the trail is level and easy

*Tuolumne River and the distant Grand Canyon of the Tuolumne*

going for the first 2 miles as it winds through a rocky, lodgepole forest. Pass a trail from the stables merging in on the right and carefully cross Delaney Creek on steppingstones at 1.3 miles. This section of trail is rather uneventful as you alternate between thick forest and open meadows that offer occasional views of the surrounding domes and peaks poking above the treetops.

At 1.6 miles the trail forks; stay left and soon cross a granite slab, guided by cairns (there are several of these along the route). Reach a broad meadow and spot the lazy Tuolumne River snaking peacefully to your left, no doubt saving its energy for the down-

stream extravaganza. Traverse several dry branches of Dingley Creek, round a granite outcrop, and gain your first view down the Grand Canyon of the Tuolumne, a spectacular chasm that stretches all the way to Hetch Hetchy Valley.

At 4 miles, cross twin bridges spanning the river, which is starting to liven up a bit. The river's awakening also signifies changes in elevation, and you begin a more noticeable descent along the rocky western bank to Tuolumne Falls. Pass a left-branching trail heading toward Tenaya Lake at 4.9 miles and soon reach White Cascade, its frothy water funneled through a narrow cleft of granite be-

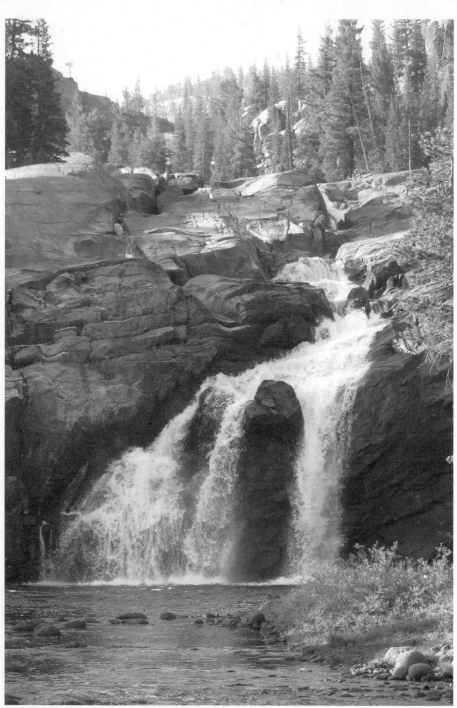

*White Cascade near Glen Aulin High Sierra Camp*

fore plunging erratically into a pool of emerald water.

A short distance farther, recross the river via footbridge and arrive at a junction leading to Glen Aulin High Sierra Camp (HSC). Turn right and cross a second bridge spanning Conness Creek and follow signs to the backpacker campground, where you can drop your gear and have a snack before continuing on. The backpacker camp has two metal bear boxes, but you should definitely carry your own canister, as they fill up fast and are quite a distance from some of the upper campsites. There is also a pit toilet, potable water, and a community fire ring for campers to share.

If your idea of a backcountry experience doesn't include sleeping on the ground and noshing on freeze-dried delicacies, you're in luck. Glen Aulin HSC is one of five outposts spaced 5.7–10 miles apart along a magnificent loop in Yosemite's backcountry. The only way to reach the camps is by foot or on horseback. The HSCs were originally built by the National Park Service in an effort to attract people to the park's high country. Now they are a wildly popular way to visit the wilderness without having to schlep a heavy pack and food. For a fee, and with a little luck (reservations are made by lottery), you can luxuriate in a dormitory-style tent cabin, eat hot meals, and best of all, take a shower.

Back on the main trail, ignore a junction heading to Virginia Canyon and climb up and over a small knoll, where the distant panorama unfolds. The river, peaceful again, slices through the forested floor, while bare walls of sculpted granite, the stone heart of the Sierra, hold it captive.

Generally following the northeastern bank of the river, the trail is pleasantly flat for 1.3 miles as it wanders through fire-scarred areas of young forests and meadows bursting with lupine. The seemingly still river is all but begging you to take a swim. If you are looking for a bit more solitude than Glen Aulin can offer, there are several fine campsites here along the river.

At 6.5 miles, reach California Falls, first in the upcoming string of impressive cataracts. The views along this nonstop series of cascades are from the side and can be somewhat obscured by the forest. You will notice several spur trails wandering closer for a better look. Take great caution if you approach, as the smooth granite underfoot is unbelievably slick, even if it isn't wet.

Under the sparse shade of a mixed conifer forest, begin a steep, stair-stepping descent past gigantic boulders that reverberate the river's pandemonium. At 7.7 miles, Le Conte Falls, caught in the throes of gravity, lurches and heaves as it slips through a maze of boulders beneath the watchful eye of Wildcat Point looming to the right.

Waterwheel Falls soon comes into view through the trees. An unsigned spur trail at 8.2 miles takes you closer (about midway down the falls). Rather than plunging, the falls are created when the Tuolumne River spills over a water-honed lip and races down a smooth granite incline, diving into deep holes sculpted into the rocky riverbed, then blasting out so fast that it curls back on itself, creating its signature "waterwheels." Several waterwheels are visible, and they are most impressive during the spring and early summer when flows are high. Linger a while, being mindful of the 1,100 vertical feet that stand between you and your tent at Glen Aulin.

---

# 40

## Gaylor Lakes

*Type: Day hike*

*Season: Late June through October*

*Total distance: 3.5 miles round trip*

*Rating: Moderate to strenuous*

*Elevation: 9,945 feet; +1,039 feet/-198 feet*

*Location: Yosemite National Park*

*Maps: USGS 7.5' Tioga Pass; Trails Illustrated Yosemite NE–Tuolumne Meadows & Hoover Wilderness No. 308*

*Fees and permits: A permit is not required for this day hike. Passenger vehicles entering the park are charged a $20 admission fee, which is good for seven days.*

*Contact: Yosemite National Park (209-372-0200 general information; www.nps .gov/yose).*

Often overlooked by tourists dashing to more notable destinations like Tuolumne Meadows and Tenaya Lake, this short hike into Yosemite's alpine environs is an eminently worthwhile excursion. Enjoy relative solitude as you marvel at the sweeping vistas above Tioga Pass, ramble past a pair of picturesque alpine lakes, and explore the remnants of the Great Sierra Mine. If you can make it past the initial butt-kicking climb, you're home free, and the wonders of this lightly visited region are all yours.

### GETTING THERE

From the Tioga Pass entrance station along CA 120, proceed through the gate and immediately turn right into a small parking area adjacent to the trailhead. If the lot is full, exit Yosemite and park along the shoulder just outside the gate and make the short walk to the trailhead.

### THE TRAIL

Set out on the well-defined path and immediately begin a stiff climb through the lodgepole pine forest. Aster, Sierra penstemon, and monkey flower brighten the grassy understory. You will rise upwards of 600 feet over the next 0.5 mile, but if you can make it past this demanding section, I promise you won't be disappointed. Your lungs and legs will soon forget their recent travail when you take in the expansive panorama that awaits.

The trail begins to level off near the top of a broad, open saddle where views of Lee Vining Canyon unfurl. Opposite, red-tinted Mount Dana casts shadows upon Dana

Prospects

WILDERNESS

USMM
NO 21

Great Sierra
Mine

BOUNDARY

To US 395
and Lee Vining

10600

BM 9734

9800

Upper
Gaylor
Lake

Granite
Lakes

30

Yosemite
National Park

Gaylor
Peak

Inyo
National Forest

BM
9769

MONO

TUOLUMNE

Lakes

CO

CA 120

CO

Middle
Gaylor
Lake

Tioga Pass
Entrance
Station
Entrance

120

BM
9943

Tioga
Pass

P

40. Gaylor Lakes

N

P  Parking

0                    1/4 mile

0              1/4 kilometer

10000

To Tuolumne
Meadows

BOUNDARY

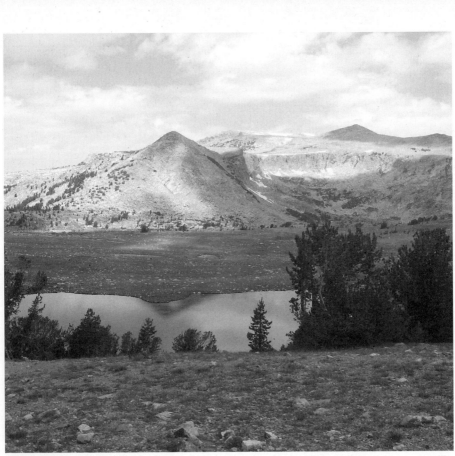

*Middle Gaylor Lake and Gaylor Peak*

Meadows, appearing almost like a golf course spreading out below. To the southwest, the meadow gives way to forest before colliding with the massive Cathedral Range rising on the distant horizon. Continue up and over the saddle, littered with chunky metamorphic rock, and spot Middle Gaylor Lake, Gaylor Peak, and a host of jagged pinnacles that form the crown of this stark landscape.

From here, begin a steep descent through scraggly whitebark pine to the lakeshore, losing precious elevation in the process. At 0.7 mile, reach the shore of Middle Gaylor Lake. Lacking perspective, the pointy tips of the Cathedral Range appear to barely poke above the lake's southern fringe. Though too cold for swimming, the lake is frequented by anglers looking to hook up with its small, but feisty, wild brook trout.

Gaylor apparently means "lake of many insects" in some ancient forgotten language. If you happen to visit during their seasonal proliferation and unless you want to be bombarded, consider packing along a bug net for the most infested parts of the trail (around the lakes). Granted, though not the most fashionable outdoor attire, it will keep the little buggers out of your mouth, and that's worth something.

The now single-track trail adheres to the northern shore as it cuts through a high-altitude grassland. Easily cross the lake's inlet, beyond which the trail bends north and continues upstream. Stick to the trail, as the subalpine meadow that gloriously surrounds you is especially fragile.

Begin a short, gradual ascent toward Upper Gaylor Lake. A variety of wildflowers color the trail as you skirt around the backside of Gaylor Peak. Look for yellow-bellied marmots sunning themselves along the trail, or listen for their characteristic whistle. These fuzzy, jumbo-size rodents are closely related to both ground squirrels and prairie dogs. At 1.3 miles, attain the shore of Upper Gaylor Lake, slightly smaller though more scenic than its downstream companion.

The level trail meanders around the west shore before ascending toward a collection of dilapidated rock edifices, the remnants of the town of Dana, an 1800s mining settlement full of hopes and dreams. The trail officially ends past several crumbling cabins. Wander farther up the hillside to explore the Great Sierra Mine, the impetus behind the town and another ill-fated endeavor by the Great Sierra Consolidated Silver Mining Company (see Hike 22). Take care when exploring the area, as there are open shafts that are extremely dangerous.

The views in this alpine wonderland are stunning, and if you're up for some more reconnoitering, the seldom-visited Granite Lakes sit just over the low rise immediately west of Gaylor Peak. This will require some freelancing over the alpine countryside, but with a good map it shouldn't be difficult. Upper and Lower Granite Lakes sit gracefully at the bottom of a large rocky bowl, a classic glacial cirque. When you are ready, retrace your steps to the trailhead.

# 41

## Chilnualna Falls

*Type: Day hike*

*Season: April to November*

*Total distance: 8 miles round trip*

*Rating: Strenuous*

*Elevation: 4,183 feet, +2,257 feet/-165 feet*

*Location: Yosemite National Park*

*Maps: USGS 7.5' Wawona, Mariposa Grove; Trails Illustrated Yosemite SW–Yosemite Valley & Wawona No. 306*

*Fees and permits: A permit is not required for this day hike. Passenger vehicles entering the park are charged a $20 admission fee, which is good for seven days.*

*Contact: Yosemite National Park (209-372-0200 general information; www.nps .gov/yose).*

Since Wawona, a Miwok word for "big trees," is located at an elevation of 4,000 feet, this makes a fantastic early season jaunt to the top of one of Yosemite's lesser-known, but no less spectacular, waterfalls. Views of this reclusive cataract, however, come at a cost—four miles of steep, relentless uphill climbing—that deters all but the brave few. If you choose to be one of the few, and I hope you do, the relatively quiet trail will reward you with outstanding views of Wawona Dome, the Chowchilla Mountains, and the South Fork Merced River coursing below. Pack along plenty of water, as the trail can get warm as summer approaches, and remember to watch for rattlesnakes. Water displays are best during the spring when Chilnualna Creek is gushing with snowmelt.

### GETTING THERE

From the South Entrance on CA 41, drive 7.4 miles north through Wawona to Chilnualna Falls Road and turn right (0.25 mile north of the Wawona Hotel). Proceed 1.7 miles past the Wawona stables, where the road narrows through a private residential area before reaching the trailhead parking lot, where there are pit toilets.

### THE TRAIL

With most tourists heading straight for Yosemite Valley, other equally transcendent regions of the park often get overlooked. One such place is Wawona, a small, quiet community located in southern Yosemite. This somewhat isolated and less visited (by

Yosemite standards) area of the park is home to the historic Wawona Hotel, Pioneer History Center, Mariposa Grove of giant sequoias, and our trailhead to Chilnualna Falls.

From the parking area, walk 0.1 mile back to Chilnualna Falls Road and up to the signed trailhead. Take the dirt foot trail (not the stock trail), which quickly narrows. Chilnualna Creek tumbles and crashes to your right as it stair-steps its way over gigantic boulders, creating an impressive cascade mere minutes into your hike. Don't be fooled, though, you haven't arrived at Chilnualna Falls at warp speed—the best is yet to come

and the only way to get there is up.

Ascend a series of granite steps and at 0.3 mile arrive at a junction with the stock trail and a placard announcing your entrance into the Yosemite Wilderness. Follow the sign to Chilnualna Falls and continue your moderate but steady climb away from the creek along the mountain misery-lined trail. A thick carpet of this fernlike flowering shrub accompanies you the majority of the trip. Sporadic wildflowers and sprigs of poison oak add to the understory of the mixed conifer forest you are traveling through.

Although your lungs are acutely aware of

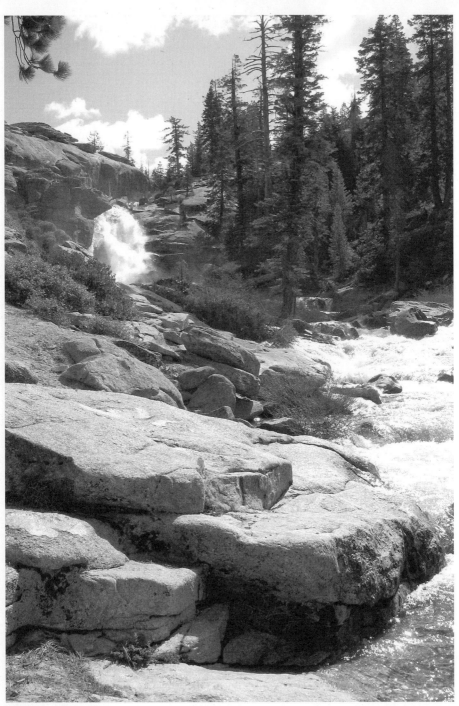

*Chilnualna Falls*

the effort being exerted, your eyes aren't fully rewarded until 2 miles into the hike, when you come to a granite overlook with views of Wawona Dome directly across from you, and the forested slopes of the Chowchilla Mountains in the distance. Catch your breath and listen for the rumble of Chilnualna Falls beckoning you to disregard your aching quadriceps and forge on.

About 0.5 mile past the overlook, get your first glimpse of Chilnualna Falls tucked in a narrow granitic chasm high on the ridge. Your view is limited from this vantage and continuously changes to include more of the falls as you switchback higher through the forest. Despite your sideways view, it is the most complete view of the largest drop in the falls.

At 3.1 miles, cross a small seasonal stream as you make your way through a shady forest of black oaks, incense cedar, and red fir offering peek-a-boo views of the valley below. The trail then opens as you make a final push to the top of the falls along a granite staircase.

From your perch atop the brink of the free-fall you admired on the way up, watch Chilnualna Creek plunge from the edge into a water-darkened chasm of rock, mist, and rainbows. Though this is not the most photogenic part of the falls (since you are on top and not in front of them) don't despair—just turn your attention upstream to upper Chilnualna Falls. A cascading wall of water tumbles hundreds of feet down the boulder-lined creek channel as it courses its way to the lower free-fall and ultimately the Merced River below.

Find a comfy spot and take a well-deserved rest along the rushing creek, or if you still want more, continue along the trail 0.5 mile farther to the top of the upper cascade. The trail will begin rising above and parallel to the creek, then veer sharply away and into a forest of manzanita before turning back toward the upper tiers. From a signed junction, walk to the waterfall's edge and enjoy a whole new set of cascades and pools before returning via the same trail.

At the junction, 0.3 mile from the trailhead, avoid the temptation to descend via the stock trail. It takes you on a circuitous route that only increases your mileage. Opt to take the foot trail and see Chilnualna Creek from a whole new vantage.

If time allows, the popular Mariposa Grove of giant sequoias, the largest inside park boundaries and just south of Wawona, is fascinating to visit. Several easy trails crisscross the grove discovered in 1857 by Galen Clark, the first guardian of Yosemite and the original proprietor of the Wawona Hotel. With fanciful names like Bachelor and Three Graces, Faithful Couple, Grizzly Giant, and Clothespin Tree, how can you resist a walk among these stately giants?

# VI. Sequoia and Kings Canyon National Parks

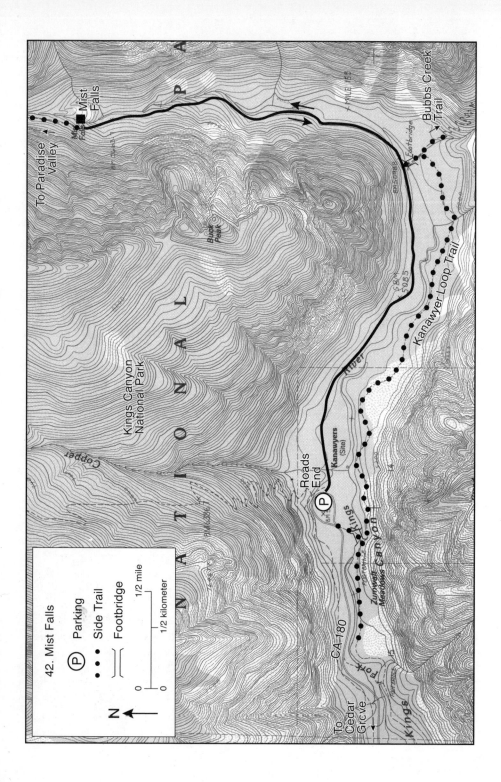

# 42

## Mist Falls

*Type: Day hike*

*Season: May to November*

*Total distance: 8 miles round trip*

*Rating: Easy to moderate*

*Elevation: 5,025 feet; +638 feet/-0 feet*

*Location: Kings Canyon National Park*

*Maps: USGS 7.5' The Sphinx; Trails Illustrated Sequoia Kings Canyon National Parks No. 205*

*Fees and permits: A permit is not required for this day hike. Wilderness permits for overnight trips cost $15 during the peak season quota period; the remainder of the year, permits are free. If you are planning an overnight in this area, be advised that camping is not allowed along this stretch of trail until you reach Lower Paradise Valley, which is 1 mile past the falls. Passenger vehicles entering the park are charged a $20 admission fee, which is good for seven days.*

*Contact: Sequoia and Kings Canyon National Parks (559-565-3341 general information; 559-565-3766 wilderness permits; www.nps.gov/seki).*

Where the blacktop ends, the adventure begins. At Roads End in Kings Canyon National Park, that couldn't be truer. The terminus of CA 180 near Cedar Grove is the farthest your car can take you into this natural playground of deep canyons, polished granite, and earth-sculpting rivers. Roads End, a widely used springboard for backpackers into the deep reaches of Kings Canyon, is where our trail to Mist Falls begins. Chaperoned by the vigorous South Fork Kings River, this popular hike to one of the canyon's most impressive cataracts is a relatively easy jaunt. Proximity to the Kanawyer Loop Trail also gives you an option for a whole different perspective on the return trip.

### GETTING THERE

From the Kings Canyon National Park Big Stump Entrance Station, follow CA 180 for 35 miles to Roads End (5 miles past the turnoff for Cedar Grove Village), where you will find ample parking, water, and pit toilets. The trailhead is located near the ranger station at the east end of the parking lot.

### THE TRAIL

Sequoia and Kings Canyon National Parks are not endowed with a plethora of stunning waterfalls like their northerly neighbor, Yosemite. Nonetheless, what the parks lack in quantity is made up in quality.

Walk past the ranger station and join the wide, sandy trail that parallels the South Fork Kings River through an open mixed forest of oaks, pines, and cedars. Quickly come to a wooden footbridge that carries you across Copper Creek. The nearly level trail wanders past fire-scarred trees and boulders that gravity brought crashing down from the granite cliffs above. Look for mule deer foraging on grasses and black-crested Steller's jays zipping about. The area also sees its share of rattlesnakes and bruins, so use caution.

The forest is open enough to grant views of the upright granite walls that form Kings Canyon, one of the deepest and most dramatic gorges in North America. Just outside the boundary of the park, near the confluence of the South and Middle Forks of the Kings River, Spanish Peak (10,051 feet) towers over the meandering river some 8,000 feet below. Like much of the Sierra, the upper reaches of the canyon were glacially sculpted (U-shaped valleys) with the lower reaches being carved by rivers (V-shaped valleys).

After bisecting a dense pocket of manzanita shrubs, the trail descends slightly into a cool forest, its understory blanketed with ferns. Trade the sandy trail for hard-packed dirt and reach a trail fork at 1.9 miles, where you veer left toward Mist Falls and Paradise Valley. The Bubbs Creek Trail is to the right and crosses the South Fork Kings River via a steel footbridge. Take note of this junction. On the return trip you have the option of crossing the river here and following the southern bank back to the trailhead.

From the junction, the trail begins to climb via a series of stone steps, rising above the turbulent river. Incense cedars, ponderosa pines, and black oaks provide shade. Bend away from the river momentarily into a peculiar stand of invasive bamboo, then cross an exposed mini-avalanche of boulders before heading back into the shady forest. Rendezvous with the frothy river once again and ascend another longer granite staircase to the top of a rocky outcrop, 3 miles from the trailhead, where views downstream unfold. The Kings River courses below, flanked by imposing granite walls on both sides. Standing sentinel in front of you is The Sphinx, an irregularly shaped granite peak that (if you squint a little and the light is just right) looks remotely like its Egyptian namesake.

Continue your ascent, passing several smaller cataracts clogged with boulders and downed logs as you close in on your goal, but don't mistake them for the real thing—you haven't reached the falls yet. At 4 miles, a sign, dispelling any doubts, marks your arrival at spectacular Mist Falls. A short spur trail takes you close to the base of the raucous cataract. As the name implies, Mist Falls is misty, so use caution on the slippery rocks if you do venture closer. Although the falls are only 45 feet high, the immense flow of water in early spring creates a frothy white, tumbling torrent that sends a cooling spray billowing into the air. As the season wears on and flows diminish, the raging torrent is tamed, and the subtle details of the cascade can be seen. You can hike to the top of the falls by following the main trail less than 0.5 mile, but undoubtedly the best vantage is from below.

When ready, retrace your steps and enjoy the views of the canyon all over again. When you reach the Bubbs Creek Trail junction (1.9 miles from the trailhead), bear left and cross Bailey Bridge. Shortly after crossing, bear right at a trail fork and head west along the south bank of the river toward Roads End. Early in the season, when flows from Avalanche Creek are high, the trail may be underwater just past the fork, and crossing can be dangerous. If that's the case, turn around and head back the way you came.

Though this is a slightly longer option (2.6 miles versus 2 miles back to the trailhead from the Bubbs Creek Junction), the trail is

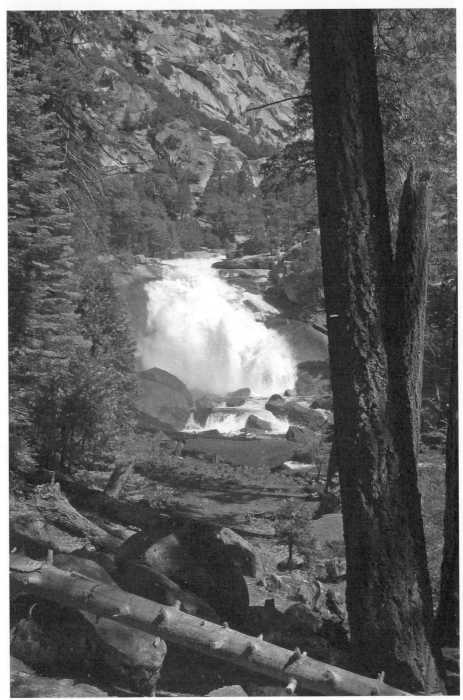

*Mist Falls*

less traveled and offers a new perspective. You will need to walk slightly downstream of the trailhead to reach a footbridge where you can recross the river and head back to the parking lot at Roads End.

If you are looking to delve deeper into the backcountry, from short weekend trips to long-distance treks, there is a plethora of backpacking opportunities out of Roads End. Backpackers can complete the breathtaking 42-mile Rae Lakes Loop, cross the Sierra via Kearsarge Pass, and even join up with the Pacific Crest Trail and hike to Canada, or simply overnight in Paradise Valley.

On your drive to Roads End, you may have noticed Boyden Caverns along the south bank of the Kings River. To date, more than 200 caves have been found in Sequoia and Kings Canyon. Most are in the western third of the parks, along a narrow bank of marble paralleling the Sierra. If you are looking for a fun diversion, stop in at privately owned Boyden Caverns, which is just outside the park. Although it's highly commercialized, a 45-minute tour, suitable for children, takes you into the cavern, where you can marvel at the amazing underground formations. Crystal Cave (in Sequoia) is the only commercialized cavern within the boundaries of the park. Note that both Boyden Caverns and Crystal Cave charge separate admission fees.

# 43

## Boole Tree

*Type: Day hike*

*Season: June through October*

*Total distance: 2.5-mile loop*

*Rating: Moderate*

*Elevation: 6,272 feet; +809 feet/-809 feet*

*Location: Sequoia National Forest*

*Maps: USGS 7.5' Hume (part of loop trail not shown); USFS Sequoia National Forest*

*Fees and permits: A permit is not required for this day hike. To reach the trailhead, you must enter Kings Canyon National Park and pay a $20 admission fee, which is good for seven days.*

*Contact: Sequoia National Forest, Hume Lake Ranger District (559-338-2251; www.fs.fed.us/r5/sequoia).*

This hike ventures into the northeast corner of the Converse Basin, former site of one of the largest stands of giant sequoias in the world. Today all that remains of the grove is a single mature specimen—the Boole Tree. At 269 feet tall, with a circumference of 113 feet, it's the eighth largest giant sequoia in existence and the largest in any national forest. Ironically, the tree was named for Frank Boole, the lumber mill superintendent who oversaw the grove's unfortunate destruction. This lightly traveled, moderately steep loop gives you the chance not only to stand at the base of this marvelous monarch, but also to witness the second growth of a new generation of sequoias and take in the outstanding view from the southern rim of Kings Canyon. The trail can be dusty and warm, so get an early start to avoid the afternoon heat and pack plenty of water.

### GETTING THERE

From the Kings Canyon National Park Big Stump Entrance Station, follow CA 180 for 6.6 miles to the signed turnoff for Boole Tree Trail (Forest Road 13S55). Proceed along the narrow unpaved road 0.3 mile to a three-way intersection and follow the signed middle path. Pass a second junction with FS13S21 and continue straight. Bisect Stump Meadow, and 2.6 miles from CA 180 arrive at the large parking area with pit toilets.

### THE TRAIL

From the information board, where the two ends of the loop trail meet, take the right fork and complete the loop in a counterclockwise direction. Enter an open forest of ponderosa pine, incense cedar, sugar pine, and fledgling sequoia and immediately begin a moderate ascent. The trail is lined with a dense carpet of mountain misery, a sticky, fernlike, leafy shrub with small white blossoms. Native Americans, who called the plant *kit-kit-dizze,* drank a tea steeped from the leaves as a cure for a number of ailments.

Eventually you parallel the southern flank of a slender meadow. At the far end of the grassy swath, at 0.6 mile, the trail bends left (northwest) and crosses its trickling inlet stream. Climb three switchbacks and a short but steep series of railroad tie stairs to the crest of a dry saddle blanketed with mountain whitethorn. Converse Mountain rises directly to the south.

Enter a jungle of twisted willows and briefly descend to a junction, simply marked "trail," at 0.9 mile, leading to Boole Tree. Turn sharply right and walk downhill 150 feet to an information placard. Continue 300 feet farther to the base of this magnificent leviathan that seems abnormally out of proportion with the surrounding vegetation. Extensive burn clefts, typical of giant sequoias, scar the thick, fibrous red bark. It's uncertain why this tree was spared the ax when

*Boole Tree*

all the other giants around it were felled by loggers in the late 1800s. By the time the 3,000-acre Converse Basin came under US Forest Service protection in the 1930s, only very young trees and this solitary monarch remained. Ironically, when commercial sequoia logging operations began, the loggers expected an extraordinary amount of timber volume from each tree. It wasn't until many sequoia groves had already been decimated that lumbermen realized that their size and age made the trees extremely brittle and the wood unsuitable for anything more than fence posts and roof shingles.

Return to the main trail and veer right. Heading north, switchback up a dry, open hillside to a ridgetop, where the trail grade levels and you have fine views of the Kings River gorge and the distant Sierran peaks. Walk along the ridgetop, passing the remains of several severed stumps and a small woodshed. Go through a cattle gate in a barbed wire fence and get your first views northward. The horizon is dominated by 10,051-foot Spanish Mountain, which lords over the Kings River some 8,200 feet below. This dramatic difference in elevation affords this section of Kings Canyon the distinction of being the deepest gorge in all of North America.

Descend the dusty trail via a series of switchbacks that zigzag across an open slope dotted with sun-loving manzanita, chinquapin, and prickly gooseberry. Occasional black oaks, ponderosa pines, and white firs provide short spurts of shade. Meet up again with the barbed wire fence and follow it along a lower ridge to more fantastic views of the canyon's deep, steep-sided walls and the Wild and Scenic–designated Kings River thrashing below. Farther west, the lower reaches of the river, which forms the dividing line between the Sierra and Sequoia National Forests, boast fantastic whitewater rafting before ultimately spilling into the Central Valley, where it is used to irrigate crops.

At the western end of the ridge, pass through another steel gate and descend a mountain misery-covered hillside interspersed with California rose, golden brodiaea, and Mariposa lily, and close the loop at 2.5 miles.

If you haven't done so already, stop at Stump Meadow on your way out. The massive stumps that litter the meadow are an eerie sight. Young sequoias are visible around the perimeter of the meadow, however, not in the meadow itself. Since a single, mature giant sequoia can draw a whopping 137,000 gallons of water out of the soil during a normal growing season, it is believed that after the grove was felled, the water table rose, creating the meadow and making the soil too wet for seedlings to become established. With their phenomenally fast growth rate, many of the second-growth sequoias proliferating within the basin have reached diameters of 24 inches or more.

# 44

## Redwood Mountain Grove

Type: Day hike or overnight

Season: Mid-May through November

Total distance: 7.2-mile loop

Rating: Moderate

Elevation: 6,218 feet; +1,465 feet/-1,465 feet

Location: Kings Canyon National Park

Maps: USGS 7.5' General Grant Grove; Trails Illustrated Sequoia Kings Canyon National Parks No. 205

Fees and permits: A permit is not required for this day hike. Wilderness permits for overnight trips cost $15 during the peak season quota period; the remainder of the year, permits are free. Passenger vehicles entering the park are charged a $20 admission fee, which is good for seven days.

Contact: Sequoia and Kings Canyon National Parks (559-565-3341 general information; 559-565-3766 wilderness permits; www.nps.gov/seki).

Redwood Mountain Grove is the largest concentration of giant sequoias left in the world. Partly because of its obscurity and partly because of the dirt road you take to get there, Redwood Mountain Grove has remained off the grid for the majority of Sequoia and Kings Canyon visitors, who would rather flock to the manicured trails within Giant Forest. This loop hike takes you into the very heart of the grove, where you can walk among the soaring monarchs in blissful solitude. The lightly used trail wanders past lush meadows, along trickling creeks, and under a shady canopy that offers fleeting vistas of the surrounding peaks.

### GETTING THERE

From the Kings Canyon National Park Big Stump Entrance Station, continue along CA 180 for 0.9 mile and turn right onto CA 198 (General's Highway). Proceed 3.5 miles to Quail Flat, and turn right onto a dirt road signed for Redwood Canyon (opposite the paved road to Hume Lake). Reach a Y-junction at 1.7 miles and veer left, following the sign to Redwood Canyon Trailhead. Find the spacious parking area with pit toilets 0.1 mile farther. Find the signed Hart Tree trailhead at the southeast corner of the parking area.

### THE TRAIL

There are two loop trails that start here, Hart Tree Trail and Sugar Bowl Trail. We take the Hart Tree Trail, which passes through Redwood Mountain Grove's eastern side. Later, I discuss how to combine the two trails to create a slightly longer loop.

Descend the wide trail (once a roadbed) into a beautiful forest where giant sequoias intermingle with other conifers and shade a rich understory of dogwood, California rose, and broadleaf lupine. Pure stands of sequoias are rarities. Most often, they are found growing alongside white firs, sugar pines, and red firs. Ponderosa pines and California black oaks often occupy drier sites within the grove boundaries. Pass an interesting cluster of four sequoias in perfect alignment, and at 0.3 mile come to a trail fork. Bear left and continue along Hart Tree Trail. The right fork will be our return leg.

Enjoy the melodious, fluty warble of the hermit thrush as you descend toward Barton

Creek. Easily cross the lush, fern-choked rivulet and begin a mild climb to the next creek crossing just before Log Cabin. The "cabin" is actually a downed giant sequoia that was hollowed out, partially by fire, and transformed into a rudimentary domicile by an enterprising human during the first half of the 20th century, when the grove was unfortunately logged (prior to it falling under the purview of the National Park Service).

Past the cabin, you climb above the creek to a manzanita-covered saddle where the forest opens briefly, offering limited views of the tree-covered slopes to the west. Sequoias are scant along this section of trail, but will reappear later. Pass a swath of singed trees and charred stumps, but notice how nature heals itself as grasses and wildflowers quickly reemerge on the forest floor.

You cross two more seasonal creeklets and climb to a granite outcrop at 1.75 miles, from which you have views of Redwood Mountain to the west and Big Baldy to the south. From here enjoy level walking before meeting Hart Meadow, which is bursting with slender grasses and elegant ferns. At the southwestern end of the meadow, easily cross the double channels of Buena Vista Creek and follow the trail on a general descent. The sequoias reappear, and you bisect

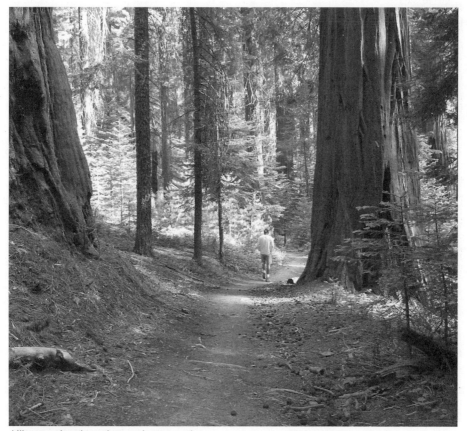

*Hiker passing through two giant sequoias*

a small stand of about six of them, giving a little perspective to their enormity. The trail then passes through Fallen Tunnel Tree, a fire-gutted sequoia (watch your head), and your descent steepens for about 0.2 mile. Walk through and along fallen sequoias, crossing East Fork Redwood Creek 3 miles from the trailhead. This crossing can be slightly difficult when flows are high.

From the creek, ascend along the southern bank and shortly thereafter reach a junction with a short, steep trail leading to fire-scarred Hart Tree, one of the 25 largest sequoias. Fire is a critical factor in the growth and vigor of giant sequoia forests. Their unusually thick bark is fire-resistant, allowing them to survive while other species perish. They actually depend on the intense heat of fire to open their small cones, allowing seeds to be released. Once released, the tiny seeds require contact with bare soil to germinate, and this is only possible when fire has cleared leaf litter and other debris from the forest floor. Fire also thins out other species that compete with sequoia seedlings for light and moisture, and it cycles nutrients back into the soil. A century's worth of fire suppression has taken its toll on sequoia populations. Realizing the role fire plays in the lifecycle of these giant trees, the National Park Service now routinely sets prescribed fires, allowing sequoia forests to reproduce and as a tool for fuel management.

Back on the main trail, watch for Hartweg's iris as the descent continues to a lushly lined, unnamed creek with a lovely ribbon waterfall that glides between moss-covered rocks into a small pool. Easily cross via steppingstones and continue through the mixed forest to the bottom of the canyon, crossing one more seasonal creek. Nearing the 4.5-mile mark, the descent steepens, and you should watch for the small, ankle-twisting sequoia cones that litter the trail. You would think such a massive tree would have equally massive cones, but the opposite is true.

At 4.6 miles, a spur trail leading to Fallen Goliath makes a small loop off the main trail and rejoins it after passing along the enormous trunk of this downed giant. Reach the low point of the journey at 5.1 miles and cross alder-lined Redwood Creek. Fortunately, a fallen tree spans the creek, creating a natural bridge—otherwise crossing might prove difficult in the early season.

On the other side of the creek, you come to a signed junction with Redwood Creek Trail. Turn right and travel upstream along the western bank of Redwood Creek, arriving at a second junction at 5.2 miles with Sugar Bowl Trail. You have the option of turning left here and creating a longer loop of 9 miles. Stay straight and follow signs to the parking area. With the creek pleasantly trickling beside you, make your way through a lush understory of dogwood, thimbleberry, and a smattering of wildflowers, the most prolific being broadleaf lupine, which grows in thickets beneath the towering sequoias. At 5.9 miles, the gently ascending trail turns away from the creek and begins a steeper climb, passing around and through the decaying corpses of several fallen giants. The main cause of death among mature sequoias is toppling due to their shallow, wide-spreading lateral root system.

Reach the junction with Hart Tree Trail at 6.9 miles, closing the loop. From here, turn left (south), retracing your steps to the parking area.

# 45

## Little Baldy

*Type: Day hike*

*Season: June through October*

*Total distance: 3.4 miles round trip*

*Rating: Moderate*

*Elevation: 7,360 feet; +764 feet/-110 feet*

*Location: Sequoia National Park*

*Maps: USGS 7.5' Giant Forest; Trails Illustrated Sequoia Kings Canyon National Parks No. 205*

*Fees and permits: A permit is not required for this day hike. Passenger vehicles entering the park are charged a $20 admission fee, which is good for seven days.*

*Contact: Sequoia and Kings Canyon National Parks (559-565-3341; www.nps .gov/seki).*

Rise above the treetops on this pleasant hike to the top of one of Sequoia's uncharacteristic exposed granite domes. The well-defined trail climbs moderately along wildflower-laden hillsides to a broad outcrop with expansive views in every direction. In fact, the view from Little Baldy's summit is so extensive that it was once used as a fire lookout. There are no facilities at the trailhead, nor is there any water along the trail. Little Baldy's exposed nature is an invitation for lightning, so be mindful of changing weather and descend immediately if storms threaten.

### GETTING THERE

From the Kings Canyon National Park Big Stump Entrance Station, continue along CA 180 for 0.9 miles and turn right onto CA 198 (General's Highway). Proceed 17.7 miles south to Little Baldy Saddle and park in the roadside pullout. The trail begins near a large sign on the east side of the highway.

### THE TRAIL

Mount a series of steps and enter a mixed forest of stately red firs and Jeffrey pines. The trail steadily rises, parallel to the highway, past hillsides adorned with scattered ferns, bitter cherry, thimbleberry, and a cornucopia of wildflowers. The hum of vehicles quickly recedes the higher you climb, and you enjoy slivers of view through periodic breaks in the trees of Chimney Rock (frequented by rock climbers) and the protruding round face of Big Baldy to the northwest.

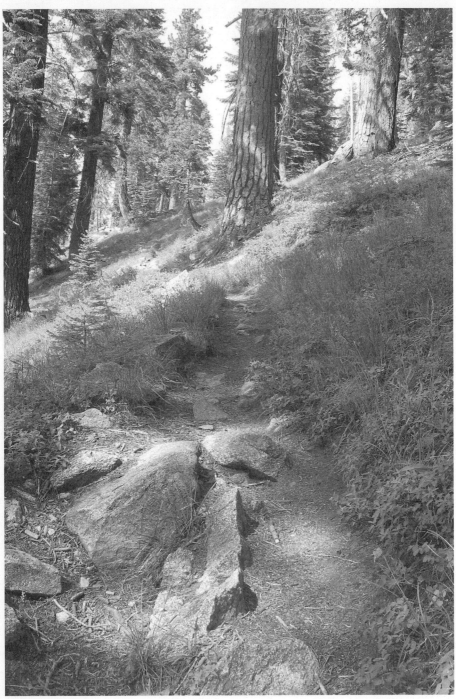

*Trail to Little Baldy summit*

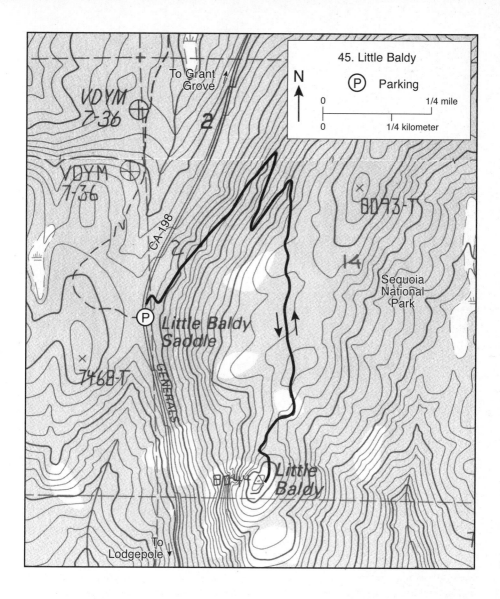

### 45. Little Baldy

P  Parking

N

0 .......... 1/4 mile

0 .......... 1/4 kilometer

To Grant Grove

VDYM 7.36

VDYM 7.36

CA-198

2

8073-T

14

Sequoia National Park

P  *Little Baldy Saddle*

7468-T

GENERALS

8074

*Little Baldy*

To Lodgepole

In late spring and early summer, wild-flower enthusiast will enjoy the fantastic array of blooms. The path is mottled with blue-eyed Mary, monkey flower, groundsel, pen-stemon, Coulter's daisy, wallflower, Indian paintbrush, and larkspur, to name just a few. In addition to the wildflowers, watch for mar-mots, chipmunks, butterflies, and birds on your quest for the summit. We even had to pause while a sooty grouse and her brood of youngsters crossed the trail.

Continue uphill via a series of long, easy switchbacks, and at the 1-mile mark reach the crest of the hillside. Enjoy level walking along a fire-scarred ridge littered with downed logs and dense clusters of saplings

---

*The Great Western Divide as viewed from Little Baldy summit*

vying for survival. The flat path comes to an end a short 0.2 mile farther, and you make a small climb, passing a rocky knoll to your right. Lose 100 feet of the precious elevation you worked so hard to attain before the final climb to the summit. From the base of Little Baldy, a short, rocky climb leads to the top and the panoramic view.

From the broad granite summit (8,044 feet), Spanish Mountain and Obelisk are visible to the north. To the east, the Great Western Divide dominates the landscape. This small side range of the Sierra Nevada separates the Kaweah and Kern River watersheds. Southward you can see the top of Moro Rock and the jutting spires of Castle Rocks. Westward, you now have an unobstructed view of Big Baldy and Chimney Rock, and in the distance through the haze, the San Joaquin Valley. When you are done admiring the view, return to your vehicle via the same path.

# 46

## Tokopah Falls

*Type: Day hike*

*Season: May through October*

*Total distance: 3.8 miles round trip*

*Rating: Easy*

*Elevation: 6,762 feet; +683 feet/-3 feet*

*Location: Sequoia National Park*

*Maps: USGS 7.5' Lodgepole; Trails Illustrated Sequoia Kings Canyon National Parks No. 205*

*Fees and permits: A permit is not required for this day hike. Passenger vehicles entering the park are charged a $20 admission fee, which is good for seven days.*

*Contact: Sequoia and Kings Canyon National Parks (559-565-3341; www .nps.gov/seki).*

This hike up glacially carved Tokopah Valley culminates at the base of 1,200-foot-high Tokopah Falls. This impressive cataract along Marble Fork Kaweah River originates high above in alpine environs, and you get a front row seat as it slides, plunges, tumbles, and careens over smooth granite faces in its quest for the valley floor. Tokopah Falls is without a doubt the most spectacular falls in Sequoia National Park. The easy trail and its proximity to Lodgepole, one of the park's major hubs of activity, negates any chance of solitude. However, by starting early you can avoid much of the crowd.

### GETTING THERE
From CA 198 (General's Highway), head east at the signed Lodgepole junction. Proceed 0.7 mile, passing the visitors center and campground entrance station to a large parking area. Walk up the campground access road, passing the Walter Fry Nature Center and restrooms to a fork in the road. Veer left and cross a bridge spanning Marble Fork Kaweah River and immediately find the trailhead on the right.

### THE TRAIL
Your course follows the north bank of the Marble Fork Kaweah River. Throughout the hike, you will notice several unofficial trails leading down to the river's edge. If your plans call for fishing or a chilly soak for trail-worn toes, take care on slippery rocks and near swift-moving sections of the river, especially during peak flow periods.

The falls lie at the east end of U-shaped

46. Tokopah Falls

Ⓟ Parking

N

0 ____ 1/4 mile
0 ____ 1/4 kilometer

Tokopah Falls 23

3538T

Horse

Marble Fork Kaweah River

Valley

Tokopah 22

MILE 1.5

8530

Marble

CAMPGROUND

SPRING

Sequoia
National Park

7592T

Willow
Meadow

Lodgepole 21

CAMPGROUND

Wolverton

Creek

Tokopah Valley, which was formed in much the same way as Yosemite Valley. As the powerful Tokopah Glacier moved across the land, it carved, scoured, and scraped, leaving in its wake towering cliffs of smooth, bare granite marred by rock fragments and boulders carried by the moving sheet of ice. At the head of the valley lie the Tablelands, a lofty plateau of stark granite flanked by Mount Silliman to the north and Alta Peak to the south.

Begin by gently climbing through a mixed forest of red firs, incense cedars, and ponderosa and Jeffrey pines. A variety of wildflowers like golden brodiaea, lupine, cinquefoil, and mustang clover soften the boulder-strewn path and fill trailside meadows. Though the trail meanders near and far from the splashing river, its soothing melody is never far from earshot. There are many spots to stop and admire the pleasing pools, cascades, and ripples created by the streambed's changing terrain. Cross a verdant meadow on a narrow path trimmed with stones and as you move farther into the valley, garner glimpses of its towering southern flank.

At 1.3 miles, an easy boulder hop takes you across a small tributary clogged with boulders and downed limbs, and you get your first good view of the Watchtower, an island of granite rising 1,600 feet above the river. Views of this hulking monolith only improve as you continue farther, and if you look closely, you might even be able to spy the trail to Heather and Pear Lakes clinging to the cliff's edge (see Hike 47).

Traverse the first of three wooden footbridges over Horse Creek to 500 feet beyond and continue across a dry wash. At 1.6 miles, as you leave the forest, the trail grade increases, and you get your first glimpse of Tokopah Falls as it stair-steps and spills down the valley's headwall. Over the last 0.25 mile, shady conifers are replaced by drier, sun-loving shrubs, and the trail becomes increasingly rocky. Watch your footing and your noggin as you cross a talus slope, occasionally passing beneath head-banging boulders. A flat bench at the base of the falls signifies the end of the trail. A sign warns hikers not to continue farther, as steep cliffs make travel extremely dangerous.

Now up close, you can only see the final cascade. Like most Sierra waterfalls, these are best viewed in spring and early summer when the rivers are swollen with snowmelt. From the falls, you have amazing views of the pointy Watchtower knob jutting from the striated southern wall, you can watch the pacified river disappear into the forested valley downstream, and gaze up at the chunky granite wall directly behind you (north).

Watch for yellow-bellied marmots sunning themselves on boulders or listen for their distinctive whistle. Marmots, relatives of ground squirrels and prairie dogs, are commonly called "whistle pigs." Their whistle is typically used to notify other marmots of approaching predators; however, I think it also serves to let the group know of incoming hikers lugging backpacks loaded with tasty vittles. Guard your food and don't give them any handouts, no matter how cute they appear. After enjoying the falls, return the way you came.

If you're traveling with young children, the Walter Fry Nature Center is a great stop for some hands-on activities (it's open from July to Labor Day). Ironically, Fry originally came to the area as a logger. After spending five days with a crew cutting down a single sequoia and subsequently counting its rings, he realized he was in the wrong business. In a matter of days, his crew had ended 3,266 years of growth! This discovery prompted him to become a park ranger and later, park superintendent.

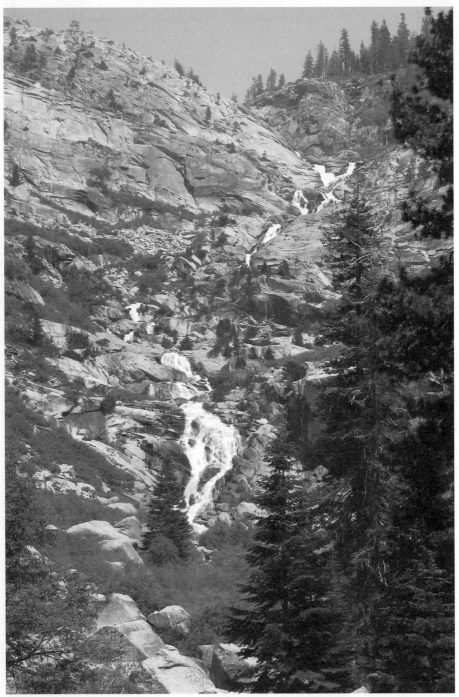

*Tokopah Falls*

# 47

## Lakes Trail to Heather Lake

*Type: Day hike or overnight*

*Season: Mid-June through October*

*Total distance: 8.2 miles round trip*

*Rating: Moderate to strenuous*

*Elevation: 7,281 feet; +2,210 feet/-229 feet*

*Location: Sequoia National Park*

*Maps: USGS 7.5' Lodgepole; Trails Illustrated Sequoia Kings Canyon National Parks No. 205*

*Fees and permits: A permit is not required for this day hike. Wilderness permits for overnight trips cost $15 during the peak season quota period; the remainder of the year, permits are free. Passenger vehicles entering the park are charged a $20 admission fee, which is good for seven days.*

*Contact: Sequoia and Kings Canyon National Parks (559-565-3341 general information; 559-565-3766 wilderness permits; www.nps.gov/seki).*

This popular route along the Lakes Trail offers, hands down, some of the most scenic hiking in all of Sequoia National Park. Climb through a hearty red fir forest to spectacular vistas from the Watchtower, a hulking monolith that looms over Tokopah Valley, and visit a tranquil subalpine lake festooned with heather and lodgepole pines. Though this hike culminates at picturesque Heather Lake, the first of a succession of lakes found along the trail, you have the option of continuing on to three other alpine gems (Aster, Emerald, and Pear Lakes). Strong hikers can make the challenging 12 miles round trip to Pear Lake in one day, but even better is to overnight at this granite-hemmed alpine beauty, where you can watch shadows dance on stark granite walls and count stars that choke the charcoal sky and color the night.

### GETTING THERE

From CA 198 (General's Highway), 1.5 miles south of the Lodgepole turnoff, head east at the signed Wolverton junction. Proceed 1.4 miles to the large trailhead parking area (continue straight at the three-way stop near General Sherman Tree). Turn left into the first parking area, where you will find the trailhead and bathrooms.

### THE TRAIL

The trail begins at the top of a set of brick stairs at the north end of the parking area. The well-used Lakes Trail gently climbs to a junction at 0.2 mile, with a connector path leading to Lodgepole. Bear right and almost

*Tokopah Valley as viewed from the Watchtower*

immediately you pass a second junction with Long Meadow Trail. The grade eases as you make your way along a dry ridge dominated by wolf lichen-covered red firs. The neon-green-colored lichen is a combination of a fungus and algae. The fungus, similar to a mushroom, is incapable of making its own food, and that's where the algae come in. With the ability to photosynthesize like a plant, the algae provide nutrients, which the pair uses to proliferate together. Wolf lichen, which is toxic, was used in Europe to poison wolves (hence the name) and by Native American tribes to make poison arrowheads, dye, and, strangely enough, tea.

Toward the crest of the ridge, you begin to hear Wolverton Creek splashing to the right. The trail briefly drops down to its northern bank and along a verdant meadow of grasses, forbs, and sedges neatly trimmed with lodgepole pines. The ascent resumes as you parallel Wolverton Creek, occasionally utilizing tree roots for stairs. The trail alternates between open grassy clearings dotted with wildflowers and dense forest with little understory. At 1.6 miles, an easy boulder hop takes you across an aspen- and wildflower-edged feeder stream of Wolverton Creek. Arrive at the Alta Peak Trail junction not long after and veer left (north)

47. Lakes Trail To Heather Lake

Parking Ⓟ

Side Trail ••••••

View ⬆⬇

0    1/2 mile
0    1/2 kilometer

N

To Pear Lake

Heather Lake

Kaweah

Tokopah Falls

Hump Route

Watch Tower Route

Fork

Valley

Tokopah

Marble

Lakes Trail

CAMPGROUND

Lodgepole

To Lodgepole

To CA 198

Wolverton

Long Meadow

Creek

To Alta Peak

Sequoia National Park

Panther Meadow

Long Meadow

SKI HUT

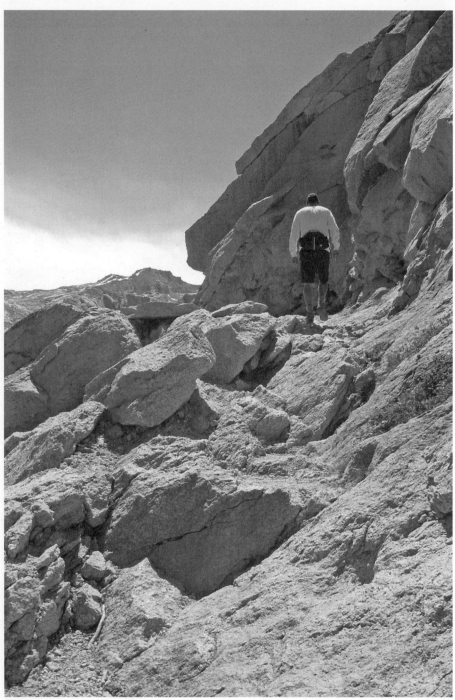

*Lakes Trail*

toward Heather Lake. Climb moderately past fern-covered hillsides and recross the same small tributary, but now higher up the slope. Arrive at the Hump Trail junction, 2 miles and 1,000 vertical feet from your starting point.

From here you have two options, which both ultimately get you to Heather Lake. The Watchtower Route is without question the more scenic path but isn't advised for acrophobic hikers, as one section traverses a fantastically exposed, precipitous rock ledge. The Hump Route is steeper, rises an additional 200 vertical feet, lacks any notable views, and the concoction of twigs, pine cones, rocks, and loose sand at your feet creates a literal slippery slope (note: walking sticks come in quite handy). Its only saving grace is that it is 0.3 mile shorter. If you absolutely can't stand going the same way twice when you have the option, ascend via the Watchtower and return on the Hump Trail. My recommendation, though, is to come and go via the Watchtower and enjoy a second helping of superb vistas.

From the junction, the trail steadily rises and the northwestward views of Tokopah Valley begin to take shape through occasional voids in the red fir forest. At 2.5 miles, the woodland briefly opens and you enter a swath of greenery surrounding a tributary of Marble Fork Kaweah River. The lush area is brimming with streamside bluebells, and a lovely little waterfall tumbles upstream. Cross with the aid of steppingstones and continue onward and upward. With each advance in elevation, notice the increasing appearance of boulders and the disappearing trees.

A series of switchbacks deposit you atop the Watchtower, an enormous granite spire towering some 1,600 feet above the Marble Fork Kaweah River coursing below. From your perch, the views are staggering. The stark Tablelands sit in repose to the east; Tokopah Falls, cradled in the heart of the valley, careens down clefts and crevices in the polished granite; and Mount Silliman rises stoically to the north.

Leave your lofty vista point and begin the final push to the high point of the journey. The trail, initially tucked beneath the trees, eventually emerges onto an exposed ledge that was blasted from the granite cliff. Rounding the uppermost corner, the viewshed expands to the south to include 11,204-foot Alta Peak and several of its craggy neighbors.

The rocky trail then heads gently uphill and rejoins the Hump Trail at 3.9 miles. Bear left and continue 0.2 mile to the shore of Heather Lake, passing a signed path leading to an open-air toilet 200 yards from the main trail. A steep arc of granite forms the backdrop of this subalpine gem, and purple mountain heather adds a splash of color to the lodgepole pine-dotted shore. Scout out a nice boulder and spread out a picnic before returning or venturing farther.

If you extend your day hike by continuing up the Lakes Trail, you will reach Emerald Lake (9,226 feet) 0.9 mile beyond the outlet of Heather Lake. Aster Lake (9,108 feet) is accessed by turning left where Emerald Lake's outlet crosses the trail and following it 0.2 mile downstream. Pear Lake (9,548 feet) is the official culmination of the trail and is 1.9 miles past Heather. Backpackers should note that camping is forbidden at both Heather and Aster Lakes. Wilderness permit-carrying backpackers can find designated campsites near Emerald and Pear Lakes.

# 48

## Circle Meadow

*Type: Day hike*

*Season: May to November*

*Total distance: 4-mile loop*

*Rating: Easy*

*Elevation: 7,063 feet; +694 feet/-694 feet*

*Location: Sequoia National Park*

*Maps: USGS 7.5' Giant Forest, Lodgepole; Trails Illustrated Sequoia Kings Canyon National Parks No. 205*

*Fees and permits: A permit is not required for this day hike. Passenger vehicles entering the park are charged a $20 admission fee, which is good for seven days.*

*Contact: Sequoia and Kings Canyon National Parks (559-565-3341; www .nps.gov/seki).*

The Giant Forest is by far the most heavily visited area within Sequoia National Park. This easy hike begins and ends by dodging the hordes of tourists who flock to see the General Sherman Tree, but if you can manage the masses, it's the middle of this ramble that makes it all worth the hassle. Wander off the paved pathway and skirt lush Circle Meadow, passing several notable trees in the process, minus the fences and the crowds. Start at the Giant Forest Museum, just south on General's Highway, and acquaint yourself with the natural and human history of the area before walking among the big trees.

### GETTING THERE

From the Lodgepole turnoff in Sequoia National Park, drive 1.5 miles south on CA 198 (General's Highway) to Wolverton Road. Turn left and proceed 0.5 mile to a three-way stop. Turn right, following signs for Sherman Tree parking, which is 0.6 mile farther.

### THE TRAIL

From the parking area, make your way to the ostentatious Sherman Tree Trailhead (there are bathrooms and water here). Follow the wide paved pathway downhill, passing several interpretive plaques, and take note of the signed Congress Trail to your left. Assuming you got an early start, explore the General Sherman Tree at 0.4 mile before it gets overly crowded.

This gargantuan sequoia not only holds the distinction of being the largest tree on earth by volume (52,500 cubic feet), but

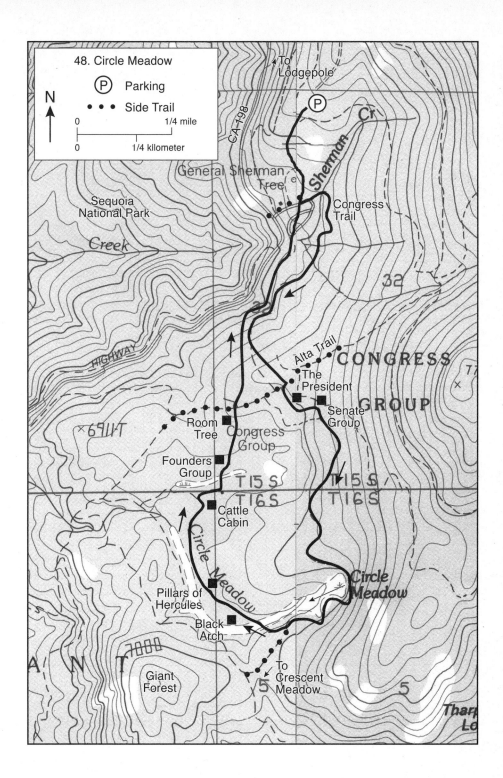

48. Circle Meadow

P Parking
• • • Side Trail

N

0 _____ 1/4 mile
0 _____ 1/4 kilometer

To Lodgepole

P

Sherman Cr

General Sherman
Tree

Sequoia
National Park

Congress
Trail

Creek

CA-198

HIGHWAY

32

Alta Trail

CONGRESS

The
President

GROUP

Room
Tree

Senate
Group

×6911'T

Congress
Group

T15 S

77

×

Founders
Group

T15 S
T16 S

T15 S
T16 S

Cattle
Cabin

Circle
Meadow

Circle
Meadow

Pillars of
Hercules

Black
Arch

To
Crescent
Meadow

7000

Giant
Forest

5

5

ANT

Thar
Lo

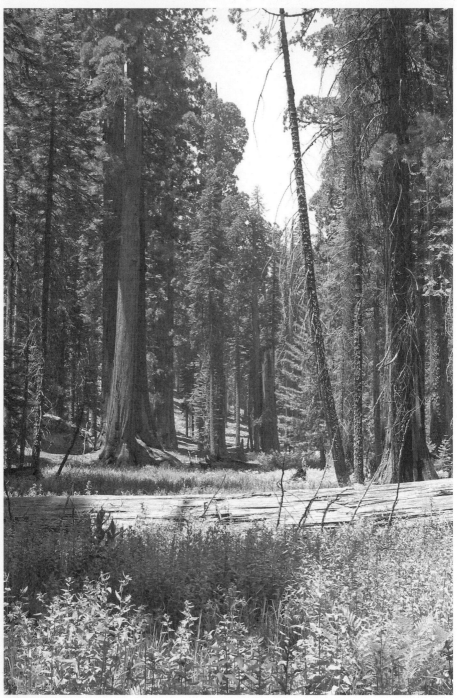

*Circle Meadow*

also the largest living thing in the world. Named in 1879 by James Wolverton, a pioneer cattleman who served under General William Tecumseh Sherman in the American Civil War, the tree stands 275 feet tall, has a trunk diameter of 36.5 feet, and is a whopping 2,200 years old. The top of the tree is dead, so instead of getting taller, General Sherman expands around the "trunk line." In optimal conditions, it adds enough wood to equal another good-size tree each year. When you're done craning your neck, wander back to the start of the Congress Trail.

The Giant Forest is crisscrossed with a multitude of well-marked paths, so it's hard to get lost. Follow the paved Congress Trail downhill to the Learning Tree and subsequently cross a pair of footbridges spanning branches of Sherman Creek. Continuing south, you pass several towering sequoias before coming to a cutoff trail on the right. Stay left (unless you want a shorter loop) and reach a junction with Alta Trail at 1 mile. Follow the pavement by bearing right on the Alta/Congress Trail and immediately come to another junction. Turn left to remain on the Congress Trail and head toward President Tree, the third largest sequoia, and later the Senate Group.

Near the cluster of sequoias named the Senate Group, find a sign directing you through the middle of this stately bunch and off the paved pathway toward Circle Meadow. The size of these trees is that much more amplified when you can actually stand next to them and gaze up their cinnamon-colored, fibrous trunks.

The trail undulates and winds through the peaceful woodland. Ferns and broadleaf lupines blanket the forest floor. At 1.9 miles, reach the southeast corner of Circle Meadow. The meadow actually forms a "C" (you are at the bottom and will follow the curve around in a clockwise direction). Ringed by majestic sequoias and other lesser conifers, the narrow clearing is filled with verdant sedges and grasses that are complemented each spring by a colorful palette of wild blossoms. Watch for bears and deer foraging in the meadow.

At 2.3 miles, come to an intersection with the Crescent Meadow Trail. Turn right and head north across the meadow. Pass through Black Arch, a fire-hollowed sequoia, and between the Pillars of Hercules, a pair of big trees flanking the trail. Continue toward Cattle Cabin, which was built by cattlemen who used the meadow for grazing prior to the establishment of the park. Past the cabin, cross the northern portion of the meadow (the top part of the "C") and stroll through the Founder's Group, a collection of sequoias dedicated to the people who helped establish Sequoia National Park. Next up is Room Tree. Climb through the low opening at the base of this giant and enter a small wooden chamber—a literal treehouse.

At 3.1 miles, you rejoin the paved Congress Trail near the McKinley Tree. Follow the path north as it descends toward the cutoff trail and later walk through a low tunnel carved in a fallen sequoia. Cross Sherman Creek via footbridge and ascend back to the bustling General Sherman Tree area, where you can retrace your steps uphill to the parking lot.

# 49

## Crescent and Log Meadows Loop

*Type: Day hike*

*Season: June to November*

*Total distance: 2.5-mile loop*

*Rating: Easy*

*Elevation: 6,691 feet; +570 feet/-570 feet*

*Location: Sequoia National Park*

*Maps: USGS 7.5' Giant Forest, Lodgepole; Trails Illustrated Sequoia Kings Canyon National Parks No. 205*

*Fees and permits: A permit is not required for this day hike. Passenger vehicles entering the park are charged a $20 admission fee, which is good for seven days.*

*Contact: Sequoia and Kings Canyon National Parks (559-565-3341; www.nps.gov/seki).*

There are many trails crisscrossing the popular Crescent Meadow area. This short, pleasant loop packs in a little bit of everything: splendid views, flower-filled meadows, a dose of history, and numerous giant sequoias. John Muir is said to have called sequoia-rimmed Crescent Meadow the "gem of the Sierras," and when you finish this hike you will no doubt agree with his observation.

### GETTING THERE

From the Sequoia National Park Ash Mountain Entrance Station, drive 16 miles north on CA 198 (General's Highway). Just south of the Giant Forest Museum, turn east onto paved Crescent Meadow Road. Follow the narrow road 2.5 miles, past turnoffs for Auto Log and Moro Rock, to the parking area at road's end. Along the way, pass through Tunnel Log, a fallen sequoia that was cut, allowing vehicles to drive through it (a bypass is available for higher-profile vehicles). You will find water, pit toilets, and bears at the trailhead. Most trailheads in Sequoia provide metal bearproof lockers for visitors to store food and scented items that might attract curious bruins. Use them—they are there for a reason.

### THE TRAIL

This counterclockwise loop begins on the paved pathway just south of the restroom building. The first leg coincides with the 49-mile High Sierra Trail. Crescent Meadow marks the western terminus of this long-distance route traversing the Sierras from

*High Sierra Trail*

49. Crescent and Log Meadows Loop

P Parking

••• Side Trail

N

0             1/4 mile

0           1/4 kilometer

east to west. The demanding trail goes up and over the Great Western Divide, eventually intersecting the John Muir/Pacific Crest Trail, where it officially ends.

Cross fern-filled Crescent Creek via a pair of wooden footbridges and bear right at a fork to maintain course on the High Sierra Trail, and trade the pavement for dirt. Immediately arrive at a second junction heading toward Bobcat Point and Moro Rock. Bear left this time and follow the easy grade uphill through

a forest of red fir and scattered sequoias.

At 0.5 mile, reach a saddle and a signed three-way junction. Bear southwest toward Eagle View. You will return to this spot after a quick jaunt to the overlook. Follow the now rocky trail 0.3 mile to a lofty perch high above Middle Fork Kaweah River. Notice the dramatic shift in vegetation on the steep, south-facing slope. From here, Moro Rock is visible to the west, Castle Rocks and the Paradise Ridge sit opposite, and the snow-capped peaks of the Great Western Divide dominate the eastern horizon.

Retrace your steps to the three-way junction and follow signs toward Tharp's Log. The trail descends quickly to another junction near the southern end of Log Meadow. Turn right and meander along the eastern edge of this verdant meadow brimming with grasses and seasonal wildflowers. Watch for mule deer and bears foraging in the meadow as you approach another junction (right) which connects with the Trail of the Sequoias. Stay straight, crossing two forks of Crescent Creek. The trail bends west as you skirt the northern end of the meadow and soon arrive at Tharp's Log and a trail junction at 1.7 miles.

Hale Tharp was the first European settler to homestead in the area, establishing a ranch among the big trees and allowing his cattle to graze in the meadow. He built a summer cabin out of a fallen, fire-hollowed giant sequoia in the 1860s that John Muir described as "a spacious log house of one log, carbon-lined, centuries old yet sweet and fresh, weather proof, earthquake proof, likely to outlast the most durable stone castle, and commanding views of garden and grove grander far than the richest king ever enjoyed." Muir was right—the sturdy arboreal domicile is still here, and holds the distinction of being the oldest structure in the park.

From the junction near Tharp's Log, briefly climb northwest. Cresting a low ridge separating Crescent and Log Meadows, you then head downhill, arriving at Chimney Tree, an erect, fire-hollowed giant, and a junction with the Cleveland Tree trail at 2 miles.

Veer left and take a short detour to Cleveland Tree, one of the larger sequoias in the Giant Forest. Return to the junction near Chimney Tree and turn left, walking along the northern fringe of Crescent Meadow. Soon you'll arrive at a trail fork and turn left, following the trail as it bends south and skirts the meadow's western margin. If you hit it right, the green carpet of grass can be bursting with a cornucopia of wildflowers including shooting stars, leopard lilies, and lupines. Close the loop at 2.5 miles when you reach the picnic area and parking lot.

If you've got time to spare, head to Moro Rock and Crystal Cave. Moro Rock (you passed a sign for it on Crescent Meadow Road) is an exfoliating granite dome offering unparalleled views of the surrounding landscape. A short but steep set of stairs ascend 300 vertical feet to the summit (6,725 feet). Even though you can expect an army of people climbing alongside you, the view makes up for the dearth of solitude.

Crystal Cave, just south on General's Highway, provides a break from the granite and forests above ground. Unbeknownst to many visitors, Sequoia and Kings Canyon include an extensive karst system. There are in fact over 200 known caves within park boundaries, Crystal Cave being the only commercialized one within Sequoia. The exquisite marble cavern is festooned with icicle-like stalactites and mounds of stalagmites that are wondrous to behold. Note that there is a separate fee required to tour the cave, and tickets are sold only at the Lodgepole or Foothills Visitors Center.

# 50

## Eagle Lake

*Type: Day hike or overnight*

*Season: Late June to mid-October*

*Total distance: 6.8 miles round trip*

*Rating: Strenuous*

*Elevation: 7,822 feet; +2,202 feet/-11 feet*

*Location: Sequoia National Park*

*Maps: USGS 7.5' Mineral King; Trails Illustrated Sequoia Kings Canyon National Parks No. 205*

*Fees and Permits: A permit is not required for this day hike. Wilderness permits for overnight trips cost $15 during the peak season quota period; the remainder of the year, permits are free. Passenger vehicles entering the park are charged a $20 admission fee, which is good for seven days.*

*Contact: Sequoia and Kings Canyon National Parks (559-565-3341 general information; 559-565-3766 wilderness permits; www.nps.gov/seki).*

A fair warning: although the hike to Eagle Lake is one of the easier treks radiating from the Mineral King area, that isn't saying much. The well-maintained trail rises swiftly more than 2,200 feet in less than 3.5 miles, but don't let that stop you. Sublime views of the metamorphic peaks surrounding the Mineral King Valley, a granite-hemmed subalpine lake, and easy brook trout fishing are just a few of the reasons to make the long journey to the seldom seen southern fringe of Sequoia National Park and venture to the tranquil shore of this high-country gem.

### GETTING THERE

From CA 198, just north of the town of Three Rivers, turn onto Mineral King Road and drive 24.5 miles east along this narrow, bumpy, mostly paved, winding road to its end at the trailhead parking area (allow a minimum of 90 minutes). You will pass the Lookout Point Entrance Station approximately 10 miles into the drive. Find pit toilets across from the Mineral King Ranger Station or on the north side of the Kaweah River Bridge just prior to the trailhead. The parking area is a favorite feeding spot for marmots that like to nibble through car hoses in search of aromatic antifreeze. We didn't have any problems, however we did see several cars wrapped with tarps or surrounded by chicken wire to keep the yellow-bellied beasties out. Check your engine compartment before driving off to make sure there are no stowaways hiding under the hood.

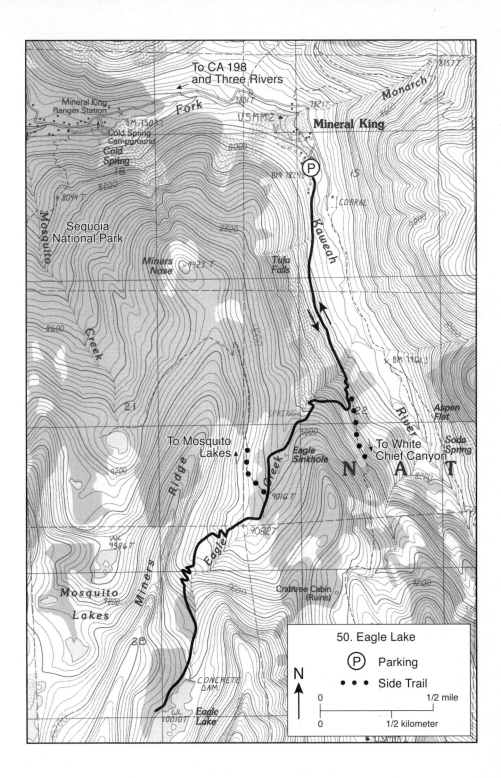

To CA 198
and Three Rivers

Monarch

81577

Mineral King
Ranger Station
BM 7503

Cold Spring
Campground

Cold
Spring
16

7801

U SMM2

Mineral King

8217

BM 7829

CORRAL

8044

Sequoia
National Park

Miners
Nose

9423

Tufa
Falls

Kaweah

5

Mosquito

Creek

8600

SPRING

BM 7101

Aspen
Flat

River

Soda
Spring

To Mosquito
Lakes

Creek

Eagle
Sinkhole

9016

N   A   T

To White
Chief Canyon

Ridge

9200

9092

WK
9586

Eagle

Miners

Mosquito

Lakes
28

8700

Crabtree Cabin
(Ruins)

9200

CONCRETE
DAM

WL
10010

Eagle
Lake

**50. Eagle Lake**

Ⓟ  Parking

•••  Side Trail

N

0                    1/2 mile

0            1/2 kilometer

## THE TRAIL

Yes, you have to work a little to get to Mineral King. That's the downside. The upside is the chance to walk into a glacially sculpted valley framed by 11,000-foot sawtooth peaks reminiscent of the Swiss Alps, to experience its wildflower-studded meadows and gaze at narrow braids of water that course down its red-tinged mountain slopes. Oh, and all this without the crowds of the more accessible regions of the park.

As the name implies, Mineral King first gained recognition in the early 1870s when silver was discovered in the valley. Though the mines never produced, Mineral King Road, constructed by a mining company to transport mill and mining equipment up to the mines, opened the area to logging, hydroelectric development, and tourism.

As early as the 1940s, Mineral King, not part of the National Parks system at the time, was considered by the United States Forest Service as a potential site for a ski resort under its multiple-use mandate. It wasn't until the 1960s, however, that wheels were set in motion when Walt Disney Enterprises, Inc. laid out an ambitious plan for a $35 million complex of motels, restaurants, ski lifts, and parking lots to accommodate the masses. Fortunately, the resort never came to fruition, due to environmental concerns raised by a coalition of preservationists, spearheaded by the Sierra Club. After years of legal wrangling between environmental groups and commercial interests, the Mineral King Valley was annexed into Sequoia National Park in 1978 by an act of Congress, which decisively ended any plans for ski runs and hordes of visitors of ever scarring this beautiful valley.

The trail commences at the southern end of the parking lot. After passing the trailhead information board and the restored Honeymoon Cabin, you begin a mild climb up the sage-covered western slope of Farewell Canyon. The Great Western Divide forms the eastern wall of this glacially carved valley. After 0.25 mile, you cross boisterous Spring Creek via a narrow wooden footbridge; upstream is Tufa Falls.

Just beyond the crossing, pass an unsigned spur trail descending left toward the river. The trail wanders in and out of small stands of red fir and past a few contorted western junipers as you continue to climb. Your eastward view includes cascading Crystal Creek, south of Mineral Peak, and Franklin Creek, north of Tulare Peak. Both spill from headwaters high above in a rush to meet the East Fork Kaweah River coursing below. After crossing Eagle Creek via some conveniently placed steppingstones, the trail steepens. Reach a trail fork 1 mile from the trailhead and turn right toward Eagle Lake.

The single-track trail climbs steeply past the junction through a denser red fir forest. About 0.3 mile past the junction, the forest opens and you switchback up a grassy slope alive with butterflies and sprinkled with larkspur, monkey flower, and bistort. At the top of the hillside meadow, reach a ridge where the grade eases and you follow the mysteriously dry Eagle Creek streambed before arriving at Eagle Sinkhole. It is here that Eagle Creek plunges into a deep crater and flows underground, leaving its former streambed dry.

With Eagle Creek now as your chaperone, stroll pleasantly along its western bank before coming to your second junction at 2 miles, this time with the Mosquito Lakes Trail. Veer left and skirt a large clearing, catching your breath along the nearly level trail before ascending again on the far end of the meadow. Glimpse a pretty cascade through the trees as you climb a pinemat manzanita-lined trail past boulders and the ever-thinning woodland.

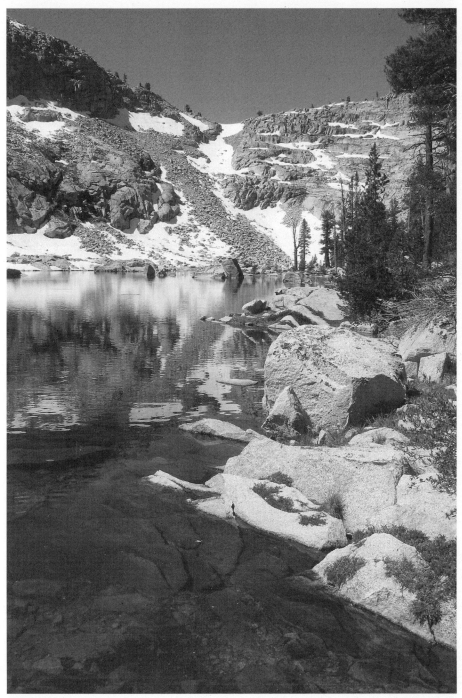

*Eagle Lake*

**Eagle Lake**

After passing a small meadow to the east, you arrive at the base of an expansive talus slope. Begin the long trek across the exposed slope by boulder-hopping the first 100 feet. Past this small section, the trail becomes more defined. Look for red penstemon and red elderberry that sprout from rocky crevices and add splashes of color to the stark granite landscape.

Of course, the higher you get in this treeless terrain, the better the view. Brooding to the northeast are metamorphic Sawtooth and Mineral Peaks, and to the southeast, Franklin Pass and Florence Peak. From this vantage it's easy to understand why much of the southern Sierra is devoid of roads. In fact, Sequoia and Kings Canyon Parks form the heart of the second-largest contiguous roadless area left in the Lower 48. The southern Sierra are so rugged that you must go north to Tioga Pass in Yosemite or south to Walker Pass in Tehachapi to cross them.

You have undoubtedly seen several marmots scurrying about during your ascent. As you cross the talus slope, you may also spot American pikas, high-altitude relatives of the rabbit that are about the size of a large hamster. Pikas live in rocky mountain areas and boulder-covered hillsides between the timberline and subalpine forest, within reach of meadows or patches of vegetation. They have small rounded ears and peppery brown fur, and have no visible tail. They use a variety of squeaks and squeals to communicate with each other and their marmot neighbors.

Beyond the talus slope, the grade eases and you pass through a thin forest of lodgepole pines underlain with a smattering of grasses, shrubs, and slabs of granite before arriving at the concrete dam that impounds Eagle Lake (10,010 feet). The lake was dammed by Mount Whitney Power and Electric Company so they could better control water flow to their hydroelectric plant near Three Rivers.

The crystalline lake is bordered by steep granite walls and decorated with lingering patches of snow well into summer. Cross the dam and explore the eastern shore, or walk farther along our trail and scout out a camping or picnic spot. If you plan on camping, the best sites are located near the midpoint of the lake on the pine-shrouded western shore.

Anglers will enjoy fishing for brook trout that I think would eat a bare hook, they are so aggressive. Though the fish are small, there is something magical about casting a line into a remote high-country lake. When you've gotten your fill, return via the same path.

# Recommended Reading

Alden, Peter, Fred Heath, et al. *National Audubon Society Field Guide to California*. New York: Chanticleer Press, 1998.

Curtis, Rick. *The Backpacker's Field Manual: A Comprehensive Guide to Mastering Backcountry Skills* (revised updated edition). New York: Three Rivers Press, 2005.

Farquhar, Francis P. *History of the Sierra Nevada* (2nd edition). Berkeley, CA: University of California Press, 2007.

Hill, Mary. *Geology of the Sierra Nevada* (2nd edition). Berkeley, CA: University of California Press, 2006.

Storer, Tracy, Robert Usinger, and David Lukas. *Sierra Nevada Natural History* (2nd edition). Berkeley, CA: University of California Press, 2004.

# Index